ENGLISH
PARISH CHURCHES
as Works of Art

Even if Hell exists (which I doubt), and even if Heaven is a reality (which I sincerely hope is not true), . . . I believe that the gift I most appreciate is the gift of seeing beauty. Why should I experience such a spurt of pleasure at seeing the tower of Staplehurst church catch the sun through fog?

HAROLD NICOLSON, *in his seventies*

ENGLISH
PARISH
CHURCHES
as Works of Art

ALEC CLIFTON-TAYLOR

Oxford   New York
OXFORD UNIVERSITY PRESS
1989

Oxford University Press, Walton Street, Oxford OX2 6DP
Oxford New York Toronto
Delhi Bombay Calcutta Madras Karachi
Petaling Jaya Singapore Hong Kong Tokyo
Nairobi Dar es Salaam Cape Town
Melbourne Auckland
and associated companies in
Berlin Ibadan

Oxford is a trade mark of Oxford University Press

First published 1974 by B. T. Batsford Ltd.
Second edition 1986
First issued as an Oxford University Press paperback 1989

British Library Cataloguing in Publication Data
Clifton-Taylor, Alec, 1907-1985
English parish churches as works of art.–2nd ed.
1. England. Parish churches. Architectural features
I. Title
726'.5'0942
ISBN 0-19-282596-8

Library of Congress Cataloging in Publication Data
Clifton-Taylor, Alec.
English parish churches as works of art / Alec Clifton-Taylor.–2nd ed.
p.   cm.
'First published 1974 by B. T Batsford Ltd.'–T.p. verso.
Bibliography: p.   Includes indexes.
1. Church architecture–England.   I. Title.
726'.5'0942–dc 19   NA5461.C487   1989   88-36928
ISBN 0-19-282596-8

Printed in Great Britain by
Butler and Tanner Ltd.
London and Frome

Contents

For
NIKOLAUS
with affection, admiration
and profound gratitude
for having
through the prodigious achievement of
The Buildings of England
added so much
to the pleasure of living

PUBLISHER'S NOTE

Alec Clifton-Taylor died shortly after completing the revisions for this new edition. The publishers are grateful to Mr Mervyn Blatch for his expert collaboration during the later stages of the book's production.

List of illustrations

Illustration Acknowledgements

There are 124 plates, carefully chosen to illustrate specific themes, and 4 illustrations in the text.

Because the possibilities are almost limitless, choosing the best illustrations has been no easy task. The National Monuments record has proved, not for the first time, a tower of strength, and I have also been fortunate in being able to draw upon the publisher's own collection for some close-ups. Mervyn Blatch took twelve photographs specially for this book (13, 15, 17, 27, 32, 36, 41, 43, 66, 112, 116 and 118).

The owners of copyright of the other photographs are as follows: Berrow's Newspapers, Worcester (70), Avery Colebrook (21), Marjorie Gayton (44), O. G. Jarman (110), A. F. Kersting (22, 28, 37 and 39), National Monuments Record (1–8, 10, 11, 16, 18–20, 24, 26, 29–31, 35, 42, 46–48, 51–54, 55, 57, 59, 64, 65, 68, 69, 77, 78, 81, 82, 84, 88, 92, 93, 94, 103–105, 107, 111, 113, 115, 117, 119, 120, 123 and 124), Oxford Public Libraries (17), the Rev. M. Ridgway (33, 34 and 108), J. Dixon Scott (106), Walter Scott (50), Mrs Edwin Smith (22, 23, 28, 38, 71, 85, 102, 121 and 122) and Reece Winstone (67). Plate 25 is from a photograph by the late Rev. F. Sumner. Plates 14, 39, 40, 45, 49, 56, 58, 60–63, 67, 72–76, 79, 80, 83, 86, 89, 90, 91, 95–101 and 109 are from the publisher's collection.

The engravings on pages 32 and 132 come from the National Monuments Record. The line drawing on page 160 is reproduced by kind permission of the artist, Mr Cecil Clutton.

Foreword to the First Edition

There have been many books about the English parish churches, and it may well be wondered what justification there an be for writing yet another. But so far as I am aware no book has been undertaken which considers them purely aesthetically. It will of course at once be objected that they were not built to serve the cause of art, and that their beauties, which, everyone will agree, are there in abundance, were a by-product of the will to glorify the Creator. In fact I suspect that this may be a good deal less completely true than was at one time believed. Several other more worldly factors certainly operated, among them the pride and ambitions of the great ecclesiastics and other rich patrons, and the very healthy rivalry which often existed between neighbouring towns and even villages. After having, over the past forty years or so, visited several thousand of England's churches, including all the finest, I feel more sure than ever that much of what can be seen came into being as an outcome of the sheer joy of creation, like so much of the best art of every kind the world over. No other explanation need be sought, for no other activity is better worth while.

Thus, when the publishers invited me to write a book on the parish churches 'from the point of view of an intelligent enthusiast living not in the heyday of the Victorian ecclesiologists but in the 1970s', I saw at once what kind of book this would have to be. Since more people would now seem to visit our churches as art-lovers, even if not always as well-instructed ones, than for any other reason, this approach requires, I feel, neither justification nor excuse. I am conscious that the book is unlikely to please everybody who like myself holds the churches in high affection. Some parts, and especially two of the longest sections, on churchyards and on nineteenth-century stained glass, may not win universal concurrence. Of course I regret this; but I have positive views on these subjects, and I feel I must voice them.

This book makes no higher claim than to present one way of looking at our parish churches. It is of course my way, but I believe it may also be the way of a good many others, and perhaps of an increasing number. Nothing would delight me more than to learn from members of the younger generation that this book had done something to crystallize their feelings about the parish churches, and to encourage them to become lifelong 'amateurs of churches' (a term which will be employed throughout in place of the unworthy 'church-crawlers').

How much this book owes to Professor Jack Simmons only he and I will ever know. His suggestions have been incorporated at every turn. With great generosity, four other friends also read the book in typescript: Elizabeth Mitchell, Norman Monk-Jones, Hilary Rogers and Robert Storrar. All four gave me wise advice and invaluable help. Samuel Carr of Batsford, who asked me to write it, has indulged my every whim.

Foreword to the Second Edition

When the publishers suggested to Alec Clifton-Taylor that there was room for a second edition, he eagerly seized the opportunity to bring certain sections up-to-date, and to make various corrections and additions.

The author had completed most of the revision before his unexpected death in April 1985. He was helped in this by Miss Judith Scott, O.B.E., F.S.A. – former Secretary to what is now called the Council for the Care of Churches – who made various comments which he adopted and expressed certain opinions, not all of which he accepted. Moreover, although the author was well aware that some of his views might not win universal approval, he did not change his stand on churchyards and nineteenth-century stained glass. Nor did he take into account recent work (such as 1979 Symposium by Cathedrals Advisory Commission and Council for Care of Churches, National Survey of Wall-Paintings or the Conservation Course now run by the Courtauld Institute of Art) on wall-paintings and the fact that they are our main national heritage of medieval primitive painting, the influence of which might have modified his poor opinion of them as part of our church heritage. And his lack· of enthusiasm for Victorian work in general and scant reference to Art Nouveau work is apparent.

This book, however, is his statement and it ill becomes us to change what some might consider the author's lovable idiosyncrasies in these fields, having regard to his well-nigh unrivalled knowledge of our

English parish churches from personal inspection and his long study of architectural history based upon a thorough training in this discipline.

Unfortunately, he was not able to tie up all the loose ends, or to repair certain omissions before his unfortunate death, some of which he was intending to make good. We have, therefore, found room for sections covering reredoses and altars, sedilia/sanctuary chairs, church bells and chests on·pp. 192 *et seq.* These perforce are not products of the author's own inimitable pen but, as a friend of more than 25 years' standing, who has enjoyed his company on countless visits to English churches and as the author of three books on churches, I have taken it upon myself – with Miss Scott's valuable help – to plug these gaps, and I must hope that Alec Clifton-Taylor would have shared any views expressed. We seemed to agree on most things.

In view of all that I have learned from and enjoyed with him, I am more than happy to have been entrusted with this contribution to a book, which I am confident will continue to give pleasure to the large body of church-lovers who particularly value this part of our national heritage.

MERVYN BLATCH
12 September 1985

Author's Note
It should perhaps be made clear that this book takes no cognizance of the rewriting of the county map of England in 1974 in interests of administrative convenience and without regard for historic and traditional loyalties.

ONE

Introduction

WHEN ONE HAS TRAVELLED extensively in the younger countries of the English-speaking world, the United States and Canada, Australia and New Zealand, in which buildings that in England would often merit no more than a cool nod have become places of pilgrimage because of their rarity, one realises all the more forcefully how immensely privileged we English are, in possessing within the confines of our small, overcrowded country a wealth of architecture which in the entire world is rivalled only by Italy and France. Dr Johnson made a nice distinction between what was worth seeing and worth going to see. Among the English parish churches alone – and there are over 17 000 of them – about 11 000 are included in the statutory lists of buildings of special architectural or historic interest. Some 8000 of these churches are still predominantly medieval, of which about three quarters are mainly or solely in the Perpendicular style. 2000 are Grade A. Most of these, and some others, perhaps only for a single remarkable feature, are worth 'going to see'.[1]

Paradoxically, some of the finest of today's parish churches were not built as such. The noblest of all, St John, Beverley, always known as the Minister, was served by a College of Secular Canons established as long ago as *c.* 937 by King Athelstan. It has been an Anglican parish church only since Easter Day 1548. Among those which until the Dissolution were monastic, seven are outstanding: Tewkesbury, Selby, Sherborne, Bath and Romsey were all Benedictine Abbey churches, the last for nuns; Great Malvern was the church of a Benedictine, Christchurch of an Augustinian, Priory. About eighty more parish churches were also formerly associated with monasteries, principally Benedictine or Augustinian, with a few Cistercian and still fewer of other orders, including three friaries. In most cases (Dorchester, Cartmel, Edington and Amesbury are the chief exceptions) only part of the church has survived; usually it is the nave, but a small number of very distinguished parish churches (Pershore, Abbey Dore and Hexham – with a new nave built in 1907–9 – are the leading examples) occupy what was once the eastern portion of a large monastic church. A full list of these churches is given in Appendix A. Some are now quite unimportant; some always were. I shall not be much concerned here with churches of non-parochial origin, and wish therefore to make it clear that generalisations in this book about parish churches usually have no application to these others, which did not become parochial until after the Dissolution. I shall also exclude parish churches elevated to cathedral rank in recent times, even though the aspect of some of them does little to belie their origins.

It has been said that the English cathedrals and parish churches constitute an architectural patrimony and a historical record unparalleled in the world. For what is now only a minority they also have a liturgical and symbolic significance which loomed much larger at the time they came into being. One of the problems of today is to try to find some common ground between these two very different sets of values. At present we still have in England the quixotic situation of an Established Church whose buildings are nevertheless neither the property nor the responsibility of the State. When in 1913 the Church of England under the leadership of Archbishop Davidson decided – with the full concurrence, it should be said, of the then Minister of Works, who was anxious not to take on the administrative problems which the inclusion of churches would have involved – to take no part in the legislation for the preservation of ancient monuments, an undertaking was given that the Church would make its own arrangements for the proper upkeep of its buildings. In many ways, it can be said, this pledge has been faithfully honoured, often at considerable personal sacrifice to Church members. But after over 60 years' experience several things have emerged.

The first is that the clergy, bishops and deans included, are not usually qualified to be the guardians of our churches as works of art or as historic buildings. And why has anyone the right to expect that they should be? They have been trained in quite another discipline. It is also evident that a great many of them, the younger men in particular, have no interest in preservation. Some, indeed, regard old churches – often 'in the wrong place, of the wrong shape, and quite impractical for maintenance and heating', one of them wrote – as 'obsolescent plant', an incubus which is absorbing far too much of the Church's resources already, and which, unless action is taken, is likely to require still more. The big 'thermometer' in many church porches records only their irritation. Another clergyman recently stated that 'if a scheme could be devised whereby these buildings and their expensive care could be the responsibility of aesthetes, there is a high degree of probability that more time, money and manpower could be devoted to building up a real church treasure, viz. a worshipping community'.

This is a perfectly intelligible standpoint for a young man in holy orders. But it is not one which can be equated with the undertaking given in 1913 by Archbishop Davidson. The truth is that the Church no longer has the resources to implement that undertaking. And as a non-churchman I would go further and say: why should it? Why should not the very large numbers of non-churchmen to whom the heritage of parish churches is precious also help to contribute to their preservation? Well, the short answer is that they do, both by an unending stream of voluntary contributions and now also as taxpayers.

Since this book first appeared, a radical change has taken place. State grants have been paid to churches as well as to secular buildings. Since 1977, when the first grants were made, more than three thousand churches have received help, to the tune of over £20 000 000. The usual rate of grant is 40% of the eligible repair costs. The great surprise is that this aid has been made available without the Church's buildings becoming subject to the planning laws already applicable to every other kind of English building except (most improperly) Government offices and all Crown property, barracks, palaces, guardianship monuments, etc. The Historic Buildings and Monuments Commission does exercise some control. Grants are only offered for structural repairs regarded by the Commission as essential, and executed to specifications agreed in detail in advance. And, to qualify for a grant, the Act of 1953 under which most of this assistance is forthcoming lays down that the building must be of outstanding architectural and historical interest, and that, whether the building is ecclesiastical or secular, any future proposals for additions, improvements or alterations must be agreed by the Commission.

At the time of writing the so-called 'ecclesiastical exemption' has still not been abolished, and for churches in use it is by no means certain that it will be. This is a highly controversial question on which the most divergent views are held. At present, it is still possible for improper things to be done to them, despite the surveillance of Diocesan Advisory Committees. There are now moves to improve the DAC system, however, and to limit the powers of Chancellors from whom the faculty or legal permit to proceed is obtained. It is to be hoped that these will soon be implemented. The Non-Established Churches (and these, of course, include the Roman Catholic Church) have no equivalent to the DAC system, and their buildings are at greater risk. If the churches accept a substantial grant from public funds, it is surely reasonable to expect that they will be willing to accept at least a measure of control.

In some cases one of the most difficult problems is to find architects really competent in the rather specialised field of church conservation. The skill of these architects varies enormously, and it makes a considerable difference if a church finds a good one. Another greatly overdue reform is for the Government to cease charging VAT on repairs to historic buildings. As the law stands at present, the way to avoid this tax is to demolish and rebuild rather than to restore and preserve. It would be difficult, one would think, to devise a more cock-eyed procedure.

In recent years more attention has been paid to regular inspection. The Inspection of Churches Measure has, since 1955, required that every parish church should be reported on by a qualified architect at five yearly intervals. This has forced Parish Church Councils to face the problem of putting repairs in hand at an early stage before serious decay begins. Sometimes patches of damp on the walls may be due to no more than a blocked gutter or a rusted downpipe, and be remediable at a very much lower cost than would be incurred by delaying.

A church in difficulty over fund-raising (of any denomination) may appeal for help to the Historic Churches Preservation Trust. This admirable body, supported by charitable trusts, commerce and industry, and many caring individuals, has assisted churches and chapels – about four thousand in all – since its formation in 1952, sometimes with interest-free loans, but generally with grants which nowadays often help to 'top-up' what has been collected from local sources, sufficiently to enable the parish to obtain much larger aid from the State.

The number of Church of England churches which in recent years have been declared redundant is now approaching a thousand. Of these nearly 250 have been demolished, while over 500 have been put to alternative uses; the best, however, have passed into the care of the Redundant Churches Fund. This was set up in 1969, to preserve Church of England churches of architectural or historic interest no longer required for worship – though they may still be used for occasional services, as well as for other events such as concerts and exhibitions. This enlightened scheme got off to a somewhat slow start but in recent years has steadily gathered momentum so that the Fund is now responsible for close on two hundred churches. Many of these are in areas of sparse population and so have to be kept locked, but kind people living nearby are generally willing to hold the key and access usually presents little difficulty. In my experience, churches in the care of the Fund have always been admirably restored (often at considerable cost, for their condition when handed over was usually poor) and are models of good maintenance. The Redundant Churches Fund is certainly proving to be a most essential element in the defence of our ecclesiastical heritage. Any church referred to in this book which is now vested in it will be followed by an (R). Part of the income of the Fund comes from the Church, part from the State. It is a pity the Non-Established Churches have not negotiated any similar arrangement.

A good many of the churches not considered to qualify for being taken into the care of the Fund are, it is fair to say, not of much account as works of art, and some demolitions have been positively welcome. In any case, we cannot afford to keep all of them. During the last few years, I have visited a church whose lofty nave was thickly festooned with cobwebs,

another with ominous cracks in its brickwork and plaster rotting off
the interior walls, a third with a tower leaning noticeably if not yet
dangerously, and a fourth with signs of neglect and damp everywhere and
the benches so covered with bird droppings that it was impossible to find
anywhere to sit down. The experience was deeply depressing. In a remote
village in Norfolk, with a churchyard knee-deep in nettles, I met the old
parson. 'The congregations,' he said 'never exceed four except at pumpkin
time (the harvest festival). The organist was so awful that I stopped organ
playing, and now the damp has ensured that we can't have any organ
music, nor any hymns either: that's one thing to be thankful for. We had
the architect's quinquennial visitation, but we can't afford to pay his fee,
let alone the £400 he recommends for essential repairs. Our Sunday
collections average 7p.'

For such churches and many others, if not worthy of substantial grants,
the future looks somewhat bleak. It must, however, be admitted that the
standpoint of those who value the churches for non-pastoral reasons is
prima facie not easy to defend. If we do not like to see the churches unused,
yet feel no call to use them ourselves, I can see only one possible way out,
which is to go back to the pre-Reformation custom of employing the nave
for secular and recreational purposes – anything from a parish meeting to
a play or a concert, from a film show to a festival of light music – and
reserving only the chancel for sacred uses. 'The nave (of Aldeburgh) is
broad because, in pre-Reformation days, the nave of a church did duty for
all the due functions of the parish', writes Ronald Blythe in his guide to
the church. 'There are records in Aldeburgh to say that ship-auctions
were regularly held in the nave as well as theatrical performances given by
travelling players. A spacious nave was also essential to the proper
management of processions.'

Even this flexibility, which is being increasingly re-adopted, would not
solve the problem of the estate churches, to which reference will be made
later. But it seems clear that, in the interests of having the building used,
compromises will have to be made on the aesthetic plane; and at least this
would bring with it one great artistic advantage, that is to say the
disappearance of pews, and perhaps another, the removal of inappropriate
stained glass. There will be more to say about both these matters in a later
chapter. Since 1968 the situation has been greatly eased by the liberal
provisions of the Pastoral Measure of that year, for there is now no longer
any difficulty about the secularisation of unwanted churches.

In this respect the city of Norwich has for many years given
enlightened leadership. With far more churches than are required for
worship, there has been a wholesale conversion to other uses. One has
long been an ecclesiastical museum, another a public hall. A third is now
headquarters for scouts, and three others are employed for storage: not

the best solution, but at least the buildings are preserved. Other cities, including London and York, have followed suit, and will have to do so increasingly in the future. Outstandingly successful has been the conversion of two of Oxford's redundant churches into college libraries. St Edmund Hall also acquired the graveyard of St Peter-in-the-East and has made of it a delectable garden: something which this little college badly needed. Old gravestones have been retained on the faultlessly mown lawns. In urban centres other uses are almost certain to be found in time for many of these redundant buildings. It is the lonely churches that are really our greatest problem.

Many parish churches, it must be admitted, are buildings of character rather than of any great architectural importance. They belong to a category which looms large in my personal records, the category that I term 'pleasantly dull'. A few, of course, are 'unpleasantly dull', but with these we need not be much concerned in this book. If they should turn out to be redundant, they can be sacrificed without a pang.

There are others, including some celebrated ones, with much more history than art. Brixworth, for example: an ecclesiologists' church without much aesthetic appeal (and in which the original Anglo-Saxon structure has been badly mauled). For the historically minded there is always pleasure to be had from a church which spreads out its whole story to be 'read' immediately one enters, like Brighstone in the Isle of Wight. The north arcade here is still Norman, with short circular piers, wide-stepping round-headed arcades and tiny round-headed windows above in pairs. In the thirteenth century a nice chancel was built, with lancet windows. In the fourteenth century the Norman south nave aisle was pulled down and another, much wider and loftier, was built in Decorated. In the fifteenth century this aisle was extended, in Perpendicular, until it was flush with the east end, and there was a new font. Under James I, as so often, they added an oak pulpit. Under the Georges, again as so often, the church quietly slept. That left the Victorians with plenty to do in the way of restoration: in came the dark stained glass and the tedious pews; off went the plaster from the walls. The twentieth century added nothing but some pleasantly 'tasteful' chandeliers. There it all is: an object lesson in the evolution of a typical English parish church, and one that can all be absorbed without difficulty by anybody who knows the language. But that evolution may be much more interesting historically than in terms of art.

Other churches, while still not being works of art, are much more in tune with the approach adopted in this book. Such a one is Stoke Orchard in Gloucestershire, formerly a chapel-of-ease of Bishop's Cleeve. This is a little building dating mainly from *c.* 1170, of rubblestone, partly rendered, with a good Cotswold stone roof; from outside it looks small and venerable. The interior is dark but, having discovered the whereabouts of the lights, one has an experience of timelessness. People have been doing things to this little building for 800 years. There are wall paintings of more than one date, learnedly restored by Mr Clive Rouse 20 years ago but still, as often in England, more or less invisible. The walls are patched, faded, flaking and confused, yet not 'dead' nor uninteresting. Only the eyes of an expert can discern what has been done, and for most of us it will not be worth the effort. It is not an aesthetic experience but something rather different: a consciousness of identity, perhaps, with those who love England for her long history and tradition. That the Georgians should have come along and slapped their nicely lettered Creed, Commandments and Lord's Prayer on top of everyone else's contribution is endearingly characteristic.

Lytton Strachey, under a cloud today as a historian but unassailable as a master of language, drew this delightful picture of the Anglican Church in the eighteenth and early nineteenth centuries, before the advent of the Tractarian movement:

'The Church of England slept the sleep of the – comfortable . . . Portly divines subscribed with a sigh or a smile to the Thirty-Nine Articles, sank quietly into easy livings, rode gaily to hounds of a morning as gentlemen should, carried their two bottles of an evening . . . The fervours of piety, the zeal of Apostolic charity, the enthusiasm of self-renunciation – these things were all very well in their way, and in their place; but their place was certainly not the Church of England . . . There were, it was true, within the Church some strait-laced parsons of the high Tory school who looked back with regret to the days of Laud or talked of the Apostolic Succession; and there were groups of square-toed Evangelicals who were earnest over the Atonement and confessed to a personal love of Jesus Christ . . . But such extremes were the rare exceptions. The great bulk of the clergy walked calmly along the smooth road of ordinary duty. They kept an eye on the poor of the parish, and they conducted the Sunday Services in a becoming manner; for the rest, they differed neither outwardly nor inwardly from the great bulk of the laity, to whom the Church was a useful organisation for the maintenance of Religion, as by law established.'[2]

The churches were used. Nearly everyone attended except in the autumn at one church in Devon, which the incumbent always closed for three months during the shooting season. In the country people often brought their animals too. Horses of course were tethered outside – vestiges of tethering rings can still be seen at Walpole St Peter in Norfolk and a fine mounting block at Lowther in Westmorland – but from medieval days dogs had always been allowed to come in. At Stanton in Gloucestershire, there are three old benches which were reserved for those farmers and shepherds who brought their dogs to church with them, and the heads of these benches show deeply incised rings made by the dog-chains. Laudian communion rails, which protect the holy table on three sides (and at Lyddington in Rutland on all four), were introduced on the Archbishop's orders to prevent dogs from defiling the sanctuary. Several churches in North Wales still preserve their dog-tongs, formerly used for the ejection of canine intruders: at Bangor Cathedral and at Clynnog Fawr in Caernarvonshire they are of iron, at Llaneilian in Anglesey of wood. I have never come across any English dog-tongs, but a pair may still survive at Clodock in Herefordshire. Some churches had an official dog-whipper, and not only in Laudian days; at Baslow in Derbyshire a dog-whip of much more recent date can still be seen. But in the easy-going eighteenth century I suspect that these whips were seldom used. Some country churches had 'Hall dog pews', provided especially for the dogs of the Squire. Even in the City of London, at St Mary Abchurch, there were, until the restoration of the church after the last war, dog-kennels beneath the high pews on the south side. The chancel now counted for very little. It was a time of extreme Low Church Protestantism, and the chief reason for attendance was to hear the sermon.

So the churches were primarily preaching-houses, and the pulpit was more important than the altar. When it was a three-decker or had a tester, the pulpit was indeed a very prominent object, and when it was sited at the east end of the central aisle, as was quite common in the eighteenth century, it dominated the church. Such a placing of the pulpit can still be seen at Congleton in Cheshire, where, although the church dates mainly from 1742, the pulpit is Jacobean brought from elsewhere, and at King's Norton in Leicestershire, where, except for the obtrusive Victorian organ, all the furnishings – which are mostly Norwegian oak, and of austere design – date from the building of the church in 1757–75. The squire had his own family pew; the grander families, as we shall see, liked to have a private gallery, often with its own fireplace and a separate entrance, through which it was not unknown for a liveried servant to enter, with sherry and biscuits, while the parson droned on. The rest of the congregation kept as warm as it could, within the shelter of the box-pews, but there can be little doubt that in winter some of the churches were extremely cold, with patches of damp and mildew on walls and floors. I trust that I may be excused for repeating here a quotation from Smollett's *Humphry Clinker* (1770) which I have cited elsewhere:[3]

'When we consider our antient churches ... may we not term them so many magazines of rheums, created for the benefit of the medical faculty? And may we not safely aver that, in the winter especially (which may be said to engross eight months in the year), more bodies are lost, than souls saved, by going to church?'

One example of what a largely medieval church looked like in the latter part of the eighteenth century has miraculously survived: St Mary, Whitby. This building is far from being a work of art, but it is most valuable, even lovable, and should now on no account be tampered with. It is not a large church, but with the help of a congeries of white-fronted galleries facing in all directions and at many different levels, it is said that it can accommodate two thousand people. The most extraordinary feature of all, which some would term blasphemous, is the Cholmley pew, perched up on four barley-sugar columns at exactly the point where one would expect to find the rood screen.

An unspoiled interior from the closing years of the reign of George III, which has also survived intact, is Mildenhall in Wiltshire, standing by the Kennet a couple of miles east of Marlborough. This little church, of no great architectural merit, was given a complete scheme of refurnishing in the Gothick taste in 1815–16. A symmetrical effect was obtained by placing opposite the pulpit a reader's desk of identical design; both have tall backs and testers. There is also a small organ in a west gallery. With its box-pews, panelled chancel and reredos, this is a cosy if slightly fussy interior, and very endearing. It seems perfectly appropriate that for many years the sole occupant of the north aisle was the mower.

By this time rafter roofs had not infrequently disappeared from view behind flat plaster ceilings inserted to accord with classical taste and also, slightly to reduce the cold. Rubblestone walls were invariably plastered. Most of those churches that had been able to afford one or more stained glass windows in the Middle Ages had probably by now seen them fall victims to iconoclasts or vandals. In the Georgian period daylight was welcome and stained glass not required, so that it was by no means unknown for fragments which had managed to survive to find their way, perhaps as a gift from a complaisant parson, into the manor house. At Tattershall in Lincolnshire much of the glass remained in the windows until 1737. Nearly all of it was then taken out by the Fortescues, whose living this was, and apparently put into storage, awaiting a customer. After about twenty years he appeared, in the person of the 9th Earl of Exeter, who carted it all off to Stamford. That explains why some of the Tattershall glass now adorns the hall at Burghley, and a good deal more the Cecil family church of St Martin, Stamford Baron. At Nettlestead in Kent nearly all the fifteenth-century glass that survived on the south side of the church was shattered in 1763 by a storm, and there can be little doubt that the releading always necessary after three hundred years had not been carried out and that the general condition of the windows was weak.

Not all the parish churches were in poor condition at the accession of Queen Victoria. Some had been well maintained; in the country it depended very much on who happened to be the squire. Where he was not interested, or where there was no squire, the church might well be shabby and neglected. The average Georgian had no high opinion of the medieval churches and, when restoration was essential, it was usually carried out as cheaply as possible; decayed stonework was often repaired with red brick, and rendered, and when this rendering decays and starts falling off, the shoddiness of these repairs is revealed. The durability of the old building materials varied a great deal; the granite churches of west Devon and Cornwall, for example, seem to have needed much less in the way of restoration than those built in softer stones elsewhere. When Warren Hastings erected his new church by Daylesford in Gloucestershire in 1816–18 (replaced in 1860 by the present building: J. L. Pearson at his worst), he re-used, so a tablet tells us, 'such of the same materials as had escaped the mouldering hand of time', but its predecessor had already 'suffered some encroachment upon it from the licence of incidental reparations'. In this it was by no means alone.

All then was not well with the churches that the Victorians inherited. Many excellent medieval buildings had been mutilated. Much needed to be done in the cause of preservation. And within a single generation, between about 1845 and 1880, the work was accomplished. It was a remarkable achievement, realised at the cost of much hard work, devoted service and self-sacrifice. There was, certainly, more money about at this time, but it was not evenly distributed; at some churches, one rich man, or often his widow, might pay for everything, but at others there was no such benefactor at hand, and when that was so, restoration was again carried out as cheaply as possible.

The leaders were the clergy, among some of whom there was a sudden swing back towards ritual and a degree of High Churchmanship which had not been seen in England since the days of Laud, just two hundred years before. This affected the church interiors radically. They were, in fact, not just preserved; they were often dramatically, even destructively, altered. For this reason today's attitude towards the Victorians, in the context of the parish churches, is an odd mixture of gratitude and indignation.

I would not wish to imply that no alteration to the fabric or furnishings of a medieval church is ever permissible. Medieval taste was by no means infallible. For example, it seems probable that colour was often used crudely and even garishly, and certainly with no artistic concern. There will be more to say about this in Chapter 6. Few people, I imagine, would wish to see the façade of Wells cathedral replete again with coloured statues, as it once was. It has been open to every generation to introduce improvements. Where is the church which does not look all the better for possessing Caroline altar rails or a Georgian pulpit? The trouble, as I see it, about the Victorian contributions is that they hardly ever were improvements, although of course the Victorians fervently believed them to be. Or rather, most of them did: not Ruskin, who all his life, to the great irritation of the clergy, opposed restoration as 'a lie from beginning to end'; not William Morris either. It was he who founded, in 1877, the Society for the Protection of Ancient Buildings, 'to stave off decay by daily care, to prop a perilous wall or mend a leaky roof by such means as are obviously meant for support or covering, and show no pretence of other art, and otherwise to resist all tampering with either the fabric or ornament as it stands; if it has become inconvenient for its proper use, to raise another building rather than alter or enlarge the old one; in fine, to treat our ancient buildings as monuments of a bygone age, created by bygone manners, that modern art cannot meddle with without destroying'. To these sentiments Morris was able to rally some of the most eminent men of his time.

By 1877, however, the worst damage had been done. Why was it such a disaster, aesthetically?

The key to the artistic failure of Victorian restoration rests in the disregard of the *genius loci*, a disregard rendered possible by the Industrial Revolution, which gave them materials of many kinds produced by machine processes, and railways to transport them with comparative ease. As a result of this, there appeared on and in our churches, for the first time in their history, all kinds of materials which looked wrong, which 'did not belong'. Pink roofing tiles, for example, produced in large numbers at Broseley in Shropshire and elsewhere. These tiles made the cheapest roof covering, cheaper even than Welsh slates, so all over the country they travelled. Stone walls utterly different in colour, texture and character, suddenly found themselves called upon to support these nauseous roofs, which effectively ruined the church's outward appearance.

The Victorians were often excellent craftsmen – indeed, the standard of their craftsmanship was far higher than that generally obtaining today – but there can be no question that they were basically insensitive to materials. How otherwise can be explained, for instance, their addiction to hard, shiny surfaces in juxtaposition with old stonework; the machine-made encaustic tiles with which church after church was refloored; the liking for brass and other gaudy metalwork; the introduction of furnishings such as reredoses, pulpits and fonts in polished marbles, alabaster and similar materials often with variegated markings? They even varnished Purbeck marble in order to obtain a gloss. Their excursions into polychromy are usually embarrassing, because of the stridency of the colours used, not only in the matter of brashness but in less obvious ways also: why point granite, for example, with nearly black mortar, as J. P. St Aubyn did all over Cornwall? This at least could hardly be in search of cheapness. At Highnam near Gloucester, which is in some ways a very fine Victorian church built 'regardless of expense' for the landowner, the architect, Henry Woodyer, added a tiled roof in coloured stripes, which could hardly look worse or more out of place. Another common example of the Victorian use of inappropriate materials is to be seen at the ridges of church roofs. There developed a particular liking for serrated ridge-tiles produced by machine in a form of terracotta, and for fussy cresting of various kinds. These never look well on a church, even if the roof is tiled, but they were also used to crown stone roofs. At Stretton in Rutland the little church has nice stone walls and a charming roof of Collyweston stone-slates, crowned with a ridge of these serrated red tiles. Such insensibility as this seems incomprehensible. The calamitous results, visually, that followed from the introduction of alien materials into our churchyards after about 1850 will be enlarged upon in the next chapter.

Where response to the *genius loci* is the criterion, the leading architects of the period themselves set a very bad example. Butterfield is a byword in this respect. As Goodhart-Rendel aptly remarked, '*defiant* is the word that fits the usual temper of this coarse-grained genius'. Pevsner, Chairman of the Victorian Society, wrote of the strident colours of Butterfield's tiles on the east wall at Amesbury, 'now mercifully hidden by curtains'. But for insensibility in this respect, as in others, the prize should probably go to S. S. Teulon, a distressing example of whose church work can be seen at St Mary, Ealing. One of the things for which Martin Briggs, in his excellent book *Goths and Vandals*, condemned Sir Gilbert Scott is 'the introduction of French and other exotic features into historic English buildings', a practice to which J. L. Pearson was also prone. Pearson was very variable; at his best he is one of the most sympathetic of Victorian architects, and his restoration of the great Saxon–Norman church at Stow in Lincolnshire was highly accomplished. G. E. Street is also very unpredictable. Many of his churches and restorations are lifeless and boring, but at Stone in Kent he did a good job in a nineteenth-century building of rare quality. Among his own churches there are Kingston in Dorset, of which I shall have more to say presently, and Toddington, built in 1873–79. This is one of the finest Victorian churches in England, a really creative reinterpretation of Gothic executed in a masterly manner; yet David Verey is quite right in saying that this big church would be more suitable in London than in a park in Gloucestershire. Even Bodley, who was responsible for some of the best of the Victorian restoration schemes, built in 1898–1903, at Long Melford of all places, a tower which, although faced with flint, manifestly does not belong to Suffolk.

Apart from their fatal abandonment of the *genius loci* as the first factor to be taken into account either when building new churches or when restoring old ones, there were two other directions, both inimical to art, towards which the leading Victorians were also drawn. One was the ecclesiological. It might be supposed that a passionate concern with the historical development of our churches and everything pertaining to them could not fail to have worked in the interests of preservation, and in some ways no doubt it did; but unhappily, all too often, it involved what Morris called 'skinning a church alive'. Up to the Victorian period rubblestone walls inside a church were always rendered (and sometimes outside too). In the lucky churches they still are (*86, 111*). But the ecclesiologists, ever eager to find evidence of earlier foundations and of the location of such features as Easter sepulchres, sedilia, piscinas, aumbries, 'low side-windows' and squints, often long blocked up, stripped off the 'dishonest' plaster and scraped the stonework in countless churches. Aesthetically the results were disastrous, so much so that within a few weeks of its foundation Morris himself gave the SPAB its popular soubriquet, 'The Anti-Scrape'. The effect of plaster-stripping on amenity is specially evident in those churches without clerestories, of which in Devon and Cornwall, Kent, Westmorland and Cumberland there are a great number; many of them are now almost unbearably gloomy.

Still more damage was done as a result of the growth of doctrinaire ideas about religious observances. In pre-Victorian days the evangelical revival had involved the loss of a good deal of furniture, especially screens. The pendulum swung sharply back. The Cambridge Camden Society, founded in 1839 and which within four years numbered among its members both the archbishops, 16 bishops, a whole cohort of clergymen and a substantial contingent of Members of Parliament, for a while exercised great influence. Not all that it did was regrettable: the removal of the galleries often clumsily inserted by the Georgians into churches quite unsuited to receive them was obviously an excellent move. But many of the 'improvements' stemming from this religious revival were very much otherwise. The installation on a large scale of pitch-pine pews, often in replacement of Georgian hardwood box-pews, of big organs sited as close to the chancel as possible, and of a welter of coloured glass in the windows are among the subjects which will be considered in Chapter 5.

But, even more radically, there were now pontifical instructions about styles. Only one style was 'correct': the Middle Pointed. The Perpendicular was dismissed as worldly; architects were enjoined to change everything possible to Decorated. No advice could have been more misplaced. At St Peter, Wolverhampton, which is late-Perpendicular, with many of the windows flat-headed, a long, dark chancel, aisleless and charmless, was added in 1865 in this prescribed style, instead of rebuilding in harmony with the nave. It looks wretchedly out of place. At Algarkirk near Boston Pevsner's experienced eye spotted the anomaly at once. 'An over-restored church (R. C. Carpenter, 1850–4), once no doubt very beautiful . . . Can the Dec. aisle windows be trusted, under their segmental arches? . . . The N. chapel, E.E. in proportion though Dec. in most details . . .' Basil Clarke cited the case of Kemerton in Worcestershire, also restored by Carpenter under the aegis of a Camden Society enthusiast. First the south aisle was rebuilt, then the north aisle, where 'the "early and rude" Norman arcade gave place to a graceful arcade in Middle-Pointed style'. At the time the result met with warm approval.

The greatest changes occurred in the chancel, which might well be extended if funds were forthcoming. This was sometimes performed with skill, as at St Philip, Birmingham (now the Cathedral) and at Blandford. But St Peter, Brighton, the large chancel of 1900–06 which replaced the polygonal apse designed by Barry upsets the proportions of the interior. For liturgical reasons changing levels were introduced in the sanctuary: two steps up here, three there, producing, artistically, an effect of fussiness. At Dinton in Wiltshire in 1876, Butterfield, in addition to reflooring the chancel with machine-made tiles, introduced no fewer than five changes of level. Hand in hand with these went a deeply felt resentment towards large Georgian monuments, which wherever possible were removed from the chancel (sometimes, but not always, justifiably) to less prominent positions, as at Walton-on-Thames, where the grandiose monument to Richard Boyle by Roubiliac now fills a dark corner of the north aisle. At Carshalton the big one to Sir William Scawen (1722), though of quality, is hidden behind a side-altar. I still find that the clergy nearly always deplore and dislike these large Georgian monuments, which, admittedly, can be 'white elephants' (literally as well as figuratively) but which, as for instance the very handsome Humfrey monument at Rettendon in Essex[4], can be far and away the finest feature of the church.

Towards the end of the nineteenth century the quality of Victorian restoration improved. Materials, thanks especially to Bodley, were handled more sensitively; colours were less strident. In particular, the Perpendicular style won a belated acceptance. Even Scott, who died in 1878, had not changed Hillesden to Middle Pointed. This, the best parish church in Buckinghamshire, belongs almost entirely to the reign of Henry VII. Scott had a special regard for it, as he was born in the next village, Gawcott, where his father was the perpetual curate. His restoration was admirable. As Basil Clarke so aptly remarks, 'This was the real Gilbert Scott, which people failed to see behind the façade of the business man running his efficient church building and restoration business'.

Still better was Bodley's restoration in 1874 of Brant Broughton in Lincolnshire. He did a great deal, including the provision of a completely new chancel, perfectly proportioned, to replace a poor structure of 1812. The circumstances here were very propitious. There was, in the first place, already surviving from the Middle Ages the larger part of a beautiful church built of the finest Ancaster limestone. The nave and the tower are late Decorated work of 1338–39; the spire and both porches are mid-fifteenth-century Perpendicular, exuberantly sumptuous. The exterior makes a gorgeous display. The crocketed spire, visible for miles across the ploughlands of Kesteven (2), is nearly 200 feet high. Only the chancel was unworthy, yet the church had fallen into a state of neglect. Then the Sutton family, patrons of the living since 1728, bestirred themselves. Canons Frederick and Arthur Sutton were successively rectors from 1873 until 1924. They were men of taste and of knowledge; they were also well-to-do and generous. They loved the church and they gave unstintingly. There are no fewer than twenty-eight windows, some very large, filled with stained glass and all is of the late Gothic or earliest Renaissance type, admitting a good deal of light. Much was the work of Frederick Sutton and was fired in a kiln at the Rectory. In itself it is of no special account, but the effect, as every window is filled in more or less uniform style, is exceptionally harmonious and pleasing. The seating is with light wooden chairs, not pews; the floor, too, is largely wood. The nave has its original camber-beam roof, adorned with angels. Bodley cleaned and renovated it, adding a good deal of decorative colour and some gilding, especially on the angels' wings. The aisle roofs also have colour and gilding, and so have the ribbed wooden 'vault' of the chancel and the rood screen. The reredos and the altar frontal are also right for the church. Brant Broughton, in a word, is a treasure, yet I seldom meet anyone who has seen it. And it owes a not inconsiderable part of its beauty to the Victorians.

Here, then, is Victorian restoration at its best; it shows what could be achieved with ample funds and a sensitive architect. Unfortunately such a combination was rare. If the Victorians sometimes saved our churches, they also did a great deal towards despoiling them. There is not a single county that does not contain churches which are potentially pleasant but, owing to Victorian bad taste, are at present dreary and wholly uninviting. Perhaps the unluckiest of all is Northumberland. Its chief church, Hexham Priory, was described by J. E. Morris in 1916 (in his *Little Guide*) as 'having been subjected, in 1858, to one of the most foolish and disastrous restorations that have ever disfigured the history even of English iconoclasm'. He continued, 'Much of this evil has been effaced at the recent happy restoration (1908–12), but much is irreparable'. Hexham has indeed recovered considerably from its ordeal of 1858, but throughout Northumberland restoration was punitive.

Specially reprehensible was the Victorian treatment of Georgian churches. These 'preaching boxes', sometimes plain but always decorous outside, often really elegant within, aroused the ire of some of the Victorian clergy, for religious reasons. So in all parts of the country these, as many now think, delightful churches were 'de-Georgianized' and spoilt. St John the Baptist, Knutsford, must have had a delightful interior when it was completed in 1744. Lord Torrington described it as 'in the Venetian ballroom stile'. Today, although it still keeps its galleries and its lovely two-tiered brass chandelier of 1763, it has a flat east end instead of the original apse, Victorian pews and some very bad glass, and is in dire need of redecoration in white. Wimpole in Cambridgeshire was rebuilt in 1749 by Flitcroft and, as Pevsner says, 'was the perfect ecclesiastical counterpart of the mansion'. But, alas, in 1887 all was changed to 'Middle Pointed'. 'Little survives inside', he adds, 'of the good manners of the eighteenth century, and the west gallery of 1887 with its elephantiasis of Gothic forms leaves one bewildered'. This gallery, built to carry an oversized organ, is indeed a monstrosity. Wimpole church as a work of art was ruined. Old Alresford in Hampshire, dating from 1753, was quite spoilt by being Gothicized in 1862. Gautby in Lincolnshire, built in 1756, could be a pleasure but is so no longer. John Wood the Younger's little church at Hardenhuish near Chippenham (1779) is still attractive externally but much marred within. George Steuart's big church of All Saints at Wellington in Shropshire (1788–90) preserved its Georgian character until as late as 1898, when it was most injudiciously reshaped and refurnished. S. P. Cockerell's 90-feet square church at Banbury (1790–97), probably never very pleasing but remarkable for its vast interior space, was cruelly treated; weak glass was inserted into every window, darkening the building to no purpose, and tawdry polychrome decoration was introduced, which now just looks dowdy. (If redecorated in white and gold, this church could be immeasurably improved.) The chancel, added by Arthur Blomfield in 1873 and no less tawdry, has simulated mosaics. These are but a few instances of what the Victorians did to the churches of their predecessors. A particular outrage was the destruction of all but the twin towers of Robert Adam's church at Mistley in Essex (1776) and its replacement in 1871 by a run-of-the-mill Gothic edifice quite devoid of character.

The lesson to be learned from this vandalism is that the really good Victorian churches must be preserved *in toto*. Not, of course, the indifferent ones: a great many were run up on the cheap and are eminently expendable. There are also a fair number of Victorian churches which were most expensively built but which none the less have very little artistic value. An example, often much admired, is Sledmere in

Yorkshire, built about 1898 by Temple Moore. This church, beautifully sited among the trees of Sledmere Park, is a faultless pastiche of the Decorated style, with every detail of the finest quality. But it is a building with no life of its own: its light is the borrowed light of the fourteenth century, and it is not enough. For example, there are gargoyles in profusion. But gargoyles no longer had any meaning in 1898. By then there were gutters and drain pipes, and people did not think in terms of grotesque monsters. So it is not surprising that they are unconvincing. But there are, scattered about the country, probably several hundred which are works of art of real importance, and, in some cases, beauty. It is much more important to keep these than to preserve the additions which the Victorians made to medieval churches, some of which, as I shall later argue, are already over-ripe for removal.

TWO

The Setting

IN NO OTHER COUNTRY in the world is the parish church so frequently the visual centrepiece, the dominant building, of a town or, still more often, a village as in England. On the continent of Europe the scale of the leading churches is generally ampler, and in particular, loftier; returning from France, Belgium or Holland, many of the English churches seem at first to be diminutive. But the setting is likely to be far more attractive. Town churches on the continent may proudly adorn a public place, but usually have no churchyards nor green areas surrounding them; they abut on to the roadway, which may even completely encircle them. It can certainly be an exciting experience to turn a corner in France or Germany, Italy or Spain, and suddenly find a huge church, of whose presence one had had no premonition, soaring up before one's eyes. But all too often its stonework will be dusty and begrimed, and all day long the traffic will be swishing past under its walls. Village churches are likely to stand in walled graveyards filled, often to choking point, with memorials of surpassing ugliness.

This continental type of setting can occasionally be found in England, most strikingly perhaps in Norwich. Here, in contrast to the Cathedral, sheltering almost secretly within its gate-guarded enclosure, the great church of St Peter Mancroft rises confidently above the Market Place and the adjoining Haymarket, to create a most imposing effect. More typical, however, of England is the parish church of All Saints at Rotherham, a noble and beautiful centre-piece (and all the more so since the cleaning of its stone) for what has become an unlovely industrial town. The cruciform church, much pinnacled and battlemented, with a splendid central tower and spire, reposes upon an elevated green platform with steep banks. This platform was formerly the graveyard. A few of the stones, now recumbent, remain: the rest have been removed, and the lawn mown. Traffic flows all round the church, but at a little distance from it, so that it has room to breathe; and not only to breathe but to make its presence felt from whatever direction one approaches. All Saints is the glory of Rotherham.

Not many industrial towns endowed with stately churches have done as well as this; among those which could certainly do better is Hartlepool.

Here no doubt finance is a problem, for this is not one of England's most fortunate towns. Our ancestors took full advantage of what was once a very fine site: they built their church on the hilly crest of a small sea-girt peninsula. There is still a big graveyard, but today it is surrounded by squalor. All the greater, therefore, is one's astonishment and delight at coming upon what is probably the finest church in the county of Durham, after the Cathedral: a glory of Early English architecture in its earliest and purest phase. Hartlepool is to put it mildly not a centre of tourism, and few people undertake the depressing drive which is needful to reach this church; by not doing so they miss an architectural gem.

At another industrial town, Walsall, the parish church stands apart, on a hilltop. It is therefore prominent in many views, and deserves to be, for this is a well-maintained and much-loved building with an unexpected and rather exciting interior: Gothick at its best.

Until comparatively recently, not only in England but all over Europe, the church steeples dominated the urban skyline, particularly where the site was hilly, as at Newcastle-upon-Tyne (1). In recent years our towns have been threatened by a new menace to the church's visual pre-eminence: the high-rise building in close proximity to it. The pullulation of privately financed high buildings erected in no coherent relationship to each other, let alone to older buildings of major architectural value, has been the greatest visual bane of our time. Until the present century such intruders could be counted on the fingers of one hand, with that 'irredeemable horror', London's Queen Anne Mansions, begun in 1873 and demolished in 1971–72, as the arch-offender. Today even so fine a town as Cheltenham has one of these arrogant intruders. Formerly the buildings which gave a town its characteristic skyline were of public, often civic, significance: the Town Hall, the Library, the Courts of Justice, the University, the Cathedral, the Parish Church. Now, not only in England but all over the world, commercial interests have been allowed to take over; and the visual impact of some of these often fine historic buildings has been gravely weakened. Even where, as at Maidenhead, there are no buildings of distinction, the upper air has been peopled with platitudes.

In our smaller towns the situation is generally happier, as visually the parish church is often of paramount importance. Countless examples could be cited. The North Riding has three that are not easily forgotten. Northallerton's big cruciform church, with its striking central tower, presides over the wide High Street to great effect. At Thirsk broad Kirkgate, with its Georgian brick houses, curves gently round to reveal, bestraddling its northern end, a sandstone Perpendicular church of exuberant character, which is an abiding delight. At Bedale only the tower is much in view, but this dominates the market place, again from

Axbridge, Somerset, Church and Market Place in 1756

the north. At Olney in Buckinghamshire, on the other hand, it is from the
north that the approach should be made. Again a stone church, but this
time with a prominent spire, provides a stately climax to a broad, mildly
curving street; move round to the other side, and you are already in the
country, facing the water-meadows of the meandering Ouse, with
scarcely a building in sight. At Hemel Hempstead the association is more
subtle, because the High Street climbs a hill, and the fine church, despite
drastic restoration, is interestingly sited on a slope somewhat below the
street, with trees and meadows on a still lower level. Thus the spectator,
standing in the High Street poised above the churchyard, has almost the
sensation of being able to clasp within his arms the central tower with its
lofty, slender, lead-covered spire. It is a delightfully intimate relationship.
At Ilminster in Somerset the view of the church from the north-east is
somewhat comparable, but the sumptuous central tower is altogether too
much of an aristocrat to countenance the liberty of an arm-clasp.

In the villages, the rôle of the parish church is visually still more
important. Even in the Anglo-Saxon period the churches were always
relatively lofty, a sure indication that they were intended to be seen above
the roofs of the surrounding dwellings. As the village developed, so did
the church, to become more often than not the focal point of the whole
community, as at Axbridge in Somerset (see above), where, although
the houses are no longer as in 1756, the church still presides. So it does at
Audlem in Cheshire. And if one can no longer be sure that the village will
look to its church as the social and religious centrepiece, the importance
of this building aesthetically remains vital (*3*, *4*). Many English villages

derive most of their character, and even their identity, from their church. How important, therefore, that it should be worthily maintained.

Anyone familiar with the Canadian prairies will know that at settlement after settlement the loftiest and therefore most prominent building is a grain elevator. In other countries villages may be dominated by enormous water storage tanks raised aloft on cradles of concrete lattice-work: poor substitutes indeed for the towers and spires which so often adorn the landscapes of England (*7, 8*). Some consideration will be given to the design of these very important features of our churches in Chapter 4. Their profusion in some parts of the country, notably the East Midlands, explains that odd word 'steeplechase'. This is said to owe its origin to the fact that in the course of an afternoon's riding there was always a steeple in sight to serve as a goal, towards which all intervening obstacles had to be cleared.

Some of the loveliest churches are the loneliest. All over England one finds them, often beautifully sited, with no habitation in sight, and many more with only a single house, although often a big one, for company. These are among the least spoiled of our churches, but as many of them no longer perform any useful function they are also specially vulnerable – and, inevitably they are nowadays all too often locked.

There is Great Walsingham in Norfolk. It stands in isolation and one feels that time has passed it by, to its infinite advantage artistically, despite the fact that in the course of the centuries the chancel has fallen and all but gone. As it is entirely free from Victorian glass, the light floods in through its large windows with their exquisite Decorated tracery, to cast into bright relief the marvellous oak benches with their traceried backs and richly carved ends. The whole place is a delight; but its value to the Church of England is less immediately apparent. Take, again, Little Washbourne, hidden in a Gloucestershire orchard; it would not be difficult to believe that people living only two or three miles away are unaware of its existence, for this church is small and secret. The structure is largely Norman; pretty well everything else here, and especially the woodwork – pulpit with tester, reading desk, box-pews, all in brown oak dusted with silver – is Georgian. The pews are anything but comfortable; the floor today is green from damp and the only lighting is with candles; the church, one suspects, is virtually unused. Yet it is a precious survival which must on no account be allowed to go. So who is to pay for its preservation? Another Gloucestershire treasure, but in this instance with a hamlet not very far away, is Duntisbourne Rouse (*5*). The little church stands on the brim of a valley; the site is so steep that it was possible to put a tiny crypt, empty and disused now, under the chancel, with its own east window. The approach is from above by a straight grass path sloping gently down. The church, by the happiest of chances, is not end-on to the path but at a slight angle to it. The beautiful little saddle-backed tower has a top stage which is Elizabethan. There is not really much to see inside; everything here is diminutive, except one's pleasure. Croxby was once much bigger. Today it stands, precious fragment, with no tower, hidden in a small fold in the centre of the Lincolnshire Wolds, with only the rather opulent-looking Georgian Hall across the road. Although so small, this is internally a solemn building, strangely impressive on account of its Norman chancel arch, massive in its simplicity. Idsworth in Hampshire in the summer months is anchored now in a sea of barley. Once it stood beside a manor house, but the construction about 1850 of the Guildford to Portsmouth railway was too much for the squire, who built a new house for himself on a hill more than a mile away; the old one, with its park, has completely vanished. Nevertheless the little church, beautifully restored in 1912 by H. S. Goodhart-Rendel (then only 25), still flourishes. Sussex has several enchanting miniatures of this kind: in particular Up Marden and Warminghurst, both of the thirteenth century. As a final example I choose Navestock in Essex, the interior of which is entirely delightful and quite unspoiled. The structure is of various dates from the twelfth century onwards, but one does not visit this church for architectural interest. One goes for the atmosphere. Except for a new pulpit in yellow oak, there is not a jarring note inside. The floors are of red unglazed tiles with good stone ledgers inserted here and there. One of the piers is of oak, but since almost the whole interior is whitewashed, this is not immediately apparent. Happily there is no stained glass; but as there are trees to east and north, and no west window because at this end there is a timber-framed tower with oak posts believed to go back more than seven hundred years, the church, though light, is not excessively so. There is a good collection of wall tablets, some most seemly and with touching inscriptions, and one leaves with the feeling of having made acquaintance with a most lovable building.

The settings of these remote and usually little-visited churches fall into a number of groups. The most exciting, no doubt, are the hilltop sites. These range from the merest hillock that nevertheless commands a wide view, as at Pyrford in Surrey, or indeed at Warminghurst, whose churchyard has a grandstand view of Chanctonbury Ring, and the gentle hill with the church at the top, as at Rettendon in Essex or Barking in Suffolk, to abrupt isolated hills like Glastonbury Tor and St Michael's Mount, neither of which has, or ever had, a church that was parochial, or St Martha on the Hill in Surrey, which is the parish church of Chilworth, but a Victorian rebuilding. A memorable hill-top church is Breedon-on-the-Hill in Leicestershire, placed inconveniently high above the village because in Saxon times its site was occupied by a monastery that had been erected within an Iron-Age camp. Saintbury in Gloucestershire is not on the ridge of the Cotswolds, but high enough to command a tremendous panorama stretching to Bredon Hill (as distinct from Breedon-on-the-Hill) and the Malverns, some twenty-five miles away. Here again is a remote church high above the village with only a footpath to the churchyard gate. On my last visit I noticed that Matins were said once a month; Evensong monthly in summer only; Communion fortnightly.

Different from any of these are Walesby and Whiston. All Saints, Walesby, is situated on an isolated spur of the Wolds of Lincolnshire, utterly remote from the village. There used to be a tarred road leading up to it, but this is no more. Today one climbs on foot by a track that is muddy after rain. From the summit on a good day Lincoln Cathedral can be clearly seen, eighteen miles away. The church, though not of any special merit architecturally, is internally spacious and unexpectedly impressive, with some nice woodwork. It is only used sporadically in summer. Whiston, in Northamptonshire, provides a memorable experience. This church stands alone on a hill-top to which, again, the only access is by field-paths. Yet it is, or was until recently, still used every Sunday, in summer at least. It was all built in the reign of Henry VIII, a spacious hall-church with a wonderful unity of design, marred only by the insertion of unworthy glass in the east window in 1858. An exterior redolent of Tudor lavishness is the prelude to a fine interior which is full of interest, and satisfying even down to such details as its dignified, limestone-paved floor and its pretty little Art Nouveau candlesticks attached to the handsome Tudor benches. Yet who visits Whiston or Walesby? Who even knows of their existence?

Churches which stand alone in the fields are less conspicuous, but may be equally inaccessible. I am thinking especially of St Ninian, the old parish church of Brougham, on the northern fringe of Westmorland. This building can be reached only by a rough track over three miles long, with five gates to open and close on the way. It was rebuilt at the close of the Cromwellian interlude. It is a long, low structure of red sandstone, with a good roof of Westmorland slate, but only a bell-cote. The windows, segmental-headed, have no tracery. The interior is simple but well-maintained, with its whitewashed walls, attractive red sandstone floor inlaid with big ledgers, a roof of gentle arch-braced form, with a king-post and collar, and plain oak furniture of excellent quality. Happily, except for one insignificant Victorian window, there is no stained glass. This unspoilt Commonwealth church is (or was until lately) used twice a month for evensong at 2 p.m., and for Holy Communion on the fifth Sunday of the month when there is one! And what would the congregation be? Two, one, or none?

Other churches standing isolated in fields include Upton in the Soke of Peterborough, another example of seventeenth-century Gothic, with

handsome stonework: Ford, Sussex, a flint church with a brick porch in
the Dutch style and a tiny weather-boarded belfry, set within a now much
depleted circle of trees, with no road of access: Stoke Charity in
Hampshire, another flint church with a pretty shingled spirelet, notable
inside for its monuments: Tarrant Crawford in Dorset, virtually
inaccessible after heavy rain because of the mud: Low Ham in Somerset,
yet another seventeenth-century church quite untouched by the
Renaissance although it was virtually rebuilt as late as 1668 and Ampney
St Mary in Gloucestershire, which has two noble cedars in its field for
company. At Brushford in Devon, another of these remote little field
churches with a service once a month, the vicar (of Wembworthy,
Eggesford and Brushford) used in summer to be seen before service-time,
mowing the grass path leading to the door.

Not far from Brushford is deliciously named Honeychurch, with seats
for no more than 33 people. This minute building has no special features,
but with its oil lamps and candles, the only lighting, it is full of
atmosphere.

Others among these isolated, remote churches seem all the more
sequestered by hiding among trees. Such a one is Shocklach in the south-
western corner of Cheshire, a little towerless red sandstone building a
mile from its village in the centre of a veritable oasis. Broomfield in
Somerset, secluded among trees, is equally out of the way. Courteenhall in
Northamptonshire is another example of a church which is both off the
beaten track and so engulfed in trees that, although almost within earshot
of the M1, a good map is needed in order to find it. Some later churches
were deliberately erected in the midst of the woods, like that strange
Gothick church of 1822 at Parkend in the Forest of Dean, which
contrives to be both cruciform and octagonal.

Elsewhere trees may provide a noble 'backcloth' for a church, as at
Northorpe in Lincolnshire, which inside and out is all that a village
church should be (apart from the organ, an obtrusive lump). The site, on a
slight eminence with big trees immediately behind, is pictorially perfect.
Among many other churches memorable for their relationship with trees,
Nynehead and Stocklinch Ottersey in Somerset (6), North Cerney in
Gloucestershire, Farleigh in Surrey and Navestock in Essex are but a few.

In the eighteenth century, the great age of English landscape
gardening, a church might be erected to serve as one of the 'ornaments' in
a private park. Usually the landowner started by demolishing the existing
church, even when, as at Well in Lincolnshire, at Nuneham Courtenay in
Oxfordshire and at Ayot St Lawrence in Hertfordshire, it was in perfectly
good repair. At Ayot it is said that when the Bishop came to hear of this
he was most indignant and forbade the work of demolition to proceed,
which is why the ruin of the old parish church still stands in the centre of

the village. Fortunately for the owner, though not for the villagers, the work of demolition had already proceeded far enough before the Bishop's intervention to have turned the old church into a 'picturesque object' in accordance with sophisticated eighteenth-century taste.

At West Wycombe in Buckinghamshire the chancel and part of the tower of the medieval church on a hill-top in full view from the Georgian house were retained, but the nave was turned into a spacious Corinthian hall and the tower was heightened and given the golden ball, large enough to contain several seats, which is still a fascinating object in the view. Nikolaus Pevsner aptly quoted Charles Churchill (who was a self-unfrocked priest):

> *A temple built aloft in air*
> *That serves for show and not for prayer.*

At West Wycombe the identity of the architect is unknown, but elsewhere the services of leading practitioners would occasionally be enlisted. At Well it has been suggested[5] that it was Henry Flitcroft who was responsible in 1733 for the little brick church on the hill, aligned exactly to the front door of Well Vale; this is not, however, an original building, for it derives very obviously from Inigo Jones's St Paul, Covent Garden, built exactly a century earlier. No matter; against a background of fine trees with the lake far below, this building, with its Tuscan Doric portico of white limestone, makes a delightful eye-catcher, especially since the restoration in 1970 of the original wooden cupola improperly removed in the Victorian period. The Georgian interior, too, is unspoiled.

At Nuneham Courtenay the architect was James Stuart, working from a design given to him by the owner of the estate, the first Earl of Harcourt. Here Capability Brown was landscaping the park in a masterly fashion; what the Earl wanted was a large and stately portico to provide a 'feature'. He certainly got it; Stuart designed a lofty hexastyle Greek Ionic portico which is said to be the earliest of its kind in England. It does not lead into the church, which has a quite independent existence behind the wall against which the portico abuts. The presence of the church is, however, indicated by the dome that is lifted above a lofty circular drum. The date is 1764. F. G. Brabant, writing his *Little Guide* to Oxfordshire in 1906, thought this church 'only remarkable as an illustration of the depraved taste of the eighteenth-century', adding with evident relief that it 'is no longer used'!

At Ayot St Lawrence the church was designed by Stuart's collaborator in *The Antiquities of Athens*, Nicholas Revett. Although not built until 1778-79, the conception is still Palladian, not Grecian, for the main building is linked by open screens with aedicules, which recall the side pavilions of many a Palladian country house. The style, however, is impeccably neo-Greek, the front of the church being a direct copy of the Temple of Apollo at Delos. It must once have been one of the finest eye-catchers in the country. Today, although Ayot House survives, trees have intervened to prevent the church from being any longer visible from its windows. Moreover the church itself, in a part of England where stone is scarce, was built only of brick, the parts facing the house being cement-rendered; and inevitably this is now in a state of decay.

By comparison the small church which Adam designed in 1769 at Gunton was much more modest: structurally little more than a box built of 'white' brick (actually pale buff, with some grey lichen) with a handsome tetrastyle Tuscan Doric portico facing towards the house, for this too was an eye-catcher. Norfolk is another part of England very short of stone (apart from flint), so the columns and west face of the church, looking towards the house, were cement-rendered to give the right illusion. A Victorian owner planted a conifer, now very large, so that the church, so shockingly pagan-looking, is today almost concealed from the mansion, which in 1882 was mostly burnt, and never rebuilt. The church's interior is charming, and very well maintained. Even the handsome Morocco-bound bibles and prayer-books of the Harbords (Lords Suffield), who built the church and the house, still adorn their stalls at the west end.

All these four churches are, as was to be expected, in the classical style, but mention must be made of at least one fine specimen in the Gothick taste: Croome d'Abitot in Worcestershire(R). Here the new house, the park and the church were all due to the sixth Earl of Coventry, the first patron and later friend of Capability Brown. Perhaps with assistance from the amateur architect Sanderson Miller, who was himself responsible for another exactly contemporary and rather similar house, Hagley Hall, in the same county, Brown appears to have designed both the house and the church at Croome, as well as undertaking the landscaping. But for the interior of both house and church Lord Coventry employed Robert Adam. The church, which is sited on a low hill, was at first intended to be classical, but after the old church had been taken down, for some reason the plans were changed. At the west end is a beautifully executed pastiche of a Somerset tower (*10*). The whole church benefits greatly from being built of the best yellow-buff Cotswold ashlar.

England has many hundreds of old churches that stand remote from any habitation except 'a great house'. To reach some of them one may have to go through the garden of the house; if the building is a parish church, as is usual, there is always a right of way. Here and there, as at Great Badminton and at Dodington in Gloucestershire, the medieval church was completely rebuilt and the new one was linked physically to the mansion. (At Badminton the new church, by one Charles Evans, dates from 1785; at Dodington the architect was James Wyatt, shortly after 1800.) Usually, however, the medieval church remained, even if, as at Chastleton in Oxfordshire (9), it found itself duly 'put in its place' by the mansion. In the eighteenth century it was not uncommon for an imperious landowner to insist on removing the entire village from the proximity of his own house; whatever the villagers may have felt about this high-handed treatment, it is undeniable that they usually found themselves much better housed as a result of it, even though they had further to go to church.

Frequently known as estate churches, this big group embraces many of the most endearing buildings in England. I select, as an example, St Mary, Nether Alderley, Cheshire, a charming sandstone building dating mainly from the fifteenth century. The Elizabethan Old Hall still stands beside the contemporary water-mill a little way to the east, but the mansion, former seat of the Stanleys of Alderley, is no more. None the less, the presence of this family, baronets from 1660, barons from 1839, is pervasive as soon as we enter the church. Perched aloft at the south-east end of the nave is their family pew (11), which the pulpit directly faces. It was a two-storeyed Jacobean addition to the church, and has heraldry along the parapet. Behind it is a room with a coved ceiling and plasterwork. It has its own entrance, and is inaccessible from the church. There are Stanley monuments, not specially notable, a bad east window of 1856 commemorating the first peer, a Stanley Mausoleum of 1909 in the churchyard, and next to it the very picturesque Old School, partly seventeenth-century and partly 1817, paid for, no doubt, by the Stanleys. The entire set-up is intensely patriarchal and has no connection with the present time, but as a piece of 'visual history' it is a precious survival.

The immense self-esteem of these eighteenth-century landowners, as reflected in the design and furnishing of their estate churches, is a source of constant entertainment. At Avington in Hampshire, built in 1768–71, the family pew occupies fully one-sixth of the total seating area of the church. At Stapleford in Leicestershire, erected a dozen years later, the spacious interior is like a large hall, with an attractive ribbed plaster ceiling, no coloured glass and three tiers of seats facing each other as in a college chapel. This still unspoiled Gothick church, in Weldon limestone, was all paid for by the Earl of Harborough, in whose park it stood. He surveyed the scene, and no doubt his employees, from the west gallery, which has a fireplace in Coade stone and over it the royal arms in plaster.

A characteristic of many estate churches is the profusion of family monuments. However interesting they may be genealogically, however enjoyable the inscriptions, these are by no means always of great value as works of art. Although often too large for the buildings which house them, the monuments of the late seventeenth century and the first half of the eighteenth are in my experience those most likely to provide real aesthetic pleasure. Jacobean monuments may be equally large but are seldom inspired and sometimes positively inept.

The most remarkable collection of monuments in an English estate church is at Exton in Rutland. The church was struck by lightning in 1843 and largely rebuilt in 1850 on a most lavish scale. It is now therefore essentially a Victorian church, but spacious, lofty and of unusual distinction. The nine important monuments range over nearly four centuries, beginning about 1390, and here, for once, it is not the Georgian monuments which are the best. The most beautiful commemorates Lady Bruce of Kinlosse, who died in childbirth in 1627 at the age of twenty-two. This is of black and white marble and not at all Jacobean in character: a work of exquisite refinement and sensitive feeling.[6] And next in merit to this, surprisingly enough, are two late-Elizabethan monuments of outstanding quality. Exton offers a rare experience for the amateur of English monumental sculpture.

Where for centuries the same family had – and occasionally still has – the big house, the monuments serve to commemorate its achievements, however slender, through many generations. There are, for example, the Knightley monuments at Fawsley in Northamptonshire, 13 of them, ranging from 1516 to 1913. It is a sad comment on taste that the latest is without question artistically the worst. The village which once adjoined this building was removed and today it stands alone upon a knoll above the lake; the Hall is now the property of a timber company and in a very sorry state; yet the church is well maintained. Steane Chapel, in the same county, is the parish church of Steane. It has (or had when I visited it) services only four times a year in summer, to which virtually no one comes, but it is a great ornament to the garden of Steane Park. This little Caroline building has the tombs of the Crewes, of whom the first (*ob.* 1633) was Speaker of the House of Commons. For continuity it is the Curzons who hold the record. The church at Kedleston, where again in the eighteenth century the village was swept away, contains memorials to members of this family stretching from 1275 until 1977, and there may be others to come. In Sussex the Ashburnhams are no more, and their house nearly so, but the family is still commemorated by two big seventeenth-century monuments in Ashburnham church. Another old Sussex family, the Shurleys, half fill with their memorials the church of Isfield, built among the trees below Isfield Place, close to the point where the tiny muddy Uck flows into the larger but equally murky-looking Ouse. There are the Bagots at Blithfield in Staffordshire, where some of the tombs carry engraved portraits; the Cottons at Landwade in Cambridgeshire, where the old Hall, built for Sir Walter Cotton about 1445, unfortunately gave place to another, much less attractive, in 1847; the Poleys at Boxted in Suffolk. Best of all, perhaps, are the St Johns at Lydiard Tregoze. The old church is no architectural masterpiece, but exceptionally rich in atmosphere, mainly deriving from its wealth of interesting furnishings and the numerous monuments of the proud St Johns. These even include a Caroline east window with the St John family tree instead of the Tree of Jesse, and a winged and painted triptych with another elaborate family pedigree. Their house now belongs to the town of Swindon.

None of these churches is visibly connected with any village; yet parish churches they all are. The same is true of many more, some, like Tawstock in Devon (8), very beautiful in their situation. This most untypical Devon village church stands on a lush hillside running down to the Taw, with the big house, Tawstock Court, now a school, a couple of hundred yards above. (Still finer are the sites of Staunton Harold in Leicestershire and Clumber in Nottinghamshire, but neither is a parish church. Each is – or was, for at Clumber the mansion was demolished in 1937 – the private chapel of a great house, and now owned and cared for by the National Trust.) Among other medieval churches of this type specially worth mentioning are Dalham and Brent Eleigh in Suffolk: Hatch Beauchamp and Brympton d'Evercy in Somerset – the latter of no special note in itself, but an unforgettable sight when seen, as it must be, in relation to the wonderful golden-brown house and the so-called Chantry House adjacent: Sandon in Staffordshire, which, though a long way from the house, still has very much the air of being the private church of the Earls of Harrowby, and Burton in Sussex, so plain and unprepossessing without but so sensitive and unspoiled within. In the later, classical manner are two churches built in the same year, 1676: Euston in Suffolk, with beautiful woodcarving in the Grinling Gibbons style, and Ingestre in Staffordshire, the most distinguished country church in England of the late Stuart period. Finally, two more very notable examples from the Georgian period, on which no expense was spared. Gayhurst in Buckinghamshire was begun in 1728; the limestone is ashlared throughout, with rusticated plinths and quoins, and Ionic pilasters on the south face of the nave. The light interior, with elaborate plaster ceilings and handsome woodwork, contains a magnificent monument to the builder of the church (another Speaker of the House of Commons) and his son.[7] Great Packington in Warwickshire stands four-square against the winds in the middle of a very large exposed park, and at some distance from the mansion. And square indeed it is, with a short, clumsy tower at each corner. The Earl of Aylesford employed as his architect Joseph Bonomi, who although an Italian was in that year, 1789, elected an A.R.A. He designed a church that is totally unlike any other in England. The material is a rather harsh red brick, with red sandstone dressings which neither match the brickwork nor provide a contrast. The exterior is frankly ugly. But the interior, which is of buff colour-washed sandstone ashlar throughout, is magnificently monumental. The plan is a Greek cross with the corners filled in. There are groined and lightly coffered tunnel vaults, and all the windows are in the form of lunettes. The building is a geometrical exercise of the most intellectual kind. The parish numbers fewer than 200 people,[8] but this church is well cared for. It is very remarkable, but perhaps one has to be a student of architecture to like it.

In their setting, these estate churches (and there are many others which it has not been possible even to mention) are among the most fortunate of any. Even where the great house has completely vanished, leaving the church in utter isolation, the scene may be very beautiful. Yet one cannot but feel apprehensive about the future of these buildings. What is to happen to them? Here and there, as at Great Packington, one finds an estate church still used for the purposes for which it was built, and when the great house has become a school or been taken over by some other institution requiring its own chapel, all will probably be well.

But the vulnerability of an unused church is obvious: to damp and decay, to dirt, and above all in these days, alas, to vandals. Adequately to protect all these pastorally unwanted churches, more particularly when the great house stands empty or has been demolished, is an impossibility. And a building which is kept perpetually locked, with no near-by cottage from which to obtain the key, loses much of its attraction for the amateur of churches. All that can be said at present is that the setting up of the Redundant Churches Fund has given new hope.

With many estate churches the churchyard presents a problem. The fortunate ones – Stowell in Gloucestershire is a good example – have no graves at all to encumber their green swards. In this respect town and village churches are in a very different situation.

Some use was made of both headstones and footstones in medieval graveyards, but the stones were small (2 to 3 feet high) and, although sometimes carved, they do not carry inscriptions. Two, with simple, incised crosses, can be seen in the churchyard at Grantham. Very few have survived; after the end of the fourteenth century they fell into disuse. If you were 'somebody' you were interred inside the church, perhaps in a special family chapel (this applied in the later Stuart and Georgian periods too); if you were not, the most you could normally expect to have to mark your grave would be a piece of wood, and usually in this period graves were not marked at all. Exceptions were chest-tombs. Burgess[9] noted at least 40 chest-tombs of pre-Reformation date. Otherwise, the only memorial was a communal one, the churchyard cross, erected as an

Newcastle-upon-Tyne in 1862
Brant Broughton, Lincolnshire

VILLAGE CHURCHES

3. Steeple Ashton, Wiltshire

4. Ecclesfield, Yorkshire

Duntisbourne Rouse,
Gloucestershire

Stocklinch Ottersey, Somerset

7. Great Ponton, Lincolnshir[e]

8. Tawstock, Devon

indicator of consecrated ground. A great many of these crosses survive, although generally much decayed. Some must once have been very handsome.

After the Reformation, the churchyard memorial in stone slowly reappeared, with the large chest-tomb as the favourite form for those who could afford it. The greatest concentration of these is in Gloucestershire; among the earliest is a big plain one dated 1653 at Standish, near Stroud. This is the tomb of a 'yeaman, Samuell Beard'; we are informed in bold lettering, still perfectly legible on the grey Cotswold limestone, that he is 'waighting for a joyfull rezurrection'. Although the heavy chest-tombs are at all sorts of angles, and it is sad to think that unless something is done soon some will certainly collapse, Standish has one of the most interesting churchyards in England. Several others besides Samuel Beard's are unusually early, including a simple yeoman's stone dated 1674 and another with two figures in full-bottomed wigs holding hands, with the date 1680. There are also some splendid eighteenth-century chest-tombs.[10]

Up on the hills not many miles away is Painswick, with a vast churchyard containing 99 carefully clipped yews, mostly planted in 1792 (*13*). At the entrance is this dignified notice:

The TOMBS in this Churchyard are of EXCEPTIONAL VALUE. They
were the work of the Forefathers of many still living here, and are
a proud Trust for the People and Children of Painswick.
It is particularly requested that VISITORS will respect them.

It is to be hoped that the implication that inhabitants of Painswick will certainly do so is justified, for this is the grandest churchyard in England: far more memorable indeed than the church itself. A number of factors combined to account for this. Painswick was a flourishing place, not only on account of wool but also, and still more, because of its famous quarries, which several centuries before had supplied much of the stone for Gloucester Cathedral. The middle-class people commemorated in this churchyard were evidently prosperous, and of course they had the stone on the spot; that was vital. There was also a gifted local family of masons and carvers, the Bryans, who worked not only in the graveyard but in the church too, and elsewhere in the vicinity. Lastly, and perhaps most important of all, it should be noted that, although delightfully varied in form, all or almost all these Painswick tombs are Georgian.

The Georgian was the great age, artistically one could almost say the only age, of the English churchyard. Wherever we encounter Georgian tombstones we can be sure of good (even if semi-standardized) design, finely lettered inscriptions and, what is at least equally important, the employment of English stone: of the local stone where, as at Painswick, it was readily available, or of a congenial and reasonably accessible limestone or sandstone if, as at Whittlesey in Cambridgeshire (*37*) or Upwell in Norfolk Marshland, local stone is non-existent. All over the country Georgian churchyards give pleasure.

> *Notice the lettering of that age*
> *Spaced like a noble title-page.*
> *The parish names cut deep and strong*
> *To hold the shades of evening long, ...*
> *And cherubs in the corner spaces,*
> *With wings and English ploughboy faces,*

as Betjeman so charmingly apostrophised 'headstones of the Georgian kind'.[11] The Cotswolds are a specially notable area, but by no means the only one. The Marshland at the head of the Wash has many beautiful grey headstones, not only at Upwell, just mentioned, but over the border in Lincolnshire too, at churches such as Holbeach, Lutton and in particular Long Sutton. Few graveyards contain a higher proportion of really beautiful headstones, but the upkeep of a churchyard as large as this one, for any but a very affluent community, is an almost impossible task, unless it is taken over by the town as a charge on the rates, as – with stringent conditions – it should be. Here and there this has already happened, especially in towns; a country example is Lenham in Kent, where a large churchyard full of handsome Georgian tombstones is admirably maintained by the local council. Among many other well-kept graveyards with memorials which give great pleasure are Hurstbourne Priors in Hampshire and Tonge, also in Kent. The latter has a lovely one, dated 1743, with an accomplished carving of a cherub extinguishing the torch of life, a very characteristic subject.

So far, then, so good; but even when all the gravestones are Georgian and all the material English, it is permissible to feel that, in relation to the church, the scale is none too happy. The large, flat-topped or sometimes crowned with a rounded bale, chest-tombs of the eighteenth century are unquestionably the best, as a foreground to a church; but they are also in a small minority. A large churchyard stuffed with small headstones and, still worse, crosses and other more fancy shapes, is tiresomely fiddling as a setting; the small stone objects are like gnats swarming round some noble animal. When the colours and the textures are also wrong, the visual effect is disastrous.

And that, after about the middle of the nineteenth century, is exactly what happened. One of the earliest examples can be seen at Northleach. In addition to a great many dignified Georgian tombs, both chests and headstones, in Cotswold limestone, there is, close to the east end of the church and therefore, since the churchyard is normally entered from this direction, very prominently placed, a single gravestone in white marble commemorating the widow of a former incumbent. As she died in 1854, this is an unusually early example of the appearance in this country of monumental marble imported from Italy, a change which boded ill for the English scene. At Northleach this single stone was a sore thumb, and more recently there have been a few others (*12*); the visual harm which they do is quite disproportionate to their size.

Fine Italian marbles had of course been finding their way into England for centuries, and were much in demand during the Georgian age for chimneypieces as well as for internal church memorials. But with the advent of the steamships and the railways it was not long before what had been little more than a steady trickle became a flood, abetted by various social changes which were taking place at the same time. Victorian piety decreed that everyone, however humble, should be commemorated by a stone, even when the family could ill afford it. So the supply of gravestones became a commercial enterprise, and a highly profitable one at that. Memorials were ordered from catalogues or selected from the local undertakers' stock by people ignorant of sculpture and totally uneducated in the arts, with which indeed it would not have occurred to them that they were in any way concerned, in commissioning their tributes to the 'dear departed'. The outcome is the churchyard as it is now to be seen in all parts of the country: an outrage and a disgrace, an insult, as often as not, to a gracious church which has done nothing to deserve such treatment, and which may well have stood for several hundred years unsullied by this rash of nasty little pimples (*34*).

Strong words, these; but the situation demands them. White marble from Italy was followed by polished black marble, polished pink granite, jet-black stove-enamelled headstones, multi-coloured chips (among which the ones dyed green are a particular abomination), reconstituted stone, cast concrete and even cement. The graces of the Georgian churchyard gave place to restless crosses, sometimes wreathed, open books, broken columns, weeping angels, bird-baths and of course a profusion of kerbs. Lettering declined sharply in quality and inscriptions attained a banality which has to be encountered to be believed. One gravestone in the Midlands bears the words 'Cheerio, see you soon'. Platitudes like 'At Rest' were placed in inverted commas,[12] and as a final insult, in the present century these commercial products are often shamelessly signed by the suppliers. (Old headstones, especially those in Swithland slate, sometimes carry the signature of the craftsman who did the engraving, but it is always very discreet.) This was not a charming folk art; it was deliberate vulgarisation by a vested interest, that of many of the firms of monumental masons exploiting the emotions of grief against the common good. Another vested interest used to be that of the Church itself. Every churchyard burial meant a fee for the incumbent and a contribution to the churchyard fund, but these are now virtually in abeyance. Cremation was discouraged (and banned altogether for Roman Catholics until 1964). After an interval of well over 1,000 years, it did start again here in 1885, but acceptance at first was slow.[13]

What, then, is to be done? With regard to the gravestones of the future (since it seems evident that for the present we must still have them), the course is clear: visual education, persuasion and control. In 1952 the Central Council for the Care of Churches (as it was then called[14]) published a handbook, 'The Care of Churchyards', which was full of wise advice and comment.

'The Council recognize with appreciation the efforts which some of our masons have made to break away from these unfortunate methods and to induce customers to buy the right thing. But the problem is not yet solved. Today the type and quality of gravestones is largely determined not by public taste but by certain conditions of production, especially the organization of the trade in imported gravestones of foreign marble and granite. Monuments more or less finished by foreign labour are imported in large quantities at an attractive price. Never was there a more disastrous system for British labour nor for the beauty of our country. It is fatally easy for our people to spend excessive sums upon unsuitable foreign material finished in a style unrelated to British traditions of memorial art, including the use of leaded lettering, with the result that the quiet beauty of many of our churchyards is gone for ever. Parish councils ought to do all in their power to persuade people to assert their independence, to employ British labour, to use British stone and to maintain British traditions of quietness and dignity in their monuments. Good memorials can be obtained at no greater expense than bad.'

And more to the same effect.[15] But persuasion is not enough. Anyone who has served for years on a Diocesan Advisory Committee will know that every so often someone appears (generally a widow) who is determined to introduce an inappropriate stone, probably because of its greater durability. Such people should be reminded that no one has a *right* to erect a tombstone or other memorial; permission is always necessary. Moreover, a churchyard is a public place, a possession of the whole community, and to add an ugly or undignified memorial is an anti-social act. So it is high time that every diocese sees to it that the incumbent is given only limited discretion with regard to memorials, and offered the protection of reference to the Chancellor by the insistence that anyone who wishes to depart from the designs and materials that are within the incumbent's discretion must first apply for a faculty from the Consistory Court.

Regulations of the kind advocated here, and in some dioceses (but unfortunately only as yet in a minority) already enforced, always arouse the bitter opposition of the monumental masons ('whose ideas of monumental design have done so much to ruin many churchyards', as one of them magnanimously admitted to me). Let these people use up their stocks of screaming white marble and glossy pink granite in those abodes of visual desolation, the cemeteries, and then mend their ways by employing sculptors of real ability to design for them, so that they can offer their clients something worthier, as their Georgian predecessors knew so well how to do.

In the meantime, some parishes in the Cotswolds, and a few elsewhere, which have tombstones of good quality close to the church, have adopted the wise practice of forbidding any new graves to be dug in that area; they are relegated to a remote part of the churchyard, and preferably behind a wall or hedge.

A very suitable material for churchyard memorials, which one would like to see revived, is wood. A few people do now ask for it again. I am not thinking of crosses, which fortunately are liable before long to tilt and rot anyway, but of the old grave-board, or 'bed-head' as it was sometimes familiarly called, which was once quite common in the stone-deprived South-East. This is a long narrow board, preferably of oak or teak, supported on short posts at the head and foot of the grave and slightly angled at the upper edge to allow the name and dates to be cut boldly. Lettering on old boards was usually only painted; often the whole board was painted white and the lettering added in black, but this is not recommended, nor is it appropriate for strong woods like oak or teak. Nowadays it can be cut very successfully and in a good style by machine, much more quickly and economically than hand-chiselled lettering on stone. That they will not endure as long as stone may well be no dis-advantage. A grave-board can sometimes be lifted aside while the grass is mown. And if it decays while there is still personal interest in the grave it can easily be renewed. When that interest passes, the names having been carefully recorded, it can be allowed to perish.

Much more difficult than trying to ensure that churchyard memorials will be better in the future is the problem of how to deal with the countless thousands, probably millions, of bad ones already in existence. This is an emotive subject on which responsible people hold widely differing views. There are some who sincerely believe that churchyards should continue to be used for memorials because that is their *raison d'être*, and that if the memorials are eyesores that cannot be helped, because they are not there to provide a good setting for the church. The monuments furnish a record of what ordinary people have felt about the inevitable human experiences of death and bereavement. And since every generation has expressed its feelings differently, the gravestones are documents (I have even seen them called fascinating documents) of changing taste and sentiment in a great context. Some go so far as to say that the memorials of the dead are sacred, and that to remove them is a sacrilege.

Such opinions should be treated with respect, but they invite a number of replies. In the first place, they would seem to take no cognizance of the church itself. If it is an old building, it stood for centuries without the gravestones which surround it today. Indeed, the medieval churchyard was used for multifarious purposes, including dancing, singing and games. There is no historical authority for crowding the churchyard with a motley collection of small inscribed stones. If people want headstones that ignore visually the presence of the church, the proper place for them is the cemetery.

To plead for the preservation of all these gravestones seems also to be ignoring the realities of our present situation. Many of them are now left mouldering and uncared for, and are only 'documents of changing taste and sentiment' in that unedifying respect. In so far as the large majority had any interest at all, it was and is purely genealogical. Most parishes just do not have the resources to maintain big churchyards full of what are often artistically insignificant memorials in various stages of neglect and decay. And why should they? The legal responsibility for maintenance rests with the relatives, not with the parish. In practice, therefore, fairly wholesale clearances are inevitable.

For the well-being of an ancient church it is specially important to remove burial mounds, which trap water and render impossible the use of a mower or even a scythe. They, like the grave-boards, were once a speciality of south-eastern England, and particularly Kent. Kerbs, too, are in every way undesirable. Where they do not enclose coloured chips (and some English churchyards fall not far short of offering 'chips with everyone'), they are likely to provide an edging for areas of undignified crazy paving, probably punctuated by weeds. They are also serious obstacles to mowing.

But, it may be asked, why should one mow? Is not a 'tidy' churchyard rather a surburban idea? It can be. It depends very much on how the work is done; and in the heart of the country mowing may not be called for at all. I recall a visit to Hales in Norfolk when in the churchyard they were hay-making, which was delightful; at Gateley, equally remote, the church seemed, as we approached, to be floating on a lake of cow parsley. At Whiston, to which reference was made earlier, the churchyard was so unkempt as to be rather romantic. Ivy covered parts of most of the

Chastleton, Oxfordshire

. Croome d'Abitot,
'orcestershire

ESTATE CHURCHES

11. Nether Alderley, Cheshire

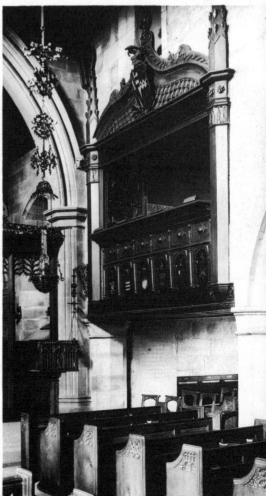

12. Northleach, Gloucestershire

13. Painswick, Gloucestershire

gravestones, and since they are of small account sculpturally this need be no cause for regret. Furthermore, with so much natural life now being endangered by herbicides and insecticides, it will often be very desirable that some parts of country churchyards should, where possible, be left to nature. In other country places the cropping of the churchyard grass is left to sheep: although they require temporarily to be wired or penned in, this practice in the right place, as at Ivychurch in that great sheep-raising area, Romney Marsh, is attractive.[16]

Elsewhere, however, and especially in towns, mowing must be the right answer. Where stones are removed the particulars must be carefully recorded; every parish should keep a stout book for this purpose. As the Council for the Care of Churches has pointed out, the parish registers have proven a far more efficient and lasting memorial of the dead than any churchyard stone. Within limits closely similar to those advocated here, the Council has been a supporter of removal: where, that is to say, the stones 'form no part of the amenity of the churchyard' and are 'very likely a disfigurement'.

It would be wrong to try to lay down any hard and fast rules; every churchyard has, or should have, its own individual personality and should be considered in this light. But, broadly speaking, to remove all stones alien to the English scene (at least from the churchyards of good churches) would seem to me a welcome first step; they should never have been put there in the first place, and may be regarded as unmannerly intruders. If likely to be of any interest, they should not only be recorded but photographed. It must be accepted that this will have to be a gradual process, since regard will need to be paid to the feelings of relatives of those commemorated even by artistically deplorable memorials. Monuments executed in a stone congenial to the locality require longer consideration. Obviously not a single Georgian chest nor bale tomb should be touched unless it is in a state of irremediable decay. Headstones should also be preserved wherever they have any artistic merit, although it may be necessary to move some of them to other positions, for stones if excessively scattered look puny. This has already been done extensively in recent years in some churchyards. The best way, in my view is to place them in groups, which in practice usually means in short orderly lines, as for instance at Finedon in Northamptonshire, where an immense churchyard has become a great embellishment to a large and handsome church. This conveys a sense of pleasing order as well as facilitating mowing (which is a very important consideration). At Finedon, where there must be at least an acre to mow, all the work used to be done – I don't know whether it still is – voluntarily by one devoted parishioner, who told me that it took him about five hours to get round. It is to be observed that those who are opposed to the removal of stones, however disfiguring, are never those who undertake the mowing, just as those who, despite pleas not to do so, persist in throwing confetti at weddings are never those who have to sweep it up, sometimes sodden with rain.[17] I have heard it argued, as a reason for not moving headstones, that if this is done the words 'Here lies' are no longer true. This is undeniable; we must learn to accept the fact that nowadays 'Here lies' may sometimes mean 'Over there lies'.

But even in the local stone a great many gravestones have very little merit. Generally, after having been recorded, they will be better removed, especially in towns – unless, that is, they are as small as the one at St Mary Redcliffe, Bristol, for THE CHURCH CAT (1912–1927). They should not be used to form a boundary wall, but the flat-topped ones are often excellent for church paths. Where headstones are sufficiently heavy it is sometimes a good plan to lay them horizontally on the ground. In parts of the North this has long been a traditional practice. Elsewhere it needs to be carried out with circumspection; but at one church in eastern England which now has a specially attractive graveyard, the rector told me that some while ago he had instructed his sexton to lay one stone flush with the grass each week, until told to stop. It has been a great success.

It is an odd fact that people who are affronted by the idea of an old church standing on a mown lawn will have nothing but praise for the Close at Salisbury, which is arguably the finest lawn in England. This we owe to James Wyatt, enthusiastically supported by the Bishop of the day. Because there were no drains to carry away the water from the roofs, the precinct, after a rainstorm, could become a swamp. Wyatt remedied this by constructing a large drain; at the same time he raised and levelled the whole churchyard and cleared away all the gravestones. The enhancement to the dignity of the great cathedral must have been immense, even though the work was undertaken some forty years before the invention of the mower. When Wyatt had finished, the effect must have been rather as can now be seen, on a much smaller scale, at Redbourn in Hertfordshire. Here the church, very pretty from the south-east, stands in an enormous churchyard which, though not mown, has miraculously remained entirely free from gravestones on the south, which is the conspicuous, side. Commenting upon the village's good fortune in this respect, I was told the reason: a stream ran here – a very shallow depression is visible – and in bad weather the soil on this side of the building is still sodden.

Today England can show a number of very gracious examples of parish churches as well as cathedrals surrounded by lawns, sometimes with big trees on the periphery. In Lincolnshire one thinks of Gainsborough and of Old Leake, where distinguished architecture has been given a majestic setting which contrasts very favourably, to say the least, with the nettles and brambles and generally unkempt appearance of a good many of that county's graveyards. The contrast also between Old Leake and the adjacent parish of Leverton, where the churchyard is crammed with recent stones of every shape and colour and of the most distressing vulgarity, is there for all to see. In Norfolk there is Attleborough, where the church now stands proudly in a very large mown churchyard with just the right number of tombstones – which is to say, rather few. It is a great asset to the town, which is equally true of Dedham; and although the tombstones are of small account, another Essex churchyard of great charm is Fryerning. The site was well chosen, with wide views glimpsed through pine trees. The mown lawns are gently undulating, and in this setting it was undoubtedly right to refrain from levelling. So also at Kirkby Stephen in Westmorland, where the church is mainly built of a beautiful grey-pink sandstone. Here the precinct is entered from the Market Place through a pretty screen of 1810; within are six tall limes, a stone-flagged path, a wide expanse of smooth greensward, and only two old gravestones. They are sufficient. The church has been given a most distinguished setting.

It is in towns that the park-like treatment of a churchyard (or, as I prefer to call it when the stones have been cleared away, the precinct) is most obviously the right one; it is there that the stones are most likely to blacken and decay, and there that the churchyard is most needed as a place of rest and amenity. The value of the work undertaken at Rotherham has already been mentioned. In the early seventies it was the turn of another and much larger Yorkshire churchyard: Knaresborough. Here there were over a thousand tombs and headstones, many of them mouldering and derelict, in an area of over five acres. This big expanse of land in the centre of the town was overgrown, vandalised and altogether wasted. It was cleared and replanned under the guidance of a leading landscape architect and with financial assistance from the Department of the Environment. The outcome was wholly beneficial; yet a few otherwise responsible people expressed strong disapproval.

Kettering is another manufacturing town which has greatly improved a large churchyard by laying many of the headstones flat, mowing, and here and there planting bulbs. At Darlington an enlightened attempt has been made to integrate the churchyard with recent building developments. In the South-East there are many beautifully maintained churchyards. At Hailsham, a specially attractive one, is a notice of which one does not question the necessity: 'We take a pride in our churchyard. Please keep your dog on a lead.'

The mention of bulb-planting at Kettering leads on to another highly controversial matter, which is whether a churchyard should also suggest something of the nature of a garden. There are some to whom a red rose in a churchyard is worse than a red rag. My own attitude here would be cautious: it depends on the kind of garden, the type of churchyard, and above all on the character of the church itself, for the building, if it is a worthy one, should always call the tune. Broadly speaking, the grander the building the less likely are flowers to be appropriate. Lawns and big trees usually enhance a church's dignity; flowers are more cosy. At Bamburgh in Northumberland, a big church in a fine mown yard with many tombstones, none in white marble, there are flowers too (lavender and so on), but only under the boundary wall. In general it is in the precincts of small country churches without architectural pretensions that flowers often look best. There are examples in the south of England, often lovingly tended. Affpuddle in Dorset is one. This little building is approached from the east across a garden laid out as a war memorial. In addition to a mown lawn, a few flowers and two fine trees, there is a clear stream to the right and a Georgian rectory to the left. A more attractive setting for this limestone church could hardly be imagined. In this type of churchyard, one likes to see a certain informality in the planting, but anything suggestive of a fruit salad of flowers would always be wrong.

Perhaps it is the county with the most beautiful churchyards of any, Gloucestershire, which also displays churchyard gardening at its best. At Sevenhampton the church stands in a yard so well planted and so beautifully kept that the maintenance, one feels, must be almost a full-time job in itself. Time and skill could hardly be expected to give greater pleasure. At Minchinhampton the lovely churchyard, with some fine Georgian chest-tombs and headstones and not a jarring note anywhere, is evidently the pride of the village, and the outcome of a truly co-operative effort; on a summer afternoon at least eight people were working there, including the rector. As for Bibury, I cannot say more – nor less – than that this is one of the most enchanting churchyards in England. (Painswick is of course more spectacular.) Some of the numerous Georgian tombstones are gorgeously carved and in excellent preservation. There is a wide expanse of grass, all faultlessly mown, and a few standard roses, which look right here. It would postulate a very perverse mentality, or so it seems to me, to go fault-finding at Bibury.

Yet the battle for a responsible use of our churchyards is still very far from having been won. I have an ever-lengthening list of places at which alien stones, glaring white marble in particular, have been allowed to appear *for the first time* within the last few years. It is not so long ago since, in reply to a Question in the House of Commons asking what action he proposed to take to stop the erection of black stove-enamelled headstones and other monuments in marble imported from abroad which threaten the beauty of English churchyards, the responsible Minister replied: 'I would deprecate any attempt to use the powers of the [Town and Country Planning] Act to interfere in a matter where personal feelings may be so deeply and intimately concerned.' Are not those who have to watch this process continue unchecked also credited with deep personal feelings? In Rutland there are five graves, very prominently sited just outside the south door of a church, which are in almost dead-white reconstituted stone, all dating from the 1950s and 1960s. And in which village? The answer is scarcely credible. At Clipsham, within a mile of some of the best limestone quarries in the country. Sights such as this cannot but imbue with a deep sense of outrage those who love and cherish the English parish churches as among the most precious portions of our heritage.

THREE

The Fabric

I T GOES WITHOUT SAYING that the materials of which a church is constructed play a most important part in the visual impact of the building and therefore in the nature and scale of our enjoyment. Owing to the complexity of her geological pattern, England is able, in her churches as in her other buildings, to exhibit a very wide range of materials, a factor which adds greatly to the interest of church visiting. Because, before the Industrial Revolution, heavy materials such as stone could only be transported with much labour and expense, most people had to build with whatever was available on or very near the site; so, somewhere or other, almost every conceivable material was used. To import stone from a distance one had either to be rich, as some of the great monasteries were, or at least to be building close to navigable water.

In the Middle Ages large parts of England were densely wooded. Timber was at once the least expensive and the most readily available material, and most Anglo-Saxon churches were built of it. So were a good many village churches in the Norman period; and in some parts of the country, northern Hampshire for example, this practice continued at least until the fourteenth century. These churches were not like the unique and, for England, freakish survivor from the Saxon period at Greensted in Essex, where the nave walls are composed of the trunks of oak trees, split vertically, with the curved parts facing outwards; they were framed structures erected on exactly the same principles as the innumerable secular and domestic timber-framed buildings which covered the land. Only a handful remain: Mattingley in Hampshire, Besford in Worcestershire, Melverley in Shropshire, Marton and Lower Peover in Cheshire are some of the best known. All were doted on by the Victorian ecclesiologists, but the truth is that every one of them has been so drastically restored as to offer today only very limited pleasure. Even where some of the timbers are original, the infilling is now all too likely to be cement-rendered, which is a great pity and, one would have thought, unnecessary. (Mattingley has brick nogging, almost all renewed.) Other churches in this group, like Betley and Rushton Spencer in Staffordshire, were largely rebuilt in stone, while Holmes Chapel in Cheshire was recased in the Georgian period in brick. Some of these rustic churches can still show robust timber arcades, yet here again there has often been drastic, if not excessive, restoration. At Nymet Rowland in Devon there is an interesting three-bay Tudor arcade of unvarnished oak, all moulded exactly as if it were stone. But this was surely for economy only; the wood in fact had decayed in places and needed replacement. Stone would certainly have lasted better.

Far and away the most exciting example of timber-framing in a church context is the west wall, the only original part to have survived, at Hartley Wespall in Hampshire (*14*). Here, to quote Pevsner, 'the huge early fourteenth-century timbers form one enormous, boldly cusped lozenge cut by a cusped middle post'. No other church has anything like it, and its bold fantasy is memorable.

If wooden churches are now rare and no longer impressive, the same is not true of belfries, of which England still preserves a considerable number; some are charming. The entirely detached and mainly weather-boarded kind, of somewhat pagoda-like form, such as Pembridge and Yarpole in Herefordshire, and the unique example, 'all roof and no walls', at Brookland in Kent, qualify inevitably for the epithet 'quaint'; but they are very likeable. There is a distinctive group of timber belfries in Essex also characterised by diminishing stages; these are all attached to stone churches and carry shingled spires. Blackmore is the most important example, with three stages, but Margaretting and especially Stock, with only two, have great charm. A feature of all these Essex spires, which are of the splay-footed type, is the boldly oversailing eaves that cast a shadow – at Stock (*35*) on weather-boarding rightly painted white – and give the steeple something of the effect of a narrow-brimmed hat, which is enchanting. Closely related to the Essex group is the tower at High Halden in Kent, which also has the lean-to aisle roofs. As so often with medieval buildings, the apparently ornamental feature was in fact a structural necessity. For in all these belfries (and High Halden carries a ring of six bells) the massive angle-posts needed more steadying than could be obtained from internal cross-bracing, and these outside shoring timbers also had to be protected from the weather. The structure is in fact absolutely logical. The main beams are grandly robust; to see these properly one has to go inside and ascend to the bell chamber. The interiors of all these belfries, with their criss-cross of huge baulks of laboriously adzed oak, are most impressive. Part of the interior of the belfry at Stock is seen in the drawing on page 67.

Pirton in Worcestershire and Marton in Cheshire have 'black and white' belfries which look very different from those just described; but basically, with their lean-to sides, they are similar. Pirton is still quite a pretty tower despite unsympathetic restoration which includes cement-like rendering and inappropriate red tiles. It was built in the Tudor period to replace an earlier central tower which had collapsed. Marton's tower, crowned by a spirelet, is very small but attractively shingled.

The remarkable timber tower at Burstow in Surrey (*15*), which also belongs structurally to this group, makes a quite distinctive contribution. Shingles are everywhere here: on the plain tower: which has a pronounced batter; on the four slender corner pinnacles; and over the entire surface of the relatively lofty splay-footed spire. All these shingles on English church towers and spires are now Canadian cedar in replacement of the native riven oak; each one is about 4 inches broad and 12 inches long and some have to be wedge-shaped. The cedarwood is thinner and smoother than oak, but also weathers to a pleasant silver-grey, and looks well.

Nearly all these timber belfries are of late-medieval date. A few of them rise vertically without any external buttressing. Of these the best is without doubt Upleadon in north-west Gloucestershire (*17*). This has an abundance of closely spaced vertical studs, all exposed, with horizontal brick nogging and a pyramidal cap. Much had to be renewed in 1966–69, but the restoration was very sympathetically carried out. This is a striking and unexpected tower, well worth preserving. A somewhat similar one at Stretton Sugwas in Herefordshire was rebuilt on a new site about a hundred years ago.

Timber was also often used for porches; it did not matter if the rest of the church was stone. Here again, inevitably, there has been a great deal of restoration, but some notable examples survive. Probably the most spectacular is the early fourteenth-century north porch at Boxford in Suffolk, with traceried 'windows' in the side openings. For me, though, the most satisfying is the south porch at High Halden in Kent (*16*), for the oak on the front is largely genuine and it is quite easy to detect the renewals. The arched entrance is formed of two huge pieces of gnarled oak, cut from a branching root and set root upwards, so that each yields a jamb and half the arch-head. The cusped barge-boards are damaged but untouched. Along the sides the cusped heads and tracery of the arcading are also original. This is a porch both venerable and grand.

By comparison, however, with the total contribution which wood has made to our parish churches, porches and even belfries are minor. It is no exaggeration to say that without wood the English parish churches could not have been built at all. Wood, it should be remembered, provided all the scaffolding, and the centering essential to the construction of every stone or brick arch or vault. Nearly all the roofs are of wood; the structure that supports the external covering invariably so. The slate, tiles, lead or (occasionally) copper seen on so many spires are simply sheathing materials for wood. The timber that is externally visible accounts for only a small proportion of the quantity used.

Hartley Wespall, Hampshire
High Halden, Kent

WOOD

15. Burstow, Surrey
17. Upleadon, Gloucestershire

18. Hales, Norfolk

19. Long Melford, Suffolk

FLINT, FLUSHWORK AND THATCH

20. Shelton, Norfolk

BRICK

21. Willen, Buckinghamshire

22. Granite: St Buryan, Cornwall

THE ANCIENT ROCKS

23. Slate: Chapel Stile, Gr
Langdale, Westmorland

24. Devonian Limestone:
Ashburton, Devon

25. Devonian Sandstone:
Harberton, Devon

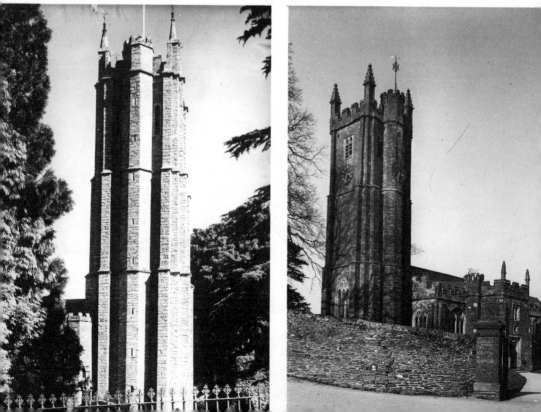

The north-west corner of the Belfry at Stock, Essex

Inside the churches there is a vast amount of woodwork, both structural and ornamental; some is of high quality. There will be plenty to say about this later.

Yet despite the splendid qualities of English oak, with its immense strength and remarkable durability, it is safe to say that, from the Norman period onwards, wherever stone – of almost any kind – was readily available, church builders used it. Even when the only stone at hand was rather soft or very intractable, it was still generally preferred to wood for church walls, apart from some towers. There are accordingly many churches in East Anglia and the south-eastern counties which look as if they had been built of 'any old thing': lumps of stone of various kinds, including chalk and conglomerates like pudding-stone, so soft that pieces can (but should not) be picked out with one's finger, knapped flints, boulders, pebbles, and later patchings in brick – these, held together needless to say with large quantities of mortar, are the materials to be seen in church walls at places as far apart as Odiham in Hampshire, Ickenham in Middlesex, Ingatestone and Hatfield Broad Oak in Essex and Tydd St Mary on the edge of the Lincolnshire Fens, to mention but a few. Nothing could look more unbeguiling either in colour or texture than these walls, but of course they were never intended to be seen. The same is true of those very different church walls in south-western and north-western districts, Devonian stone in South Devon, Silurian on the fringe of the Lake District. There the stone, of great antiquity, was so hard and so difficult to break that it was sometimes used in big amorphous chunks, also with a great deal of mortar – far too much, in fact, to make a good-looking wall. Masonry as rough as this was always plastered over and lime-washed. Unfortunately, after years of wear and tear, this 'overcoat' has often become very shabby; parts have rotted away, or the whole has been removed, discarded and not replaced.

The nature of the rendering applied externally to rubbly walls varies a good deal according to periods and to locality. The only generalisation that can be made is a depressing one: the more recent the work, the more likely is it to be aesthetically disagreeable. Roughcast should not be too rough, and in particular should contain no, or very little, cement. It was always an advantage if, as in South Devon, there was plenty of lime available locally, as well as the right kind of sand. Although their wall surfaces look a little too soft and wavy, as if modelled in clay, churches such as Stoke Gabriel or Ipplepen show roughcast at its best. At the former it is slightly pink, which 'sings' to the red sandstone employed for the window surrounds, quoins and other details. But all too often roughcast looks commonplace, particularly when the finishing coat has been omitted or when it has been neglected.

A covering material which should never be applied to churches – nor, some would say, to anything else – is pebble-dash. Here too there is a variation in quality, that composed of very small pebbles being the least unacceptable, but usually its texture is coarse and lumpy and its colour most unattractive. Its indiscriminate employment at Uffington has done much to spoil what in other respects is externally perhaps the most comely church in Berkshire, and it has made the interesting little church at Gatton in Surrey look suburban.

Naked cement is the worst of all; yet replacement of the original plaster rendering with cement has been the fate of many parish churches in the South-East. Even the addition of a coat of white – or ochre – wash would improve their appearance a little. But neither outside nor in should the rendering be removed – as in the Victorian age it often was – and not replaced. There will be more to say about the 'scraping' of internal wall-surfaces presently.

Much the most common material for churches in Norfolk and Suffolk, and frequently to be seen all over the south-eastern counties, is flint. In this region we take it for granted, yet in a world context it is a decidedly eccentric building stone. Nodules of flint are a product of the chalk, and as they made ploughing more difficult they could be gathered from the fields for the asking. Where the chalk reaches the sea the flints were dislodged and washed smooth. Their small size made then easily portable; but their highly irregular shapes imposed the need for plenty of mortar: too much, sometimes, to be aesthetically acceptable.

Flint walling varies greatly in quality. It can be, as at Hales in Norfolk (*18*), very rough and ready. But if care is taken to select stones of about the same size and to lay them carefully in courses, even uncut flints can be most attractive. A fairly recent example (1953–55) is at Bawdeswell in Norfolk. Here the early Victorian church of All Saints was a casualty of the last war, and has been replaced by a new one of Georgian inspiration, rather suggestive of a Colonial style church in the United States. Appropriately, considering the location, the principal facing material is flint: uncut flints, white, grey-blue, pale brown, dug from a pit some ten miles away, carefully selected for size and laid in courses, herringbone-wise. The effect is excellent. The architect was Fletcher Watson of Norwich.

Usually, however, the best flintwork is to be seen when the flints are knapped (that is to say fractured) and especially when employed in combination with smooth-faced white or nearly white limestone, in the manner known as flushwork. This is an East Anglian speciality, and nearly all of it belongs to the late fifteenth or early sixteenth centuries. Regarding its character and technique, I will not repeat here what I have described in some detail elsewhere;[18] suffice it to say that, decoratively speaking, it is the displays of flushwork which are the show-pieces, externally, of these churches. It was a rich man's art, and lavish structures like Long Melford (*19*), Southwold and Eye have the most, but a great many churches in this part of England have some, if only on the porch. A delightful and unusual example of flushwork may be seen at Stratford St Mary on the edge of the Constable country. This is a drastically restored and very flinty church; but all along the base of the north aisle, outside, runs an inscription, partly in Latin and partly in English, in Gothic script, the letters boldly cut in limestone, with carefully knapped flints to set them off. Above, on the buttresses, is more lettering, and higher still a complete alphabet. How they must have enjoyed themselves!

All the same, seen in quantity it must be admitted that flint soon palls, especially when, as is unfortunately all too common, it has been insensitively repointed. Worplesdon in Surrey provides such an example. All over the South-East are flint walls which, although constructed with much skill, are no pleasure to contemplate: a jumble both of shapes and of colours, black, grey, brown and white – often a good deal of white, which can be shrill. It is safe to say that the builders would not have made much use of this most refractory substance except where nothing better was available.

Visually it is a far cry from small flint nodules and pebbles to hunks of granite that may weigh a hundredweight or more, but this was another intractable material which can be seen at many churches in Cornwall and in the adjoining part of Devon. These granite churches have an entirely distinctive quality which makes an excellent addition to the overall picture of our parish churches. It is a stone with a very grainy texture, so does not lend itself to much undercutting (hence an absence of shadow) and is ill-suited to fine detail or, despite the freakish Tudor display at Launceston, to any sort of decorative enrichment. But it will often sparkle delightfully in the sunshine after rain. The usual colour in Cornwall is a light silver-grey, but it may be of a pale oatmeal shade, as at St Buryan, or with a tinge of pink, as at St Ive, where the stone came from the Cheesewring quarry on Bodmin Moor.

So hard is most of the Cornish granite that the task of cutting it in pre-industrial days must have been extremely laborious and difficult. Until the seventeenth century therefore, if not later, most of it was not quarried but gathered from the hills and moors, where huge blocks lay about for anyone to take who could shift them. They were known as 'presents' of moorstone. Gradually the masons learnt how to dress their 'presents' sufficiently well for church-building, and the last phase of our Gothic architecture saw some noble achievements in granite. Huge, carefully masoned blocks can be well seen at St Buryan (22). Yet when one looks at ornamental details – the pinnacles, for instance, here – one soon becomes aware of the intractability of this stone when it tries to emulate freestone. At St Neot the porch has a ribbed vault in granite which, through the absence of crisp mouldings and the shallowness of the cutting, misses all the beauties of a similar design executed in limestone. In the classical church at Falmouth, built in 1662–64 and dedicated to King Charles the Martyr, the lofty Ionic columns are of granite, but for the capitals they had to resort to plaster.

Somewhat similar to granite is the quartz-porphyry known as elvan, the stone used at Probus, which has the finest church tower in Cornwall. Yet even this cannot equal the limestone towers of Somerset by which it was inspired.

On the Lizard peninsula the church walls have a distinctive colouring that is due to the presence of serpentine, a stone found nowhere else in the country. Some, mixed with granite, can be seen at Mullion, but there is more at Landewednack, with its joyous dedication to St Winwallo. This church, constructed of huge blocks only roughly squared, is very much a country cousin, but the stone colours range from light grey (the granite) through grey-green and blue-green to rust-brown and fawn: a truly delightful patchwork.

Except in the north of the county, an old Cornish church that is not built of granite is almost certain to be of slate-stone. This metamorphic stone quarried from the Devonian rocks actually covers a larger area of the county than the granite. Except that both are extremely hard, no two kinds of stone could look more different. Slate fractures easily, usually into long, thin pieces that tend to be wedge-shaped, splitting to points. Quarrying was often unnecessary, for quantities of slate lay about as scree below every rock-face and could be easily collected. Compared with granite, the colours are more varied and warmer: browns, purples and greens as well as greys. But, as can be seen for instance at Creed in Cornwall or, equally well, at Chapel Stile in Great Langdale (*23*) and other Lake District churches, the impression conveyed by slate-stone is by no means as monumental. Building with slate requires a good deal more mortar than working with granite.

Most churches in Cornwall and South Devon had roofs of excellent local slate, often from the great quarry at Delabole, near Camelford. Some still do. But, for reasons of cost, others have substituted Welsh slates when the original roof needed attention. The contrast between the two can be well appreciated at Torbryan, near Newton Abbot. Here the nave preserves its original Devon slates, small in scale, roughly cut, comparatively thick and pleasantly lichened. The chancel now has thin, smooth Welsh slates, wrong here in scale, wrong in colour, wrong also in texture. It was a big price to pay, visually, for a picayune and, on a church as good as this one, unjustifiable economy.

And so to the sedimentary rocks, the limestones and the sandstones. At least four out of every five English parish churches of medieval origin – and all the cathedrals – were built of one or other of these stones, a fact for which we can be profoundly grateful. But of course both of them vary a great deal: there are many kinds of limestone, many kinds of sandstone. Not all are equally durable, nor equally pleasing to look at. Moreover, a good many of them are unfortunately no longer obtainable even for repairs. The cost of stone today is such that there are now many architects who have never used it and would not know how to do so if asked. It is good therefore to be able to record two very welcome developments in the nineteen-seventies relative to the churches. One was the setting up by the Council for the Care of Churches of a Standing Joint Committee on Natural Stone, composed in part of architects and in part of representatives of the stone trade, for the purpose of establishing an information centre on the availability and properties of British stone and of providing courses for architects and teachers of architecture in the use of stone. The other was the establishment, in the little redundant limestone church at Orton in Northamptonshire, of a school of masonry with residential courses for masons.

Whatever the stone, the character of the masonry plays a tremendous part in the total visual impact of any church. Most of our churches are constructed only of rubblestone, which may be roughly coursed but is often not. The size of the individual pieces varies enormously as between one kind of limestone or sandstone and another. Structurally the essential characteristic of the sedimentary rocks is that the matter of which they are composed was originally deposited, generally by the action of water, in layers, with the result that they are usually stratified. Some of these strata are very narrow, perhaps no more than a couple of inches thick; when this occurs the stone is only obtainable in very thin pieces, and the mortar-courses have to be very close together (*64*). This is particularly noticeable wherever a church has been built of Blue Lias limestones, as in Somerset. Small stones make for intimacy rather than dignity, as can also be appreciated in central and west Devon, where most of the churches are built of sandstones from what are known as the Culm Measures, peculiar to this region. Bampton, King's Nympton, Chulmleigh, Tawstock (*8*), Monkleigh: all these and many others have hard walls, rubbly and much fragmented, saved aesthetically by their pleasantly muted colours, mainly dark brownish-red and grey, spotted with plenty of silver-green lichen. The carboniferous rocks of the North, on the other hand, can often be hewn in enormous blocks, the size only being limited by the maximum weight that it was practicable to lift; and there can be no doubt that this endows, say, the gritstone churches of the North Pennine region with a feeling of strength which is not only impressive in itself but well attuned, also, to their boldly contoured landscape setting and more rigorous climate.

Limestones or sandstones which are of sufficiently fine grain and homogeneous structure to admit of being cut freely, in any direction, either with a saw or mallet and chisel, are known as free-stones; they were the stones always in demand for the best work, for it was on them that

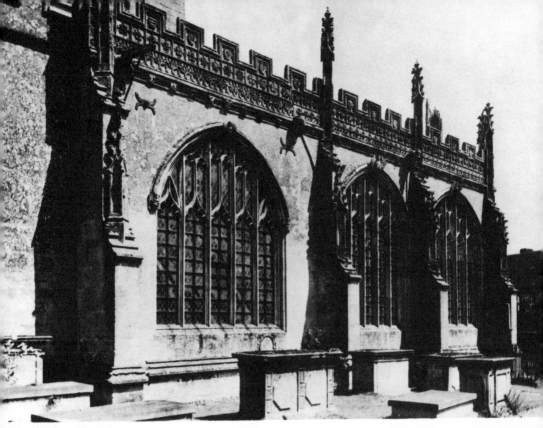

Bromham, Wiltshire

THE LIMESTONES

Eaton Bray, Bedfordshire   28. Bristol, St Mary Redcliffe

29. Crediton, Devon; South Porch

30. Nantwich, Cheshire: Sed

THE SANDSTONES

31. Pott Shrigley, Cheshire

32. West Chiltington, Sussex

ashlar masonry depended. For ashlar the blocks could be comparatively thin, since they were only needed as a facing material, but the face had to be perfectly smooth and the edges carefully squared, so that they could be laid in absolutely level courses with the minimum of mortar. The larger the blocks the better. In favoured parts of England the quality of the ashlar masonry is often very fine indeed, so that the comtemplation of a church wall can in itself be a source of deep pleasure (*42, 47*).

Freestone of high quality readily lends itself to carving too, and to a profusion of ornamental enrichment wherever it was required (*26* and *28*). This was a property of which our medieval masons were not slow to take advantage; were it not for our good fortune in possessing so much of this splendid stone many of the finest achievements in our church architecture and sculpture would have been impossible.

In hilly and moorland areas we have miles of drystone walling, and very delightful it is. But a church cannot be built without mortar, which implies pointing, a matter of great visual importance. The quality of stonework can be enhanced, or quite seriously impaired, by the choice of mortar and by the way it is handled. Mortar should be as inconspicuous as possible: not much lighter than the stone to which it is to be applied, and *never* darker. With some materials, as has already been explained in discussing flint and slate-stone, the mortar is bound to be prominent; with ashlar, on the other hand, one should scarcely be conscious of it at all. Pointing, which means the manner in which the mortar is applied, should be as unnoticeable as the nature of the stone renders possible. There is plenty of well chosen and well pointed mortar to be seen in the English churches, and in the Cotswolds almost nothing else (*12*), but unhappily bad examples are also not rare. Two examples of how not to do it can be seen in Lincolnshire: at Stixwould and (internally) at Fishtoft. At both the mortar is much too dark. At the former it has been splodged over the arrises of the stonework in a careless, insensitive fashion, while the latter, a 'scraped' interior, is an example of ribbon-pointing, the worst possible form, in which every stone is surrounded by a ring of cement-mortar defined by two aggressive-looking trowel-lines. Some of this hideous pointing can also be seen at Nantwich (*65*: on the buttress to the left of the window).

Ashlar masonry is always the best for town churches. In the London area most of the medieval parish churches were built of Kentish Ragstone, a rough, brittle, cretaceous limestone from the Lower Greensand which cannot be ashlared. Unfortunately this stone also found favour with the Victorian architects in London. Not only is its rough, rubbly wall-surface all too prone to collect and harbour dirt and cannot be cleaned as ashlar can; for a city this masonry is also too rustic-looking. It lacks dignity. Ashlar, on the other hand, carries an air of distinction and refinement (*51–53*).

In country districts an ashlared church might in some areas appear too urbane, too dressy; but this is emphatically not the case in the Cotswolds, where ashlar walling, often even for country churches, was almost taken for granted. Here, of course, the abundance of beautiful stone was a great natural asset. Cotswold stone is all oolitic limestone, and although many other kinds of English stone are tougher, none can quite equal it aesthetically. Many of these churches belong to the fifteenth century, a time when the wool trade had brought riches to the region, riches which men were very willing to spend on their churches. Some, like Cirencester, Chipping Campden (*47*) and Northleach (*12*), are sumptuous; but at many of the village churches, too, we find a handsome porch, ornamental parapets, pinnacles, gargoyles (*62*), dripstones over the windows dropped down a few inches and neatly returned, nicely finished set-offs to the buttresses, image niches and many comparable enrichments and refinements. Even if there is not much to see inside, an old Cotswold church, in its generally attractive setting, can almost always be relied upon to give pleasure. The stone will probably be cream or honey-coloured, or a stronger yellow if from the Guiting quarry; with any luck the roof will also be of the local stone, the slates skilfully laid in courses of gradually diminishing size; and the masoncraft will be impeccable. At Polton, Butterfield, using Cotswold stone for walls and roof, became almost human. (But even here he could not resist shiny and partly polychromatic floor tiles.)

Southwards from the Cotswolds into Wiltshire (*3, 26*), Somerset (*39–46*), and Dorset, north-eastwards through Oxfordshire and Northamptonshire (*64*) to Rutland (*33*) and Lincolnshire (*117*), the pageant of fine limestone masonry continues; for this is the Jurassic limestone belt, the region of the oolite and the lias, and in town after town, in village after village, the parish church is a delight. Not always, of course: here and there misfortunes have occurred; but the fact that the limestone belt throughout its whole length has remained remarkably free from industrial development has been greatly to its aesthetic advantage. So numerous and so fine are many of these churches that it would be invidious to select examples here, but reference will be made to some of them in the chapters that follow. Among the kinds of stone employed, special mention must be made of the pale cream and buff-coloured oolites of the Stamford area, weathering sometimes to a most distinguished grey, and the stone slates from Collyweston with which churches in these oolites are so often roofed; this group of quarries, Barnack, Weldon, Ketton, Clipsham and Ancaster in particular, made a splendid contribution to our church architecture. Very lovely also are the iron-tinted liassic limestones, of which Ham Hill in Somerset and Horton in north Oxfordshire are deservedly the best known.

Yorkshire is a county generously endowed with building stone of many kinds, including Jurassic limestone, but it is the magnesian limestone churches which make the most memorable impact. This is a material unresistant to coal smoke, and ill-suited to industrial towns. But at a number of small town and village churches in South Yorkshire, where the air is relatively unpolluted – Tickhill (*48*), Conisbrough, Sprotborough, Asksey, Hatfield, Campsall, Womersley, Darrington, Sherburn-in Elmet: these are some of the best – the stone is still creamy-white and so captivating that the status of the church as a visual focal point is assured. Even Portland stone, the whitest of the oolites, cannot rival the positively milky-looking surface quality of the stonework on the rain-washed south and east faces of some of these South Yorkshire churches.

Whiteness is a characteristic of several other kinds of limestone, from what is geologically the youngest, the Chalk, to one of the oldest, the Carboniferous. Chalk was used for masonry here and there all over the South-East, for want of any better material. It can be well seen in the west of Berkshire, for instance at Ashbury and at Compton Beauchamp, which has a good stone-slated roof. At Uffington they have unfortunately deemed it necessary to smother it with pebble-dash. On the Buckinghamshire bank of the Thames, a short distance upstream from Windsor, is the small, surprisingly remote church, embowered in elm-trees and generally locked, of Boveney, unusual in that the chalk-stone is galleted with flint: that is to say, each block is surrounded by a rustic necklace of flint chips which, with a purely ornamental intention, were pressed into the mortar courses while they were still soft. Since the weathering properties of chalk have often proved unreliable, it is usually seen to best effect internally, as at Eaton Bray in Bedfordshire; here the chalk-stone from near-by Totternhoe, on a spur of the Chilterns, has decayed a good deal outside, but within there is an Early English north arcade of exquisite beauty (*27*): almost a miniature Wells. The richness of the carved capitals, clustered piers and arch-mouldings was certainly prompted by the ease with which chalk can be cut, especially when freshly quarried. At Burwell in Cambridgeshire the big church is faced externally with flint, but the basic material is the local clunch, employed with excellent effect to produce a spacious, noble, very white interior (*104*). The westernmost limit of the Chalk is around Beer in the eastern corner of Devon; in the late-Gothic period Beer stone was used for several churches in this district.

Carboniferous limestone is the building stone of central Derbyshire and of an extensive but for the most part sparsely populated area in the six most northern counties. Generally it is light grey and used in rather small, rubbly pieces; ashlar was not attempted. A town church in this stone is

Holy Trinity, Kendal. The little, lonely churches of the northern dales were often made to look still whiter by being limewashed. Their sturdy construction, with a good deal of mortar, is in tune with their setting.

Still older are the Devonian rocks of the South-West, which are by no means all calcareous. Limestones from this geological formation were used all along the southern fringe of Dartmoor; their small-stoned, rough-surfaced masonry is well seen at Ashburton (*24*).

The sandstones are even more varied than the limestones: there can be few English counties which do not possess churches built of one kind of sandstone or another. These sandstones differ greatly in their weathering properties, but all too often, through the centuries, they have shown a propensity to spall and to crumble: in some dioceses, Worcester, for example, and Coventry, Lichfield and, perhaps above all, Chester, the maintenance of the stonework of the sandstone churches has been a severe drain on church finances. The most durable sandstones are the most ancient employed for building purposes, the Carboniferous and the Devonian, which are generally between 300 and 400 million years old.

Carboniferous sandstone, either from the Coal Measures or Millstone Grit, is *par excellence* the building material of the northern churches, from Durham Cathedral downwards. By comparison with most of the other varieties it lacks charm: when freshly quarried it is usually dun-coloured, but with the years it darkens considerably and sometimes turns blotchy. Because of its close grain and high silica content this kind of sandstone resists the smoky atmosphere of industrial cities better than any of the limestones, even Portland, but in such conditions it becomes black. The grime clings to the slightly rough, compact surface so tenaciously that it can be very difficult to remove, though this is sometimes attempted. From the standpoint of endurance this is a great asset, but it cannot be said to add to its charm.

On the fringe of industrial areas, as at the notable West Riding church of Ecclesfield (*4*), the stonework still tends to be grimy. In country districts the colouring is sober, but this is in harmony with Pennine austerity. The churches in this part of England are not spectacular, but, partly because of the big scale of their masonry blocks to which reference has already been made, they do convey an impression of enduring strength.

In the south-western counties carboniferous sandstone is much less important, but was used in small rubbly pieces for many churches in central and west Devon and north Cornwall, where the source, as already indicated (cf. p. 72), was the Culm Measures.

The Devonian sandstones occur in parts of Somerset and Cornwall as well as Devon; belonging to the same geological period, although very differently constituted, are the Old Red sandstones of Herefordshire and the areas adjoining. Some Devonian sandstone is dark red or brown, as at Harberton (*25*), but like many of the sandstones, some is multi-coloured. At North Molton, where the church stands high above the village, the colours vary almost from block to block: grey, fawn, dull pink, and an abundance of silver-green lichen produce an engaging harmony of colour. And in this respect Dymock, on the Gloucestershire–Herefordshire border, is still better, for it stands just at the point where the Old Red and the New Red sandstone formations meet, and has drawn stone from both. So there is a blending of the most subtle shades: purple-pinks, blue-greys, fawns, even light chocolate. A slight acquaintance with the geology of the country helps to explain what might otherwise seem to be curious and unaccountable phenomena.

New Red sandstone embraces two series with close resemblances: the Permian and the Triassic. Permian can be seen in places as far apart as Crediton and Penrith. The big stately church at Crediton in Devon, red without (*29*: the south porch), offers a wonderful colour experience on entering: an exquisite blending of pink and blue-grey. The Triassic stone is, however, far more widespread; this was for centuries the principal building stone of the whole of the west Midlands, and important also in Nottinghamshire and the Vale of York, in coastal Lancashire and Cumberland, in Somerset and east Devon.

The New Red sandstone could be ashlared without difficulty, and sometimes sawn into very large blocks; but all too often, owing to their friability and lack of structural cohesion, they stand up very indifferently to the onslaughts of the weather. The north-west tower of St John, Chester, dating from Tudor times, fell in 1881, and was not rebuilt. The ruin is interesting as illustrating the state into which this sandstone decays if left unrestored. Its surface today is shockingly fretted. Exterior carving in this stone usually has about a century of life and no more. Nantwich is another fine Cheshire church at which, because of the weakness of the stone, the carved and masoned details, where not replaced, have become badly blurred (*65*), so that we need to go inside (*30*) to appreciate how all this carved enrichment must have looked when it was first completed. In Staffordshire, Worcestershire and Warwickshire it is often the same story. So, like the cathedrals of Chester, Lichfield and Worcester, most of the churches in the west and north-west Midlands have suffered greatly from restoration, with consequent sacrifice of 'patina', or have lost all their pristine crispness of detail.

The contrast between the Carboniferous sandstone and the Triassic, and more specifically between Millstone Grit and the New Red sandstone, can be vividly appreciated if the large majority of the Cheshire churches are compared with the few near its eastern border, like Pott Shrigley or, particularly, Astbury, which are built of gritstone. The mainly Perpendicular church at Astbury is notable not only for its architectural splendour but also for its stonework; after nearly 500 years the external details are still comparatively crisp. At Pott Shrigley (*31*) the main fabric consists of small pieces of buff-coloured rubblestone from the Coal Measures, in much better condition than the grey, buff and red Triassic sandstone which was introduced for the dressings because it was so much more easily cut.

It is for their colours that the Triassic sandstones are so much the more enjoyable. The New Red is of course by no means always red; at Lapworth in Warwickshire, where it has weathered to a lovely texture, it is grey. At Martley in Worcestershire, the church tower is a rich red ochre, dusted with blue-grey lichen, which is enchanting and most uncommon, while the walls present a blend of pink, fawn and grey-blue. Elsewhere, to the reds, pinks, buffs and greys, lichens often add fortuitous patches of green.

This charm of colour also characterises many of the younger kinds of sandstone, most of which are less prone to fail after exposure to the vagaries of our weather. Delectable, but unhappily specially vulnerable in this respect, are the greensand stones of east Lincolnshire, around Spilsby. West Keal, on the rim of the Wolds, commands a tremendous prospect, with Boston Stump visible in the distance across miles of fens. How can I describe the fascinating colours of the stonework of the porch? There are sage greens, brownish greens, tweedy browns, greys and other less definite shades all most subtly blended. Halton Holgate and the nave of Burgh-le-Marsh were also built of this beautiful stone that today shows many weak and crumbling areas of walling as well as incongruous patching.

Another delightful cretaceous sandstone is that quarried in the Weald of Sussex and Kent. The colours are a gentle blend of greys, browns and fawns, once again with a generous sprinkling of lichen. This can proliferate excessively, and when it does it should be dealt with. But usually it is not only quite harmless but a visual asset to be cherished.

The most eccentric sandstones are also the youngest: sarsens, found in Wiltshire, Berkshire and Surrey. They are also known as greywethers and as heathstones. Occurring in boulders of amorphous form scattered about on the downs and heaths of this part of England, they did not need quarrying, but were very difficult to work. Four Surrey church towers, Chobham, Pirbright, Worplesdon and Ash, show sarsens to excellent advantage. Predominantly grey, the colours also include blue-grey, fawn and coffee brown: there are colour variations even on the surface of a single block. The chunky, roughly square blocks could be laid in courses only with great difficulty, but this was achieved at Pirbright. Sarsens are in no degree urbane, but they have a primeval appeal which to many is fascinating, and a countryman's strength.

Many of these churches had, and happily a considerable number still preserve, sandstone roofing slates. These have not the delicate refinement of the best roofs of the Cotswolds and the limestone belt, but their great slabs, formidably heavy, and therefore laid at a lower pitch than the limestone slates, have a tremendous presence. The stone may endure for several hundred years, but unfortunately the life of these roofs is also dependent on the supporting timber framework, which in time is likely to give way under the weight. When this has occurred the temptation to economise by substituting Welsh slate or red tiles or some other inappropriate material has often proved irresistible. At Fletching in Sussex, for example, the dull-red tiles on the chancel provide a wholly unworthy foil for the splended slabs of Wealden stone that cover the nave.

There are some lovely roofs still to be seen in Sussex and parts of the adjoining counties; the slabs are often known, generically, as Horsham slates. In course of time they turn dark brown. This stone can be over-attractive to moss, as is evident at West Chiltington (*32*), where most of it ought to be removed. The single great roof, covering the aisles too and sweeping down low – almost a 'cat-slide' – is not uncommon in the South-East. The Welsh border counties preserve fine sandstone roofs from older rock formations, while in the North, where they speak of flagstones, and occasionally of 'thackstones', this kind of roof has a long and honourable tradition, despite the often sombre colouring (*31*).

Because the English church roof is often so prominent, the choice of its material is hardly less important aesthetically than that of the walls. The range of choice has been extremely wide. The stone roofs are unquestionably the best, and even among these not much has yet been said of the blue and green slates of the Lake District. Unfortunately, however, they were the product of a region in which, in medieval days, castles and pele towers were in far greater demand than churches, and the scope of their employment was therefore limited. The Victorians set to work to remedy this, and even brought Westmorland slates to roof the chancel at Clipsham, where they look as painfully incongruous as the gravestones of reconstructed stone in the churchyard referred to earlier.

When they were first built, even some of our major churches, including cathedrals, were originally thatched. The relative lightness of this material was particularly suitable where the walls were only of flint, and in any case there was nothing else readily available. In Norfolk there are still over fifty churches with thatched roofs, and in Suffolk nearly twenty. As the thatch used in this area is reed, which is in every respect the best, these roofs give great pleasure (*18*). There is a specially elaborate one at Thurton, in south-east Norfolk, with three tiers of ornamental patterning. At one time there were a great many humbler church roofs of straw thatch in the south-eastern counties, especially Hampshire and

Berkshire, but survivors are now rare. Thatch is of course a country material; it is not suitable for towns, nor is it to be found there.

The other roofing materials, apart from shingles, are tiles and the metals. Of the latter, lead has always been much preferred to copper in England, and for that we can be grateful. A green copper roof can make a dramatic impact, and in the right place can be decidedly effective, but the usually quieter, less insistent character of lead seems more amenable to the English scene, whether urban or rural. I say usually so, because some old lead roofs have become white to the point of shrillness; the immense expanse of lead on the roof of the nave of Ely cathedral is a prime instance, specially prominent because of the steepness of the pitch. A parish church example is Ottery St Mary in Devon, where the prominent lead roofs reflect far too much light for the comfort of the pleasing but fairly low-toned red, buff and grey sandstone (cf. also *44*). Employed on spires, lead had to be laid at a very steep pitch, but otherwise its particular value to the medieval builders was for the precisely opposite reason: it was the only material with which they could satisfactorily cover a nearly flat roof. In the Perpendicular period, when churches were liable to rise a good deal higher, roofs of steep pitch were often no longer required and were regarded as an unnecessary extravagance. Lead, although expensive, was a godsend to these builders. From below these late-Gothic lead roofs are usually invisible, a fact of considerable aesthetic importance which will be considered further in the next chapter.

Lead is visually very responsive to the weather. When wet it reflects the sky; sunshine on a wet lead roof can be delightful. But it has to be said that lead, it may be felt, is often a roofing material of negative rather than positive virtue. It lacks textural interest and does not make good eaves (*21*). On a longish roof, too, the upward moving rolls that link the strips of lead seem less apt than the horizontal lines of stone slates or tiles. Sometimes, however, old lead will acquire a silver hue that has great charm. This is due not to the presence of silver in the lead (for where this occurred it was always extracted during the smelting process) but to an insoluble lead carbonate commonly found on lead subjected to long exposure. With grey limestone as with flint its colour is always better than that of tiles. At Dennington in Suffolk, an imposing flint church, the lead roof of the nave may well be preferred to the chancel roof of grey Welsh slate.

At a number of other flint churches, which include Merton in Norfolk, West Hendred in Berkshire and Hemel Hempstead, the nave is roofed with lead and the chancel with red tiles, so comparison is easy. The verdict is not in doubt. The lead is preferable for colour, the tiles for texture. The ripple of dark red and blue tiles at Merton, though not ideal for colour, is texturally rich. But tiles of course vary very much in quality. South

Cerney, a big stone church on the fringe of the Cotswolds, was re-roofed in 1862 by the architect J. P. StAubyn with machine-made pink tiles, a shocking example of Victorian insensitivity to materials. Machine-made tiles are always unworthy, and their colour, nearly always an anaemic pink, is invariably wrong. Hand-made tiles are greatly preferable, and at their best (which means in the South-East) beautiful alike in colour and texture. Yet for most church roofs there are two reservations even about tiles of the highest quality. For a building as large as a church they are too small; their mesh is too fine; and there are very few varieties of stone with which, for colour, tiles are congenial. A white or whitened stone church is the best for red tiles. Better still is brick.

Brick made a late appearance as a material for church-building. In the eastern counties bricks were used occasionally in combination with other materials from the end of the twelfth century, most notably in the second quarter of the fourteenth century for the infilling of the nave vault of Beverley Minster, of which few people are aware because it has always been plastered over. About the same time, the church of the Holy Trinity, Hull, was being constructed, from the east end to the crossing, wholly of brick. But it was not until the Tudor period that brick became an acceptable alternative material for church-building, and then only rarely.

In Norfolk, after endless flint churches, it is a delight to arrive at Shelton (*20*) and be confronted with early Tudor brickwork of exquisite quality: a deep pink, enriched with the usual Tudor diapers in dark blue. The clerestory is even faced with limestone, a great extravagance in east Norfolk, especially inland, but the miserable little tower, of flint, was unfortunately retained from the earlier church. All the rest is brickwork of *c.* 1485–90. Shelton, a gift to the parish from the local squire, is more like a college chapel than a normal village church, and the interior is very handsome. Lutton, in the south-eastern corner of Lincolnshire, is perhaps about the same date. The west tower and spire are of stone, but almost all else here is brick, even the pretty cusping of the clerestory windows. Within, however, the mistake has been made of applying a cold whitewash to the entire structure; it would have been much more effective to have left details such as capitals and arch mouldings in what Horace Walpole once termed 'their natural brickhood'.

Otherwise the principal examples of Tudor brickwork in churches are in Essex. Three entire churches, East Horndon, Layer Marney and Chignal Smealy, show very well what could be achieved in brick at this time. Layer Marney, with a whitewashed interior much more sympathetic than Lutton's, and an appropriate roof of red tiles, is a delightful church. Chignal Smealy, whose north aisle was added in 1847 with considerable skill, using old bricks, is smaller and, it may be felt, excessively red; a coat of limewash (slightly warmer than dead white) would be an improvement to the interior, which is at present too 'bricky'. Apart from whole churches, Essex has about 20 brick towers, some like Rochford and especially Ingatestone, decidedly imposing. At Fryerning the tower breaks out into an ornamental display at the crown, with corbelled arches, stepped parapets and pretty octagonal corner turrets crowned by stone balls. Tudor porches in brick are also characteristic of Essex: two south porches, at Sandon and Pebmarsh, are specially elaborate. Sandon even has, all in brick, an ogee-headed niche over the entrance, as well as stepped battlements and, within, a ribbed vault.

Few churches were built in England in any material between 1540 and 1660. The political climate of this period was unfavourable for church-building, and except in a handful of places there was no call for new churches, as there were medieval survivals in great profusion. But after the Restoration their architectural style fell out of favour with the *cognoscenti*; the desire arose for churches designed in the classical mode, and for light, airy buildings better adapted to what was now the principal reason for church going, which was to hear a sermon. In London the Great Fire gave Wren the opportunity to build churches which exactly met these requirements; the more expensive ones were faced with Portland stone, but the plainer ones were of brick (see pp. 110–112).

The later Stuart and Georgian periods saw the use of brick for churches in many parts of the country. The most enjoyable are, once again, in the South and South-East, none more so than Farley, on the Wiltshire–Hampshire border. Here, in 1688–90, Sir Stephen Fox, who knew Wren and may well have received help from him in the design, built a comely classical church, set back today behind a well-kept lawn entered between good brick piers surmounted by stone vases. The mellow brickwork, pinkish red with a scatter of blue diapers, is perfect; as Pevsner points out, the bricks here were still laid in English bond, which at this date is a sure sign that the bricklayers were local men. The quoins, parapets and other dressings are of whitish limestone. The windows are all round-headed and nearly all have kept their plain glazing. Across the road are ranges of almshouses, also in brick, the gift of the same donor. Farley, still little known, is one of the architectural delights of England.

Not many classical churches built of brick afford as much pleasure as this one. At many of them the brickwork, although technically excellent, is decidedly plain; indeed, as at Willen in Buckinghamshire (21), built in 1676–80 by Robert Hooke, a professional colleague and close friend of Wren, all the adornment of the exterior depends upon the stone dressings. As the eighteenth century advanced, brick was employed more and more for churches, because in most parts of the country it was now substantially less expensive than stone. But it would be idle to pretend that it was or is the equal of stone either in dignity or in the opportunities which it offers for ornamental enrichment. Apart from some fine plasterwork on the ceilings, the best Georgian interiors owed far more to their furnishings, in the metals and especially in wood, than to their fabric. In later Georgian and still more in Victorian times, brick was seldom much more than a utility material, selected for its cheapness.

The part played by the metals in relation to the church interior will be considered later. Externally it takes various forms, of which far the most important has already been touched on: the use of lead, and much less frequently of copper, for roofing, including spires. From the sixteenth century onwards lead was increasingly employed for down-pipes; the rainwater heads sometimes carry dates. In addition, we are perhaps apt to overlook the fact that no church glazier could work without lead. The glass that fills church windows is held together by grooved bars of pliant lead known as cames, which in larger windows are attached at intervals to iron bars, in order to withstand wind pressure. Where a window is filled with stained glass, the external effect counts for very little, although where the glass is mainly or partly old, there is no easier way of ascertaining which parts are modern replacements than by stepping outside. The old glass will all be in some degree corroded[19]; the restored parts will be smooth and clear. But even what looks like no more than a jumbled mosaic is much more agreeable than plain sheets of glass, which are occasionally inserted on the outer face of stained glass windows for purposes of protection (the practice known as 'plating'). These unarticulated sheets of glass always look very bad, and should be avoided. Fine-meshed iron cages as a protection for stained glass are also highly undesirable, since, as can be seen all too often, in time they always rust and stain the stonework. If protection of this kind is deemed essential, only rustless metal should be used. But the sole windows which make much external impact, other than for their tracery, are those filled with leaded lights in regular diamond or rectangular patterns. Far the most effective are the plain rectangular leaded lights of the windows of classical churches, with fan-shaped pieces under the arched heads. These are the only church windows which, for their glass and leading, can look just as attractive from outside as from within.

Wrought iron can sometimes be seen on towers, providing elegant support for the weather-cock (66); a few churches are also the lucky possessors of Georgian gates. In this respect none is as fortunate as Malpas in Cheshire, which has, in addition to several good smaller ones, two magnificent pairs (1725 and 1765) which were brought from Oulton Hall, a demolished Cheshire house. These are an exquisite embellishment to the church precinct. A handsome gate at Tetbury in Gloucestershire, used to be, but happily is no longer, so marked by creeper as to be largely invisible. There are plenty of English buildings, churches included, on which an overcoat of creeper, or, better, a variety of climbers, is perfectly acceptable if not positively desirable. But there are others, with gates and gate-piers too, which deserve more consideration.

FOUR

The Exterior

AFTER THE SETTING and the materials, the form. It is now time to consider the architectural composition of some of our parish churches, and certain features of external adornment. In a book of this size the treatment will have to be extremely selective.

One vision of the perfect English parish church, viewed from outside, might be a cruciform building of the finest stone, with high roofs, a central tower and spire, and carefully disposed ornamental enrichment, set upon a broad and perfectly manicured expanse of lawn, unencumbered even by Georgian tomb-chests: in fact a smaller edition of, or variation on, the cathedral of Salisbury. But, some will say, how self-conscious! If you feel like that, don't worry: there is no such church, satisfying all these conditions. But cruciform churches with central towers and spires we have, although in small numbers: Hemel Hempstead from the twelfth century, Darlington from the thirteenth, Patrington from the fourteenth, are some of them. Although the first has had to encounter formidable restoration, the second to suffer continual pollution from the Teeside chemical factories, making it very dirty outside and in,[20] and the third to see itself surrounded by a vast scatter of dreadful tombstones (34), each is still a great ornament to its locality. For Hemel Hempstead, see p. 32. The fine spire here is Georgian, and so is Darlington's: towers and spires are of course especially vulnerable to the effects of weather, and the Darlington spire had to be rebuilt in 1752. The work was well done, and indeed the distinguishing characteristic of this rather lofty, austere church is its unity of architectural style. The aisle and tower windows are Decorated and the chancel was rebuilt in 1865, but essentially this is a stately example of Early English, with a profusion of lancet shapes.

Patrington is a remote place 16 miles east of Hull, and therefore little visited except by amateurs of churches, but, probably because the patron of the living was the Archbishop of York, it has one of the great parish churches of England, one which would be certain of a place on any expert's list of the dozen finest (34). Here again the spire is not coeval with the church, but about 100 years later; yet what strikes and delights us first about Patrington is, as at Darlington, its stylistic consistency. This was a glorious creation of the Decorated period, with big traceried windows, a profusion of boldly crocketed pinnacles to crown the buttresses, and transepts with aisles, a rare and gorgeous indulgence for a parish church, for these are not even to be found in every cathedral. Only the biggest window here is Perpendicular, and artistically inferior. With a cruciform building the aesthetic value of a central tower and spire, and of the lofty roofs and pointed gables in relation to the spire form, will be immediately apparent from the illustration. The geometrical basis of the composition is a somewhat elongated pyramid. The crowning feature, an absolutely plain spire leaping towards the sky through a rich Gothic diadem, is an original conception of considerable charm.

Cruciform churches with central towers but without spires are found in many (although not all) parts of the country; in fact, on the road to Patrington we pass two very imposing ones, Holy Trinity, Hull, and St Augustine, Hedon. In this type of building, especially as the roofs are often nearly flat, one no longer thinks of a pyramid as the basis of the composition, but again the central tower acts as a focal point for the whole design. Externally there can be no doubt that the centre of the church is visually the best place for the tower. This is even true of little Norman churches without transepts, such as Iffley in Oxfordshire and Stewkley in Buckinghamshire. Apart from their paramount aesthetic value, towers were very important in the Middle Ages because they housed the bells, which, especially in the country, were the people's time-keepers. In summertime the 'alarm-clock' in a village was the ringing of the Angelus at 4 a.m.

Yet however aesthetically satisfying a central tower is externally, it soon came to be realised that internally it could be an obstruction. Its massive piers often meant narrowing and sometimes lowering the arches, as at St Peter, Wolverhampton, where in all directions views are partially blocked. At Yatton in Somerset the bulky central tower stands above a cavernous tent, effectively separating the four areas of the church into four distinct compartments which, it might be said, hardly seem to know one another. At Cricklade in Wiltshire, where the tower is huge if also poorly designed, the arches are not low, but the eyes of a congregation assembling for a service focus not upon the altar nor the east window, but upon the bell-ringers, pulling and guiding their ropes, for they have to stand right in the centre of the church. At Langford in Oxfordshire the Norman central tower is so obstructive that the chancel is now seldom used, for the high altar at the east end, as in these other churches mentioned, is invisible from most parts of the nave.[21]

So, if funds were forthcoming, these central towers were sometimes removed; other obligingly collapsed. A wit once observed that when inspecting a church of which some parts are Romanesque, which in England usually means Norman, the first question to ask is 'When did the

. Ketton, Rutland

34. Patrington, Yorkshire

SPIRES

. Stock, Essex

36. Hemingbrough, Yorkshire

A FINE MID-FIFTEENTH CENTURY
SPIRE

37. Whittlesey, Cambridgesh

tower fall?' And it is indeed true that the story of our oldest churches includes a melancholy number of tumbling towers. Nor were they all central; at Dunstable Priory *both* the Norman west towers fell on the same day, during a storm in 1222. Sometimes, as at St Mary, Beverley, the collapse was caused by later builders raising the Norman tower to a height too great for its piers to carry. (The upper part of this central tower gave way in 1520 and fell through the nave during a Sunday service, killing a number of people.) Nevertheless, from the fourteenth century onwards, new churches were nearly always planned with their towers at the west end.[22] At Wymondham in Norfolk, where after endless wrangles the parishioners were granted the use of the nave of what was a Benedictine abbey church, the central tower, octagonal and now only a shell, was built about 1400 by the monks (not in fact over the crossing but two bays to the west of it) while half a century later the townspeople erected their own much bigger square tower at the west end. Thus, as the monks' church has all but gone, this parish church now has a tower at each end, the two being of sharply contrasting forms; the effect is curious, but certainly distinctive.

The western tower had the advantage of greater stability, standing, on all sides except the east, on the whole of its walls. The central tower, on the other hand, could only be supported at its four corners, which called for a great deal of buttressing. How to fit in the buttresses sometimes posed awkward problems.

When the west end of the church came to be regarded as the normal position for the tower, it was of course possible to plan the rest of the church as a single entity, with nave and chancel linked together by continuous arcades and a single roof. This is what we may take for granted in grand East Anglian churches like St Peter Mancroft at Norwich, Long Melford (*19*), Southwold, Blythburgh and Loddon; but in fact they are exceptions. Village churches less famous than these may have it too: Denston in Suffolk, for instance, or North Cadbury and Norton-sub-Hamdon in Somerset. Whenever it occurs we are invariably delighted, for these are stately buildings. Yet in England such an arrangement is quite uncharacteristic. The explanation is rooted in history. At first by custom, and later by law, the rector was responsible for the chancel and the parishioners for the rest of the church. While the parishioners were often very willing to spend money on carrying out their responsibility, the rectors were not. Very broadly the reason for this was that rectories with the greater part of the endowment, the tithe, were often either appropriated by monasteries or were treated by the patrons, the kings and great landowners, as a form of property which could be used for endowing colleges or charities or for rewarding services. The kings' administrators, for instance, who were usually clerics, would be granted rectories as a form of payment. The monasteries and the rectors, who were absentees, were obliged by law to ensure that vicars or curates were provided to serve the churches and that the chancels were kept in repair. But they were not interested in doing more than this. The inhabitants of the parish on the other hand, if they prospered, took pride in rebuilding their part of the church on a more lavish scale. Although this gives a simplified picture of a highly complicated subject, here is the essential reason why the chancel of so many English parish churches is architecturally quite unworthy of the nave.

Hence the characteristic silhouette of an English parish church, viewed from the south, is 'two steps down' as the eye moves east: a west tower, with or without a spire, a lower nave, and a chancel lower again. There are churches, particularly in Somerset, where the diversities between these three parts might almost be regarded as comical. At Leigh-on-Mendip, for example, a proud west tower is attached to a modest nave that leads into a chancel so insignificant that on a dark night it could be mistaken for a potting shed (*41*). Occasionally a generous benefactor would pay for the provision of a new chancel on a more sumptuous scale, as at Sandiacre and Norbury in Derbyshire and at Checkley in Staffordshire, but in the nature of things this could not happen very often.

At a number of churches, including a few of importance, the siting of the tower is eccentric. Two grand instances are St Mary Redcliffe, Bristol, where it is at the north-west corner of the church, and St Mary the Virgin, Oxford, where it is in the centre of the north side; but the majority of these non-axial towers are in the three south-eastern counties, especially Kent, together with London, Wren's buildings included. In the medieval churches there is no common explanation for these unexpected placings, but in the Victorian period asymmetrical composition could be a deliberate and conscious process, as at Fretherne in Gloucestershire. This church was due to the local 'squarson', the Rev. Sir Lionel Darell, 4th baronet. It is incredibly, indeed oppressively, sumptuous. Much thought, much care went into its creation, and obviously large sums of money, but internally it is a building without sparkle, humour or grace. The tower, as at St Mary Redcliffe, is at the north-west corner, and although these asymmetrical sitings add variety to the exterior, the trouble with them is that from some angles they are unsatisfactory. The view of Fretherne from the south-east is fine, with an exquisitely detailed east end in the foreground and the roofs piling up one above the other to the richly crocketed spire as the culminating point at the back of the composition. But from any other direction it is not so good, and at St Mary Redcliffe this is equally true. With the Wren churches, often very poorly sited, the steeples are so fascinating that one tends to look at them in isolation and to forget altogether about the rest of the building.

In this chapter our concern is with formal questions, but these can seldom be dissociated from materials. This is well illustrated when we consider the incidence of round towers and apsidal east ends. The one material in which it is as easy to build a curving wall as a straight one is flint: indeed it is easier, because straight walls demand angle-turns, and for these stone is required, which is often absent from the flint areas. So it is no surprise to find that the great area for these rounded forms is East Anglia (*18*). Most of these towers and apses date back at least to the twelfth century, and some to the Saxon period. Of the round towers, some of which have a polygonal top stage later than the rest, the total number surviving in England is now about 175. Of these no fewer than 119 are in Norfolk and 41 in Suffolk. Surprisingly, perhaps, a round tower makes visually quite a good terminal feature for a square-ended church.

Completely detached towers in England are comparatively rare. Here it was not a question of the materials of building, but of the foundations. Swinging bells exert a considerable pull on the walls of the tower in which they hang. The foundations therefore need to be firm. There are certain regions where this poses a problem, notably the Norfolk Marshland at the head of the Wash, famous among amateurs of churches, for fens do not make the best foundations. The towers of two of these, West Walton and Terrington St Clement, are detached. The former has a robust and richly detailed three-stage tower, mainly erected about 1240, some 60 feet away across the churchyard. The material is not flint but Barnack limestone brought from near Stamford by water in flat barges. With its massive corner buttress, octagonal on plan, this is a memorable tower, despite a weak parapet and corner pinnacles which were added later and are unfortunately out of character. But it bears no architectural relationship to its church.

It seems probable that originally, like its not very different neighbour Long Sutton, West Walton had a lead-covered spire. For this tower was built at a time when a spire, wherever it could be afforded, was added almost as a matter of course. Until the Victorian period, however, this was only true of the years between the early thirteenth and the late fourteenth centuries.

The spire appeared in embryo in the Romanesque period: a low pyramid, like the one at Old Shoreham in Sussex, which is a renewal but illustrates the type. It is without aesthetic interest: in fact, the tower would look better without it. It was erected for the purely practical purpose of draining off rain and snow from the top.

The true spire appeared first in France. One of the first, as well as one of the grandest, crowns the south-west tower of the cathedral of Chartres; it is a stone spire, hollow inside, rising to the then prodigious and still remarkable height of 345 feet. It was completed about 1165.

In England there are no spires from the twelfth century, and not many survivors earlier than 1250. One of the oldest, of about 1230, is that of the Priory church of St Frideswide at Oxford, which since 1545 has been the Cathedral. It is rather squat and has been a good deal restored – the present corner pinnacles are all Victorian; but it is a good sound design, of a type first evolved in Normandy. Somewhat loftier, but obviously deriving from it, is the excellent spire at Witney, built some twenty years later. It is significant that both these places should be only a few miles downstream from the Taynton limestone quarries.

By this time the urge to build spires had taken hold of many of our church builders. Unlike the tower, with its bells, the spire served no useful purpose. It became a glorious extravagance. But the dramatic significance of this form, steeply heaven-pointing, was something not to be resisted; and as spires and towers play a greater part in most people's awareness of the parish churches than any other single feature, it seems worth discussing them in some little detail.

Round spires would have been quite acceptable, but in stone they were very difficult to construct. It therefore came to be taken as axiomatic that the shape of a spire, on plan, should be octagonal. This at once raised another problem: how was the transition between the square top of the tower and the spire's octagonal base to be effected? There was no structural difficulty: it was easy enough to build arches across the angles at the top of the tower. The problem was an aesthetic one, concerned with appearance. Broadly speaking, in our medieval parish churches, the difficulty was surmounted in one of three ways: either by the introduction of pinnacles at the four corners, by means of the broach, or by setting the base of the spire within a parapet, to which pinnacles might or might not be added.

Oxford and Witney are examples of the first type, and there are three more in the western part of Oxfordshire, all of the same period; but this kind of spire is not at all common in England. One other famous and early example of the type is the leaning tower at Long Sutton in Lincolnshire mentioned above. The stone tower is crowned by a big wooden spire sheathed with lead. The top stage of the tower has octagonal angle turrets which provide a perfect base for the candle-snuffer pinnacles. Compared with Witney, this tower is less sophisticated, but very likeable, with the strips of lead arranged in herring-bone patterns.

The broach type also first appeared in the early part of the thirteenth century. A broach is a sloping half-pyramid (or elongated half-pyramid) of masonry introduced at the base of each of the four oblique sides of an octagonal spire, with the object of throwing off the rain and snow which would otherwise fall on the tower's four angles. From the purely practical standpoint, the broach was most successful, but aesthetically the merits of this form are more questionable. The change in the angle of the spire's silhouette at the apex of the broaches can be unpleasing.

Later in the thirteenth century, and in the first part of the fourteenth, designers of broach spires liked also to incorporate a profusion of gabled dormers known as spire lights or lucarnes, as can be well seen at Ketton in Rutland (*33*). Here an excellent Early English tower of *c.* 1240 received, nearly a century later, a most elaborate stone spire with gabled lucarnes which achieve considerable prominence. Their function was not to light but to ventilate; other than this their intention was certainly decorative, and a further adornment was added in the form of a statue under a canopy at the apex of each of the four broaches. The result is certainly lavish; and it is not without significance that in the Victorian period Ketton was one of the most generally admired spires in England. Today one has reservations. These lucarnes and canopied statues introduce a note of fussiness which to some eyes will no longer be welcome. Still more than the broaches themselves, they can be regarded as excrescences which mar the spire's clean silhouette. Yet there can hardly be a sizeable town in the country which does not possess at least one Victorian church with a spire of this type.

In the Gothic age broach spires of stone appeared in small numbers in various parts of the country, but particularly in the east Midlands, the region in which church-building was at its most active during the Decorated period. The chief concentration is in the area bounded by Northampton, Huntingdon, Lincoln, Nottingham and Leicester. The most pleasing are those, like Spaldwick in Huntingdonshire, with small, neat lucarnes only on the four cardinal faces of the spire, the diagonal faces remaining plain. Another refinement is seen at Whatton in Nottinghamshire, where the lucarnes lean backwards against the faces of the spire, and so have very little projection at their apex.

There is another concentration of non-parapeted spires, several hundred in all, in the villages of Surrey, Kent and especially Sussex, but they are of wood, usually covered with shingles that have weathered to a delightful silvery hue. These are spires of a more modest type, without lucarnes, which is no cause for regret, but often somewhat drastically restored. The majority belong to a variation of the broach form known as the splay-footed spire. In this type, the alternate faces are splayed out near their base to cover the corner, and the intermediate faces taper away to a point. Shingles again provide the normal covering. West Chiltington in Sussex (*32*) is typical. Such spires are not architecturally ambitious, but they strike a homely note that is very appropriate to the unpretentious churches of the Weald (*15*). Horsham has one of the loftiest: a spire which towards the top has warped quite noticeably, though not of course on the scale of the famous twisted spire at Chesterfield. It should be added that, although not very common, there are examples of splay-footed spires in stone too, as at Elton in Northamptonshire.

Many of our medieval wooden spires have not survived owing to their liability to storm damage. Lightning conductors in the Middle Ages were unknown, and although a relic of a saint in a little casket was occasionally placed just below the top of the spire, it was not, in truth, quite such an effective safeguard.

Our grandest spires are all of the parapeted kind: the third type. After about the middle of the fourteenth century, until the end of the Gothic age, this was to oust the others altogether. The reason was at least partly practical. When the top of a tower terminated in a platform providing a pathway round the base of the spire, its construction, and the erection of scaffolding for the purpose of effecting repairs, became very much simpler and less costly. But in addition to this, the parapet offered new opportunities of an artistic kind. Some wonderful variations were achieved.

At its most basic I know no better example of this type of spire than Hemingbrough in the Vale of York, east of Selby (*36*). It is 120 feet high, which is exactly double the height of the tower. Of studied plainness, it leaps up dramatically, like a rapier pointed at the sky. On its very top is a gilded weathercock. The probable date is about 1430. The one weakness, to my eye, is the parapet itself, which seems too frilly for the starkness of this sweeping spire. But at least there are no corner pinnacles, and here their omission is artistically right.

Another type of parapeted spire which certainly needs no corner pinnacles is the so-called Hertfordshire spike. This is an interesting example of a local development in spire design, virtually confined to Hertfordshire and the counties contiguous with it. From the flat roof of an often quite massive tower rises a cheeky spirelet, of timber covered with lead: dignity crowned by impudence. Hertfordshire has come in for some good-natured teasing for her 'candle-snuffers', 'extinguishers' or 'needles', as her critics have variously termed them. Yet, although they disobey all the canons of good proportion and scale, these little spires are sometimes rather witty, and personally I cherish them.

Usually, however, corner pinnacles are not only an asset but aesthetically essential for parapeted spires, as can be fully appreciated at St Mary Redcliffe, Bristol. St Mary the Virgin, Oxford, even has a double tier of clustered pinnacles; although much rebuilt in 1895, this is a grand essay in the art of spire composition.

After the end of the fourteenth century, far fewer spires were built. This was partly because tower design in the Perpendicular period reached such a stage of perfection that the spire became aesthetically superfluous, and partly because men's attitude to religion tended to become more matter-of-fact and less transcendental, which also operated in favour of towers rather than spires. There was a third reason. In the fifteenth century, as was noted in the last chapter, church walls grew ever loftier, but, for reasons of economy, the roofs became much flatter. With a nearly flat roof a tower harmonizes much better than a spire. This can be seen at Whittlesey in the Isle of Ely, a typical mid-fifteenth century spire; the uninteresting flat roofs of the church do nothing to lead the eye up to it, hence it is best seen from the west (37). The tower is elaborate; the spire admirably proportioned, with three diminishing tiers of lucarnes which, very properly, are allowed scarcely any projection. The angles were now enriched with crockets. These, besides being markedly effective, served a practical as well as a decorative purpose, as steps for the steeplejack. Crockets are not at all unusual in the Perpendicular period. Then there are the four little flying buttresses that link the spire itself to the corner pinnacles. These may perhaps help to steady the pinnacles in a high wind, but for the spire itself they have no structural significance: their justification, once again, is purely aesthetic. Sometimes, as in Lincolnshire at Gosberton and Billingborough, such buttresses are so slender as noticeably to weaken the total effect, and are therefore of no benefit. But at Whittlesey the device is successful because the little buttresses, although pierced, are sufficiently robust. Louth, 'that queen of English spires', as Francis Bond called it, designed by 'a genius among masons', also has these linking buttresses, generously conceived and leading to corner pinnacles of exceptionally lofty and sturdy form. This is both the loftiest (about 295 feet) and the last (1501–15) of our medieval parish church spires, and a most noble design.

For religious reasons the taste for spires was very strong again in the Victorian period. Many of these spires are over-fussy; some are built of unsympathetic materials. But the best are splendid. To mention only two, Henry Woodyer's spire at Highnam near Gloucester, with two tiers of crocketed pinnacles and leaf ornamentation as well as roll mouldings running up the eight angles, is a most sumptuous creation, perfectly proportioned.

But these do nothing to invalidate the proposition that to one style only, the Gothic, does the spire truly and naturally belong. And even in the Gothic age the vogue for the spire was by no means universal. It is an architectural form which has never made much headway in the Mediterranean countries. Italy has always much preferred the dome, as befits both her classical inheritance and the strength of her Catholicism, for the dome, with its splendour and magnificence, is emotionally somewhat aloof: an essentially authoritarian form.

Moreover, in England itself the incidence of medieval spires is, and always was, very uneven. Those parts of the country which did not become rich until the fifteenth century were less likely to build them. In the whole of Somerset, a large county, there are fewer than two dozen medieval spires, and most of these are unimportant. In Norfolk and Suffolk they are hardly less exceptional. They are also uncommon in Devon and Cornwall and very few and far between in the distant north.

Towers, on the other hand – towers without spires, that is – are everywhere: towers secular as well as sacred, smiling or solemn, slender or sturdy, simple or sumptuous, romantic or even, though much less often, classical. I believe that no country possesses so many towers that reach a really high standard of design. And of course nearly all the best are associated with cathedrals, abbeys and priories, and parish churches. The numbers are extraordinary. Between 1350 and 1535, in addition to about 1100 new churches in the Perpendicular style with towers, it has been calculated that some 2300 churches already in existence either had their towers heightened or were given new ones. In contrast to the Norman towers they were now very well built, and nearly all of them survive. It is a marvellous legacy. Because of their prominence they impress themselves upon the imagination even of people who have never thought much about architecture nor made any study of it. As often as not, it is by them that one remembers best, or recalls most easily, a city, a town or a village. Our church towers, far more even than our spires if we think of the country as a whole, are part of our scenery.

Despite the collapses referred to earlier, a considerable number of English Romanesque church towers do survive, a few even going back to the Saxon period. Of these, Earls Barton in Northamptonshire, built late in the tenth century, is easily the finest. This tower exhibits the well-known Saxon 'long and short' work at the quoins, but in addition the whole face of the tower is adorned with stone panelling – flat strips of stone variously arranged, which perform no structural function, and apparently represent an imitation of timber-framing.

In the mature phase of Romanesque, towers grew much more impressive in scale, as can be seen for example at Tewkesbury. But in England, as everywhere else at this time, there was a tendency to cut up the wall surfaces into aggregations of small components; this can be very attractive, certainly, yet it implies an excessive concern with surface decoration at the expense of more vital qualities, and is not really very architectural. The most strongly designed of our Norman parish church towers is at Castor, near Peterborough (*38*), to which, in the fourteenth century, a short stone spire was added, that is entirely suitable. Thanks to the excellence of the local Barnack limestone, this tower is in an excellent state of preservation.

With the arrival of the Gothic style a bolder phase of tower-designing developed, cluminating in the really brilliant achievements of the fifteenth and early sixteenth centuries. Not until one has made a study of these is one in a position to formulate any sort of aesthetic in relation to the design of towers.

There are, I believe, four highly desirable requirements for a fine tower. The horizontal divisions should be subordinate to the vertical. There should be strong angle-buttresses, for, on large towers, these are of great importance visually no less than structurally. The tower should get richer as the eye moves upwards, with the horizontal divisions becoming progressively loftier. And lastly, the summit should be reconciled with the sky: a vital point, for, if the termination is too abrupt, as at Lavenham, the eye will register an uncomfortable jolt, like a vehicle coming to a sudden halt. Other factors which should certainly not be overlooked comprise the arrangement of the windows (including those unglazed windows in the upper parts of towers which are really sound holes), the position and prominence (or lack of it) of the stair-turret, and the relationship of the tower to the rest of the church. Some readers may be surprised that this last is not placed amongst the essentials; but, as was seen at Whittlesey a few pages back, it is in fact perfectly possible, and in my view legitimate, to consider a tower for itself, apart from the building to which it is attached, although a good relationship between the two is obviously preferable. In Somerset the passion for building towers gathered such momentum that the resources which elsewhere might have been devoted to other parts of the church all went as often as not into the tower; thus in the county it is not unusual to find towers which, for all their beauties, are quite out of scale with the rest of the building. The extreme case of Leigh-on-Mendip (*41*) has already been cited. The disparity is odd, even hilarious. Yet it hardly interferes at all with the appreciation, for its own sake, of this memorable tower.

It is almost inevitable that any individual consideration of English church towers should begin in Somerset. Francis Bond expressed the view that the high reputation of the Somerset towers depends upon 'the exceptional splendour of the relatively few', and that 'the greater number fall below the average of East Anglia'. It is certainly true that the majority of Somerset towers are smaller, and to that extent less imposing, than the East Anglian group. But size is not a major determinant of a tower's beauty. And the remarkable fact is that, wherever Somerset characteristics occur in other parts of England, as at Chittlehampton in Devon, Probus in Cornwall, St Neots in Huntingdonshire and Titchmarsh in Northamptonshire, these are the very towers which stand out high above their neighbours for sheer quality of design, even if, as is certainly true of Chittlehampton and Probus, the builders appear not to have given much thought to the *genius loci*. (The one exception to this dictum is Great

Driffield in the East Riding, a fine tower with some strong Somerset characteristics which yet does not surpass all its neighbours.)

Through the years there have been a number of attempts at a classification of the Somerset towers, beginning with E. A. Freeman's as long ago as 1851. Freeman's classification is not very helpful, because it is founded on the character of the stair-turrets, which are not a basic feature in tower design. In the present century there have been R. P. Brereton's valuable paper printed in the *Archaeological Journal* for 1905, Francis Bond's somewhat brief treatment in the second volume of his *Introduction to English Church Architecture* (1913), F. J. Allen's very detailed survey in *The Great Church Towers of England* (1932), in which no fewer than eighty Somerset towers are illustrated, A. K. Wickham's perceptive pages in his *Churches of Somerset* (1952) and a valuable reclassification in the introduction to Nikolaus Pevsner's two volumes on Somerset in *The Buildings of England* (1958). The reader is referred to at least three of these sources: Allen is the fullest, Pevsner and Wickham the soundest. There are, in my view, 13 parish church towers in Somerset which, for quality of design, are undoubtedly in the highest class, and in the whole of the rest of the country there are hardly more than that.

One wonders how many people every year go to Wells for the Cathedral without also seeing, perhaps even without realising that there is, waiting to be seen, hardly five minutes' walk away, one of the best parish church towers in Somerset (and incidentally also, at 142 feet, the second highest). St Cuthbert has a number of notable features, but the tower is its great glory (*39*). As with the lovely central tower of the Cathedral, the two upper stages are treated as subdivisions of a single stage of great loftiness, which gives the tower an emphatic verticality. This is what is also seen at Wrington, Evercreech and Batcombe. Of these the gem is Evercreech (*40*), a design of exquisite refinement: one of the most perfect in England.

Four of the loveliest towers are all within a dozen miles of Taunton. North Petherton (*43*), on the Bridgwater road, is marred only by being partly built of Blue (really slate-pencil grey) Lias, which marries none too happily with the brown top stage and dressings. It is none the less a masterpiece of good proportion and in the handling of profuse ornamental enrichment. The treatment of the buttresses is specially noteworthy. There are several ways of designing buttresses. They may project diagonally from the angles; they may clasp the corners; they may take the form of corner turrets; or they may be arranged as here, projecting from near the corner of each face, yet set back sufficiently to allow the actual angles of the tower to be seen. This is the most usual method in England, and perhaps aesthetically the best. At North Petherton a tall crocketed pinnacle adorns every set-off, and, at the stage below the parapet, the pinnacles are set diagonally. All the windows of the tower are filled with that elaborately pierced stone tracery which was a Somerset speciality and an addition of great elegance, unfortunately absent at St Cuthbert, Wells. The crown is opulent.

The other three specially fine towers in the Taunton neighbourhood have much in common, although the materials differ. Ile Abbots, Staple Fitzpaine and Kingston St Mary are decidedly smaller than North Petherton: none is quite 90 feet high. Ile Abbots (*45*) was partly rebuilt (extremely well) in the last century, yet preserves to an unusual degree its original sculpture. Kingston St Mary (*46*), although the roughest, is perhaps the loveliest of the three. This tower is not built, like all its fellows mentioned here, of Jurassic limestone (oolite or lias), but of Keuper (New Red) sandstone, quarried from under the Quantock hills close by. Only the dressings are ashlared: the main walling is less urbane, but has a countryman's strength. The harmony of blended colours, reds, browns, greys, greens, is enchanting: even the mortar is, most appropriately, reddish.

The tower of Kingston has not the grace of Evercreech, but it combines sturdiness of form with the utmost luxuriance of decoration, and is in many ways a model of good tower design. In the management of the buttresses, in the subordination of the horizontal divisions to the vertical, in the proportions and arrangement of the bell-chamber windows with their pierced 'Somerset tracery', in the increasing richness as the eye mounts, and in the reconciliation of the summit with the sky by means of an elaborate and beautiful crown – in all these respects, Kingston is everything it should be. In the middle stage, the windows are flanked by niches which once contained figures. Above, the introduction of crocketed pinnacles is extremely successful. And on the skyline there are, in addition to the median pinnacles, little crocketed spires at each corner, surrounded by four tiny spirelets. All these rise above an embattled parapet pierced with quatrefoils to form a splendid crown.

The other five Somerset towers to which I would accord the highest accolade are Leigh-on-Mendip, Mells, Chewton Mendip, Huish Episcopi and Ilminster. Leigh-on-Mendip (*41*), of local grey oolite, is one of the most beautiful of all the Somerset group. It has triple bell-chamber 'windows' in two tiers, the upper with 'Somerset tracery', the lower blind. Except that none of these has a hood-mould, this tower seems to me almost faultless. Mells suffers by comparison from having no decoration on the parapet, but is otherwise very similar to Leigh and a little bigger. Chewton Mendip (*42*) is the loftiest village church tower of them all (119 feet to the top of the pinnacles) and was one of the last to be built. It is a very noble tower; at the crown the designer must have looked for his inspiration to Glastonbury, which meant, as we shall soon see, to

Gloucester. The church attached to it is completely insignificant, which is equally true of Huish Episcopi. This tower (*44*) suffers even more than North Petherton from excessive polychromy; the whitish grey lias provides too shrill a background for the nutty-brown Ham Hill stone. But in its design it wears an air of great authority. The horizontal stages are boldly differentiated, yet are not so strong as the verticals, and although the ornamentation is profuse, this remains, as it should, strictly subordinate to the overall form. Ilminster, referred to in Chapter 2, is of Ham Hill stone throughout and differs from all the others in being a central and not a western tower as well as in having a big stair-turret at one corner.

Outside Somerset the grandest towers, *pace* Francis Bond, are not in East Anglia but in Gloucestershire and in Yorkshire. In the former, as in Somerset, the quality of the masonry is often superb, thanks to the Cotswold stone. Just as the central tower of Wells gave a lead in Somerset, so did the tower of Gloucester Cathedral here.[23] Characteristics of the Gloucestershire towers, all stemming from the Cathedral, are the very pronounced horizontal divisions, achieved by allowing the strongly designed string courses to thrust their way round each of the buttresses, the diagonal placing of these buttresses, and the elaborate pierced parapets with very lofty corner turrets. Both at Thornbury and at St Stephen, Bristol, there is a late crown of sensational exuberance clearly derived from the Cathedral, but in both cases the rest of the tower is comparatively plain, so that the eye is insufficiently prepared for the outburst at the summit. Perhaps the most beautiful tower of this group is not in the county at all, but at Great Malvern in Worcestershire; here the Priory has what is really a reduced version of the Cathedral tower, and still better proportioned. There is even one tower of obvious Gloucester origin in Somerset: St John, Glastonbury. It does not have diagonally placed buttresses, but another Gloucestershire characteristic, surface panelling, is present here, as also at Chipping Campden (*47*). This tower has one unusual detail: the manner in which the subsidiary pinnacles spring from ogee arches placed in front of the parapet, an arrangement more curious than beautiful. But in other ways this stylish, stately tower, admirably proportioned and beautifully sited, is a typical Gloucestershire creation.

The sandstone counties to the north of Gloucestershire do not possess many towers of the first quality, and one at least of their finest, at Worcester Cathedral, is in constant need of repair. But among the parish churches Ludlow has a tower which, if somewhat lacking in subtlety, is of striking height, and unforgettable within (*120*). No one should neglect, on entering a church, to stand directly underneath the tower and look up. Now and again, especially in Somerset, he will find a charming fan vault in stone. Of this Bell Harry at Canterbury provides the supreme example. Elsewhere there are many variants. The best effects are always obtained where the tower is central and of the 'lantern' type: that is to say, with windows lighting the space above the tower arches. At Ludlow the roof above the lantern is only of wood imitating stone (like the celebrated one at Ely), but wooden ribs, eight of them tiercerons, and trefoil-headed arches have combined to produce a stellar pattern that is wholly delightful.

Cheshire has at Gawsworth a plain tower with an exquisite crown. But the best tower of the Cheshire type is, again, just outside the county itself, at Gresford in Denbighshire. This mining village has a glorious church of buff-coloured sandstone, with a tower that is a design of rare beauty, dating from 1482.

Yorkshire has some towers of splendid quality. In the West Riding the best is Tickhill, with niched and canopied sculpture in the middle stage (*48*). The exuberant crown has, in addition to eight crocketed pinnacles, a pretty fringe-like parapet that has no parallel in the South; the effect is produced by erecting a little crocketed arch over each embrasure. Halifax, a noble church of soot-black gritstone, has a tower of quite a different kind, slightly pinched at the top but quite rich too, and strangely satisfying. In the North Riding the fifteenth-century tower at Coxwold (*50*), built of buff-coloured New Red sandstone, is distinctive in being octagonal from the ground, which, comparison with Lowick and Fotheringhay and some others suggests, is from the design standpoint far more satisfactory than modulating from a square to an octagon some way up. The face of each of the long delicate buttresses at Coxwold is not flat but brought forward to a chamfered edge. Another wholly octagonal tower, no less effective, can be seen in the East Riding at Sancton, west of Beverley; but here the church to which it belongs has been rebuilt.

It is, however, in the East Riding that the Yorkshire tower-builders surpassed themselves. As noted earlier, the influence of Somerset (in general character if not in details) is very apparent at Great Driffield, but at Beverley, Hull, Hedon and elsewhere the style is different. The finest is Hedon, a central tower (*49*). As is not unusual in Yorkshire, the belfry windows are large: so large as to leave no area of wall between window and buttress. This, and the array of sixteen rather small, delicate pinnacles – not what one would expect to find in the vigorous North, but in fact another Yorkshire characteristic – detract somewhat from the appearance of strength. But these are minor criticisms of what is, by any standard, a very lovely tower, splendid alike in scale and in its finely controlled decoration.

Lincolnshire is less famous for towers than for spires, but, in Kesteven especially, there are some fine towers that never had nor needed them. A

late and sumptuous example, built in 1519, is at Great Ponton, on the A1
(7). In its gorgeous crown and in its scale in relation to the rest of the
church, this tower recalls Somerset, but the bell-chamber windows, each
with a central mullion continued upwards into the arch, are a good
instance of local (and here rather infelicitous) mannerism to be found at
three Stamford churches and at several others in the neighbourhood.
None the less, this is a grand tower for a modest village church, which we
owe to a combination of one rich man's generosity and the fact that Great
Ponton is right on the Jurassic limestone belt, so that the beautiful silver-
grey oolite was readily available.

Norfolk and Suffolk have some very imposing towers which are seldom
out of scale with the churches, because the buildings themselves are
frequently so large. But flints, as we have seen, although immensely
durable in themselves, are no stronger in a wall than the strength of the
mortar in which they are embedded. So in East Anglia the corner
buttresses sometimes project considerably, and have a pronounced batter.
At Stoke-by-Nayland this is so marked as to mar quite seriously the
tower's effect. Elsewhere the buttresses take the form of massive corner
turrets, which may be square on plan, as at Lavenham, but are more often
octagonal, as at Eye and Redenhall. Another East Anglian characteristic,
which was probably derived from the Netherlands, is the stepped form of
the parapet's battlements.

The best towers of Suffolk and Norfolk are admirably robust, but they
lack the generous and smiling exuberance of the leading Somerset and
Severn Valley examples. The window arrangement is more haphazard,
and the shortage of good materials meant that the decorative beauties of
the West, such as pierced stonework, or crocketed pinnacles on the
buttresses and on the skyline, usually had to be omitted. To compensate to
some extent for these ornamental deprivations, the best towers do have a
good deal of flushwork, mostly in the form of tall, thin tracery patterns.

With the superb exception of Canterbury, the chalk and clay lands of
the South-East produced little that is memorable in the sphere of tower
design. Some of the modest rubble-built towers of Sussex and Kent are
likeable enough, but they cannot be said to achieve architectural
importance. Even Tenterden, the best church tower in Kent, would
attract little attention in Somerset.

In Devon and Cornwall, on the other hand, the towers, if usually
austere in form, achieve at their best a remarkable dignity. They tend to be
very tall, as at Totnes, Ashburton (24) and Harberton (25). Many of them
have a prominent stair-turret in the middle of one side: a good example of
a pronounced local characteristic. The turret itself is octagonal in form,
and rises sheer. The very hard stones that characterise these two counties
(22) do not lend themselves to rich and detailed carving like the fine

GOTHIC SPIRE ON A NORMAN TOWER

38. Castor, Peterborough

39. Wells: St Cuthb‹

SOMERSET TOWERS

40. Evercreech   41. Leigh-on-Mendip   42. Chewton Men‹

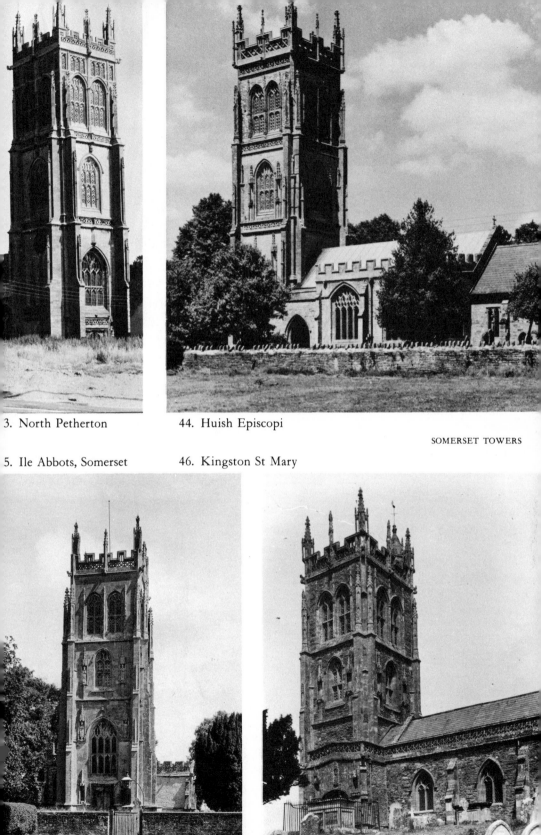

43. North Petherton

44. Huish Episcopi

45. Ile Abbots, Somerset

46. Kingston St Mary

47. Chipping Campden,
Gloucestershire

OTHER TOWERS

48: Tickhill, Yorksh

49. Hedon, Yorkshire

50. Coxwold, Yorkshire

oolites, and anyway there was not the money here to pay for it. But the lofty austerity of these towers looks specially right where the scenery is of the moorland type. For boldness of outline the best of these towers are highly successful, and to an eye attracted by the stark acerbities of modern architecture there will probably be no church towers in England that will seem so congenial.

A good many of the cathedral builders treated themselves to three towers: a fine extravagance, with no functional justification, for which we can be perpetually grateful. The parish church builders, needless to say, could scarcely ever indulge themselves to that extent, although at Melbourne in Derbyshire, an exceptionally ambitious church for its date, they contemplated doing so even in the twelfth century. In the event, the west towers were not carried up above the nave roof, and the central tower was heightened, disproportionally, in 1602, so this is not a successful three-tower grouping. The only other three-tower parish church compositions, both in Yorkshire, were not built as such. Selby was a Benedictine abbey until the Dissolution. Its central tower collapsed in 1690 and its west towers, as at Melbourne, would seem not to have emerged above the level of the roof in the Middle Ages. There was a devastating fire here in 1906 and the central tower had to be rebuilt again. The upper stages of the west towers, which are still rather on the short side, date only from 1935. At Beverley Minster, a collegiate foundation from Saxon times until the mid-sixteenth century, the central tower was never carried up; in the eighteenth century it was given a very peculiar dome of ogee form, which in 1824 was removed. So, as at Westminster Abbey, the central tower makes very little impact. The two western towers, on the other hand, are a delight, and markedly superior to the pair at York Minster. The date, once again, is the fifteenth century. If considered singly, these towers might be deemed too slender for their height, but of course they were always designed to be seen together. They are exceptional in being rectangular, not square, on plan, so that at the crown, ingeniously, they have two median pinnacles on the east and west sides, and only one to north and south, making a cluster of fourteen pinnacles for each tower. Beverley Minster has one of the best designed façades in England, the cathedrals not excepted. Its towers are in the top class.

The rectangular towers of Beverley Minster can easily be justified by reference to the church's plan, but what of the polygonal – usually octagonal – stages with which at least sixty of our medieval towers terminate? A few – Coxwold and Sancton have been cited, and another is Stanwick in Northamptonshire – are octagonal from the ground. Where a spire was wanted – and here a spire was added about a century later – the octagon provided an ideally shaped base for it. But on a square tower the transition to the octagon itself poses a problem, and the right proportions between the square and octagonal stages of a tower were evidently very difficult to achieve. Towers of this form seem to be more successful at the centre of the church than at the west end. One of the best is certainly Nantwich: it is perhaps a little small for the church, but it is a design of great charm and accomplishment. On the other hand, the octagonal top stage of Boston 'Stump', fine in itself, does not seem very happy there. This is the highest spireless tower in England (not less than 272 feet: the figures given in books for the heights of towers and spires seldom exactly agree): an extraordinary and wonderful tower, visible for many miles across the fens and even occasionally from Norfolk, 40 miles away across the Wash. Wonderful, yes, but not a great work of art. After the second stage it was originally intended to add a spire. This was never built, and it remained – a stump. After well over a century the third stage was added: and then, early in the sixteenth century, the fourth, the octagon. The tower was therefore designed piecemeal, and looks like it. It is perhaps worth adding that its composition is much less inept than that of the belfry at Bruges, which enjoys even greater celebrity.

In medieval architecture a clear distinction between the tower and the spire is almost always possible: we can see where the tower ends and the spire begins. With Wren and his successors the situation is more complicated. Sometimes the division is still quite clear, but not always; hence the employment of the comprehensive word steeple.

Most of Wren's churches were built on confined sites offering little or no scope for impressive elevations. That is why his special genius found its main expression in two other directions: in the planning, and in the design of the steeples. Within a limited range, these London steeples show extraordinary resourcefulness and variety. Almost all of them ascend in a succession of diminishing stages, so what one looks for are the basic differences in shape and proportion between the various tiers. Sometimes Wren used, in one tier, curved forms, which might be either convex as at St Magnus the Martyr, or concave as at St Martin, Ludgate. But more enjoyable are the designs of telescope form, on which he evolved many variations. At St Stephen, Walbrook, the successive tiers are square on plan. At St James, Garlickhythe (51), the steeple was not finished until 1717, which was thirty-four years after the church. As with some of our Gothic steeples, the base of the spire is a little small for the tower; but it is a charming design. There are three tiers, of which the lowest has pairs of columns projecting diagonally at the corners. From their entablatures, with the aid of Wren's favourite ornamental vases, the eye is led on to the cubical stage above, and then in similar fashion to the tier above that, and so to the lofty finial.

Wren's two masterpieces among the parish church steeples offer a fascinating contrast. St Bride, 223 feet high, is his loftiest, and undoubtedly the most beautiful of the telescope type, though, like some of the Somerset towers, it is out of scale with the church. But the church is hemmed in and little seen, whereas the steeple, partly no doubt because its general form is easily grasped, is among the best known and most highly cherished in London. 'A madrigal in stone'.

I say its *general* form advisedly, for how many people, even Londoners, have ever observed that the topmost of the four stages is quite different from the other three? The four curved pediments at the top of the tower prepare our eyes for the delights that are to follow, beginning with an inset section crowned by urns. Then come the four successive tiers of openings of diminishing size, which incidentally produce a very successful counterpoint of strong blacks and whites. Typical of Wren's subtlety is the fact that the depth of the stone base to each tier of openings (all but the top tier arched) increases as the eye mounts. And then we reach the octagon, with only four piercings, and finally a delicately tapering octagonal spire.

It is perhaps true that this steeple is more telling at a distance, and especially from the Thames, than close to. It is certainly less varied than some of Wren's steeple designs. But it is also more spirelike, and the transition from the square tower to the spire-like section above is beautifully contrived.

The other masterpiece, St Mary-le-Bow, was a comparatively early work, completed about 1677. There was no shortage of money here, and it cost the most of any. It is unique in Wren's *œuvre*. The upper stage of the tower is adorned with pairs of Ionic pilasters – two pairs to each face: and then, at the point of transition, come the big corner ornaments, which help so much to give this steeple its flowing and compact line. After this we reach the airy circular storey with its corona of Corinthian columns, and then the famous inverted consoles (or brackets) which provide the vital link with the small upper stage, which is also circular. These consoles seem like springs, coiled back at their lower ends, and serve to impart a fine note of energy into the design. Thus, in addition to being structurally useful in helping to take the thrust of the upper stage and spirelet, they also offer great aesthetic satisfaction. The steeple of St Mary-le-Bow is a complex and fascinating design of which one never grows tired, and among Wren's many steeples is surely his greatest.

A smaller, later steeple of great originality, if not one of the most immediately appealing, is St Vedast, Foster Lane, almost within a stone's cast of St Mary-le-Bow. The base is slightly rectangular, the next storey is concave, the one above that convex, and finally comes the stone spire with its four sides distinctly hollowed out again. This is therefore a very sophisticated design, relying for its effect hardly at all, for once, upon ornament; the appeal comes solely from the way in which the forms themselves are handled: the forms and, under favourable conditions, the light. For with so many contrasts of surface direction, some concave, some convex, to say nothing of the unusual placing of the projecting pilasters across the four corners of the steeple, the play of light can be a vital factor. Those who prefer Hawksmoor's steeples to Wren's are likely to cherish the steeple of St Vedast above any other by the master. It has greater precision and a more mathematical quality. It also has, in my opinion, less geniality and less poetry.

It is probably not overstating it to say that Wren and his immediate successors gave London the most beautiful skyline of any city in the world at that time. In his well-known picture, *The City of London from Richmond House*, painted in 1746, Canaletto shows no fewer than 36 steeples, some white, some grey, clustered around the great dome of St Paul's Cathedral. Some of Samuel Scott's pictures tell much the same story, though with less sensibility. Now, alas, that skyline has gone for ever. But the London steeples should still be thought of not only individually but collectively, for, in designing each one, it seems certain that Wren thought also of its place in the general scheme. One of the great unifying factors was the wonderful Portland limestone, which Wren was personally responsible for introducing, on a large scale for the first time, into London.

For three of their best-loved steeples the debt of Londoners is to James Gibbs, and also, as with Wren, to the superb qualities of Portland stone. St Mary-le-Strand, in the happy phrase of Elizabeth and Wayland Young, 'swans charmingly down the Strand with St Clement Danes in its wake'. St Martin-in-the-Fields, a brilliant design whatever one may feel about the relationship of steeple to portico, was the favourite prototype of the many charming wooden steeples of Colonial America. It was also this which provided the obvious inspiration for Henry Flitcroft's richly detailed steeple at St Giles-in-the-Fields. Thomas Archer, at St Paul, Deptford, ingeniously succeeded in overcoming the visual anomaly of a steeple 'riding on the roof' of a church of temple inspiration. From the west, the best viewpoint, the steeple reiterates at each stage the curved motif of the imposing semicircular portico (*53*).

The churches of Nicholas Hawksmoor awaken entirely different responses from those of his contemporaries. They are among the most curious and original buildings in London. As John Summerson has said, he regarded every one of them as 'an essay in solid geometry', and to some people today they make a great appeal. To me his churches seem brooding and intensely introspective. The steeples are highly original. The spire with which he crowned the façade of Christ Church, Spitalfields, exerts a strange power, but the steeple of St Anne, Limehouse (*52*), far surpasses it, surely, as a work of art. No greater contrast could be imagined than that between Hawskmoor and John Nash, whose curving portico, with the spire above, is all that one normally sees of All Souls, Langham Place. This was just a picturesque point of focus in a grand piece of town-planning. Around its curving front the eye easily pivots, at the point where a respect for the rights of private property rendered necessary a slight shift in the axis of the street. Nash managed it with ingenuity and wit.

The Georgian attitude towards towers and spires was usually, needless to say, purely aesthetic. The first Lord Berwick offered – was indeed anxious – to pay for the addition of a spire to the tower of Wroxeter church in Shropshire, a parish with which he had no connection, simply in order to improve the view from the windows of his house, Attingham Park. (The parish would have none of it.) At Worplesdon in Surrey, in 1766, the fifteenth-century tower was given a pretty little cupola brought from the rectory stables. It was, and is, an excellent addition. Out in the country Georgian towers and spires were usually built to be 'pretty objects', adornments of the landscape. In that respect some of them were near-follies, like the tower of Galby in Leicestershire, which combines Gothick with Chinese motifs! But there were some notable successes. At no period did the building of spires cease, but it was clearly felt that they would be more acceptable in the context of classical architecture if they were made to look like obelisks. Three steeples of this kind in the Midlands are well worth seeking out: Over Whitacre in Warwickshire, 1766; Tardebigge in Worcestershire, 1777; Saxby in Leicestershire, 1789. The churches are all small, with plain interiors, but their steeples, growing progressively more graceful, are charming. At each the great interest is to note how the transition has been managed from the tower to the spire. Each solution is different, and all three are successful. Incidentally, Saxby, which stands alone (apart from the former rectory) in a sequestered spot, was built and paid for by that Earl of Harborough whom we have already met at Stapleford (cf. p. 39). Before he succeeded he had himself been a local rector: a situation redolent of the eighteenth century.

In the cities the scale of the churches was usually much bigger and the architecture more ambitious. A specially distinguished steeple, in which the obelisk motif again appears at the apex, is that of All Saints, Newcastle-upon-Tyne (54). This dates only from 1790: the architect was a local man, David Stephenson, and for this lovely work he was paid a mere £300, on a contract worth £27,000. The site, on a steep hill overlooking the Tyne, is dramatic (1); no less than with the country churches, the importance of All Saints is above all scenic. The steeple is an exceptionally well designed example of the telescope type. Redundant as a church, the City Council purchased it with the intention of restoring it for use as a music centre, but after fifteen years nothing has been done, and at the time of writing (1985) the condition of the building, which is always kept locked, is said to be deplorable.

In the period of 'incorrect' Gothic before the advent of the Camden Society, tower-building continued in strength: two of my favourites are St Peter, Brighton, an *œuvre de jeunesse* by Barry (1828) and Christ Church, Cheltenham (1840) by the Jearrads. Both these excellent towers are of great scenic importance to their towns. St Peter, facing not west but southwards towards the sea, commands the whole length of the Steine, while Christ Church closes the vista down a broad leafy avenue nearly half a mile long: an exquisite sight in the second half of October. Victorian church towers were usually less adventurous, but still there is the occasional thrill to be had; Cattistock in Dorset by George Gilbert Scott, Jr. (1874) is an example. This tower was built at the expense of the incumbent and his family on a very bold scale, and well rebuilt in 1950–51 after being accidentally burnt in 1940 by soldiers using it as a look-out.

In sum, then, although in certain areas the towers and still more the spires show a family likeness, what is far more remarkable about them is their great variety. If it may seem to some readers that I have devoted a disproportionate amount of space to the steeples, that is the explanation. One of the reasons why, architecturally speaking, travel in Italy is so much more rewarding than in Greece is precisely because so few Greek churches have a campanile. England without her towers and spires would be immensely impoverished visually. As it is, one cannot travel far along English roads, one cannot even look for long out of the window of an English train, without a feeling of gratitude to their designers and builders for adding so much beauty and character to the English scene.

In order to relish the many other formal and decorative delights of our church exteriors we must approach more closely. As we walk along the church path we can often learn a good deal, not only about the stylistic history of the building but about such factors as whether it enjoyed, at any period, rich patronage and whether or not it has undergone drastic restoration.

There has always been a direct relationship between changing styles and changing fortunes. Where are the grand Perpendicular churches? Almost without exception in the rich wool districts. The heavily wooded or 'backward' counties, like Sussex or Herefordshire, had to be content with their dark little Norman churches, of which some still survive. No grand campaign of rebuilding took place here in the fifteenth century. In Sussex, however, and even more in Surrey, Berkshire and elsewhere, the rebuilding did occur – in the Victorian age.

The Norman exteriors, large and small, were sometimes greatly enriched with mouldings and small figurative carvings. After over 800 years, it is inevitable that the majority have had to undergo drastic restoration; at some places, mouldings and carvings would today be scarcely recognisable had they not been recut, and, having been recut, they may no longer be enjoyable. This of course is true of Romanesque churches everywhere; there has been a great deal of restoration in France; while in Germany, partly owing to the friability of so much of the stone but also, it may be suggested, because of an element in the German character which demands that things shall be 'just so', scarcely any original Romanesque work is to be seen anywhere (a fact which is glossed over in all the guidebooks).

The most perfectly preserved small Norman church in England is at Kilpeck in Herefordshire, thanks to the toughness of the local Old Red sandstone. Even this is, of course, by no means unrestored, but the glorious corbel-table, in particular, is mainly original and includes some of the most entertaining small carvings of the entire Middle Ages (58, 59). The sole doorway is also in a boldly sculptured frame notable for strong Viking influence, which is rare in England.

Speaking generally, the best preserved external features of Norman date are the carved tympana above the doorways, because they have often been protected through the centuries by a porch. Herefordshire has a number of interesting examples, crude but lively, notably the Samson and the lion at Stretton Sugwas (56) and the St George and the Dragon (the saint's face unfortunately lost) at Brinsop. George Zarnecki has shown that both these derive from Parthenay-le-Vieux in Poitou. One of the most memorable of these doorways is at Dinton in Buckinghamshire (57). The tympanum here has the Tree of Life, the fruit of which is being consumed by a pair of semi-leonine creatures with forked stylised tails, while on the lintel a formidable dragon is assailing the Archangel Michael. This placid-looking little winged figure is about to thrust a large cross between the jaws of the Satanic monster. The state of preservation is remarkable.

Throughout the thirteenth and the first half of the fourteenth centuries, particularly on the limestone belt, some of the carvers were still enjoying themselves enormously when the corbel-table was reached, as can be seen, for example at Adderbury in Oxfordshire (60). Often, however, the individual carvings were now smaller, as instanced by the innumerable little heads at Grantham.

The Early English period was the time when mouldings were at their purest and most effective, as can be seen in the surrounds of many doors and windows. Grouped lancets are a beautiful feature of some of these churches; Ockham in Surrey and Blakeney in Norfolk have groups of seven, of graded heights.

Windows are frequently better seen and appreciated outside the church than in, because of the poor quality of the stained glass. In Decorated buildings an external view is specially important: the first half of the fourteenth century was the great age of window tracery. Some of the designs of this period are exquisite. At Nantwich in Cheshire (*65*) the richly traceried chancel windows also have crocketed, ogee-shaped gables, producing a most sumptuous effect. In contrast to the starved-looking character of much of today's concrete, these moulded stone windows convey a fine sensation of quality. A good many can be found in Lincolnshire and Northamptonshire: Sleaford, Heckington and Higham Ferrers are all distinguished in this respect. The last is particularly notable for its reticulated tracery (*64*).

The most lavish churches belong to the fifteenth and early sixteenth centuries. A sure sign of luxury, to be sensed immediately upon entering a churchyard, is when the clerestory windows run along in a continuous range. They look best when each is recessed, and therefore strongly 'framed', as at Long Melford (*19*). Perpendicular clerestory windows are seldom of any interest in themselves: it is as a range that they make their impact, somewhat on the analogy of the Georgian terrace. They are intended, that is to say, to be seen not as separate entities but as a whole. As such they are resplendent. Many of the great wool churches have them.

At Chedworth, yet another Cotswold church set in a well-kept churchyard with beautiful Georgian tombstones and chests, the south side, with fine big windows and a collection of king-size gargoyles (*62*), is pure Perpendicular, carried out in perfect ashlar masonry; after this it is a surprising experience to step into a Norman church! This south side is in fact no more than a façade, due to the munificence of a local wool merchant or possibly the lord of the manor. Perpendicular churches can admittedly be too glassy, like Tattershall in Lincolnshire, where, incidentally, damage to glass by high winds is a continual burden on a small parish. At Holy Trinity, Hull, where the nave is like a vast conservatory, they may well have tried to use as little stone as possible in order to reduce the weight on somewhat insecure foundations. The big windows that characterise this style, and its last Tudor phase in particular, make for handsome interiors flooded with light and can also, if adequately 'framed', enhance the exterior too. This is well seen at four churches in the South-West, St John, Devizes and Bromham (*26*) in Wiltshire, Cullompton and Tiverton in Devon. All these had chapels or extra aisles added in the Tudor period towards the eastern end of the south side, in each case in a mood of uninhibited extravagance. Call them *nouveaux riches* if one must: one would have to be very puritanical not to enjoy them.

All these late Perpendicular buildings have nearly flat roofs, covered with lead, invisible behind parapets. Since these were now functionally essential, full advantage was taken of their aesthetic possibilities. Usually

. London: St James,
rlickhythe

. London: St Paul, Deptford

52. London: St Anne, Limehouse

54. Newcastle-upon-Tyne: All
Saints

55. Charney Bassett,
Berkshire

56. Stretton Sugwas,
Herefordshire

57. Dinton,
Buckinghamshire

58. Kilpeck, Herefordshire

59. Kilpeck, Herefordshire

60. Adderbury, Oxfordshire

MEDIEVAL FUN AND GAMES

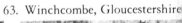

61. Adderbury, Oxfordshire   62. Chedworth, Gloucestershire   63. Winchcombe, Gloucestershire

64. Higham Ferrers,
Northamptonshire

65. Nantwich, Chesh

66. Colyton, Devon

67. Blythburgh, Suff

they were battlemented; sometimes, as at Bromham, they were enriched with plenty of carving; elsewhere they might be pierced, for with a nearly flat roof the sky, from below, might be visible through the apertures. Boldly crocketed pinnacles shot up at frequent intervals, to endow each church with a resplendent skyline. It was in the exact sense of the word a spectacular achievement. The prosperous merchants who paid for most of this work might be competing against each other: they certainly were at Tiverton and Cullompton. And why not?

We are now, perhaps, half-way across the churchyard; it is from here that this late-Gothic showmanship is at its most effective. Approach more closely, and the more sensitive and less mass-produced carvings of the earlier phases of Gothic architecture will undoubtedly make a great appeal. In a book of this length I can hardly begin to do justice to the superb exterior adornment of a big Decorated church like Heckington in Lincolnshire. The abundance of carved detail is extraordinary, but the scale of the architecture can stand it. Even a single buttress (and there are many such) carries four gabled niches for statuary (now lost), two facing south/north, one east and one west. Every gable has a little head or figure at the apex and two more at the base, as well as a profusion of crockets. The east end of both nave and chancel are flanked to the north and south by octagonal turrets, which have carved heads at every angle. There is a frieze of heads, some vividly animated, at the cornice level of every wall, and there is a grand assemblage of gargoyles. Heckington is a specially fine example, but only one among hundreds upon which the medieval masons exerted their skill and, one feels, gave expression to their high spirits. One never ceases to wonder at the fertility of invention which these men displayed, nor at the very high average level of their craftsmanship.

An entire book could be written on gargoyles, 'yelling their soundless blasphemies and derisions to the wind'.[24] In the days before lead down-pipes, which only began to be used in the Tudor period, rainwater was thrown clear of the church walls by means of a projecting spout. In due course, as so often in the Middle Ages, the opportunity was seized of endowing a purely functional member with an interesting decorative form. That was the origin of the gargoyle; and, although the English examples are not quite as bold as some of the French, they became a lively field of sculptural activity, in which the later Gothic phase was just as accomplished as the earlier: perhaps more so. They offered scope for the expression of a wide and uninhibited range of feeling and experience. Some, like the big animals at Wrington, or the set at High Ham, which includes musicians, a deaf man, two monkeys, and a man throwing a weight, are full of geniality. Others, as at Adderbury (61), are more fantastically conceived. The bawdiest known to me is at Glinton in the

Soke of Peterborough, but this too is genial! At Winchcombe, on the other hand, a more macabre note is sounded. This wool church has about forty splendid grotesques (*63*) which, strictly speaking, are not gargoyles because no water-channels run through them, but are executed in exactly the same manner. Coates near Cirencester has on the corner of the tower a carving of terrifying realism. The creature represented, of which we see only the head, shoulders and arms, is an anthropophagus. He has already eaten his victim down to the waist, so that the buttocks are now in full view. When, later, iconoclasts smashed 'holy' images wherever they found them, they were apparently content to leave this inviolate.

Some churches are greatly enriched by their porches. Cathedrals and abbeys had them from early times; that at Malmesbury, with famous Norman sculptures, is an example. Hardly any parish churches had them before the fourteenth century, and a good many of the early ones in the non-stone areas, as we have already noted, were of wood. The need for a porch, and the larger the better, arose because of the variety of functions, some of them secular, which came to be performed there. Legal agreements, for instance, were often signed, and given effect, in the porch. Bond quotes the case of a bequest of £5 in 1712 in the diocese of St Asaph, the interest from which was to be used for the purchase of flannel for four old men and four old women, who were to draw lots for it, or throw dice, in the church porch. And to this day, of course, election notices, lists of voters and so on, can make a porch look tattered and untidy.

The most magnificent church porch in England is at Cirencester, but this is a special case, since it was built independently, by the monks of the nearby abbey. In the seventeenth century it was large enough to serve as the Town Hall. Gloucestershire also has, at Northleach, a more normal kind of porch, of superlative quality. Like all the grandest examples, this one has an upper chamber – often, but wrongly, described as a parvise. (A parvise – Latin, *parvisus* = *paradisus* – was an atrium or forecourt.) This upper room served a variety of purposes; it was a kind of safe deposit for books and legal documents, and the treasury of the church; it was sometimes used as a schoolroom and occasionally, as at Grantham, for the exhibition of relics; while at Titchmarsh in Northamptonshire in the seventeenth century it was fitted up as a family pew. It could also be the abode of the resident sacristan, which would explain the fireplace in some of these rooms, including Northleach. (This chimney-flue is carried up through a buttress and a pinnacle.) Away from the limestone belt, East Anglia can show a number of very distinguished porches. Woolpit in Suffolk is outstanding. Porches were placed on the south side wherever practicable, unless the town or the village lay mainly to the north; there were no hard and fast rules about this. A west porch, however, is rare. The most notable example is at Melton Mowbray, in an exuberant Decorated style, with possibly more ball-flower ornamentation to the square foot than anywhere else in England!

Many of the cathedrals have a Lady Chapel as a separate part of the building, usually projecting beyond the east end. For a parish church to have a Lady Chapel of this kind was extremely unusual, and postulates a very munificent patron, like Bishop Grandisson of Exeter at Ottery St Mary or the Clopton family at Long Melford. The latter, for all its internal attractions and the fine quality of its external flushwork, is not well integrated with the rest of this magnificent building.

Church delights are unending. There are, for example, the weather-vanes. These are often a pleasure. The detached belfry at Brookland in Walland Marsh, referred to in the last chapter, has an excellent one dated 1797 and representing, appropriately enough, a mallard in flight. At Great Ponton in Lincolnshire it is a viol. At Kingsclere in Hampshire it is – yes, a bed-bug, and a very handsome one too, with a big lozenge-shaped body, a little tortoise-like head, six legs like fleurs-de-lis and a tail much the same. The story goes that King John – or some say Charles II – had once to spend a night here at the inn and was so badly bitten that he decreed that for ever after the church should advertise the fact on its tower. But the great majority of these weather-vanes are cocks; the central tower at Colyton in Devon, with its octagonal crown, has a proud bird with a solid tail well designed to catch the wind (66). St Mary Redcliffe, Bristol, had a specially fine one perched on the stump of a spire which was all that was left after a storm in 1446. When the present spire was completed in 1872 the cock went to Winchcombe in Gloucestershire, where it can still be seen in all its gilded splendour.

There are also a large number of church clocks, a few of which are of great horological and antiquarian interest. The one at Rye in Sussex, with a long pendulum swinging to and fro inside the church, dates back at least to the time of Henry VIII. Tower clocks have been described as 'probably the most frequently used yet least considered pieces of church property', and not all of them are in good condition.

> ... Oh! yet
> *Stands the Church clock at ten to three?*

There is a learned book on this subject, but it is mainly concerned with mechanical problems and has little to say about the visual aspect. A clock-face can be an embellishment to a tower, but is not always so (38); the best colours are nearly always black and gold, but blue and gold can sometimes look very well too, as on the smoke-black tower at Halifax. A few clocks have only a single hand: perhaps the best known is at St Margaret, Westminster. Another, dated 1796 and a few years ago skilfully repaired, is at Garsington in Oxfordshire: here too the swinging pendulum can be seen inside the church, under the west tower. The adjacent village of Chislehampton also has a one-handed clock, and so does Groombridge in Kent. The largest clock of this type, which is some 300 years old, is at Coningsby in Lincolnshire; here the huge dial is painted on to the surface of the stonework.

Because they are usually without much specifically architectural interest, very little has been said in this chapter about the humbler churches, Norman, Gothic or even Georgian (although some did figure in Chapter 2). Any amateur of English churches will have visited a great many of them; will have smiled, perhaps, at the black iron stove-pipe poking up through the roof, and at the collection of gardening tools in the unused north porch; will have left no contribution in the box because nobody has bothered to secure its lid. Individually there may be little about most of these rustic buildings that is worth saying; yet collectively they are a great treasure, part of the very warp and weft of England, which, once lost, can never be replaced. Lost, therefore, they must not be; in popular places, like Culbone near Porlock, Bonchurch near Ventnor, or Martindale on the inaccessible bank of Ullswater, they have long been a quarry for people on holiday; and the turn of others may be coming. As works of art I believe that there is a tendency in some quarters to over-praise them; but to those who care about English history and who cherish the English scene, these venerable little churches can be deeply endearing.

Nor would it be right, even if it were possible, to ignore the associational values of a great many churches. If we try to look at a church without thinking of the human beings involved in it, we may be losing something essential to the total experience. Combe Florey in Somerset may not be much of a church visually (though there are many worse), but when we learn that it was here, in reluctant exile from London, that Sydney Smith spent, as rector, the last sixteen years of his life, the building at once takes on a new significance. For what peals of laughter must once have issued from that vestry, perhaps even from the pulpit! In more solemn vein, who could not be moved by the story of Nicholas Ferrar and his short-lived religious community at Little Gidding in Huntingdon-shire? The little church still owes its unusual character to this strange, 350-year-old episode. It figures in the 'starred list' in Appendix B, but whether it should do so on purely visual grounds is difficult to decide. There are many places at which it is not possible clearly to separate the elements which comprise the total experience. It must be added, however, that in their responses to churches many people are not visual enough, and some not at all. And this may be simply because they have never at any time been helped to look.

FIVE

The Interior (1)

BECAUSE OF ALL that they contain, the interiors of the parish churches seldom make such a positive architectural impact as the exteriors; from the first moment of entering, there is so much besides the architecture to compete for our attention. That, incidentally, is why there will have to be two chapters on the interior.

Stylistically a large number, perhaps the majority, of pre-Victorian parish churches are an amalgam, which has been the pretext for a good many very desiccated pages of guidebook writing. As often as not, at the end of a long analysis of what is early EE, what is later EE, who did what in Dec., why that bit was altered to Perp. and the other bit left as it was, and a lot more in the same vein, one's instinct is to exclaim, 'How much does all this matter?' For the purposes of this study what counts is whether or not the end-product is, or is not, a work of art. This entails an analysis of the building's aesthetic character, *as we see it today*. And in this the contents play at least as large a part as the architecture.

The successive styles do, of course, embody some very positive and consistently recurring characteristics. In the Norman churches there are those slow, solemn rhythms which can always be associated with the round arch. The massive piers, generally earthbound arcades, very high proportion of wall to window, and rather low roofs all enhance this feeling of 'high solemnity' which even rich ornamentation, usually non-figurative, does little to dispel.

> *I do so like a Norman nave:*
> *One can hide behind the piers and misbehave;*
> *Whereas one has to be so particular*
> *In Perpendicular!*

But the fact is that in a Norman nave, so far from being tempted to eschew decorum, we are much more likely, moved by the evident seriousness of purpose and devotion of these not always skilful builders, to experience sensations of reverence. And if we are unlikely to feel playful in these buildings, we should recall that for their creators, too, life was no party; rather was it 'nasty, brutish and short'.

With the first Gothic churches, known as Early English, the rhythm changes to something much brisker and more staccato. There is now a sense of animation in the architecture; piers and arches become multiform, and light and shade dance and flicker over the assembled clusters of shafts, sometimes bi-coloured, while the sprouting stiff-leaf – no particular leaf, but now so universally employed as to have become one of the hall-marks of the style – expresses a sensation of bursting life. The lancet windows, often deeply recessed between nook-shafts and in other ways most elaborately framed, sweep up to sharp points and make another important contribution to the bounding vitality of the style.

The Decorated, the Middle Pointed so beloved of the Victorians, is softer. By comparison with the sharp definitions of the Early English, the profiles of piers and arches now tend to become blurred, the carving of capitals and other ornamental details more exuberant, and sometimes very naturalistic. This was a blithe phase of English church building, and far the best for window-tracery, some of which is now a delight, particularly in the later or Flowing period, when the early geometrical shapes break into motion, and the Catherine wheels begin to turn. This was also, as we have seen, the great age for spires. The interiors of the churches were now full of colour and gilding, and the services abounded in elaborate ritual.

The Perpendicular period is more mundane and less numinous, which of course implies no aesthetic criticism of it. It is, however, unfortunate that this long final phase of our Gothic architecture, which lasted more than 200 years, takes its name from the tracery of its often very large windows with mullions that are all too liable to shoot straight up into the curves of the arches in what one feels to be a very insensitive way. The windows are in fact the least agreeable feature of this style, which comprehends, as we have already seen, some towers of miraculous beauty and exterior features of great magnificence. Perpendicular churches can look mechanical and mass-produced; the term 'business man's Gothic', applicable to interiors like those of Lavenham or Thornbury, is not unjust. Nor is it, speaking generally, a good period for sculpture. But, in addition to the wonderful towers, this was the great age for church woodwork of all kinds, including the creation of some of the most beautiful roofs ever made, a subject to which we shall be returning in the next chapter.

From the restoration of the Stuarts to the battle of Waterloo the story of English church buildings is overwhelmingly London's. In the country at large few new churches were required; indeed the problem was more often to maintain those that were already there. The Middle Ages had bequeathed an enormous legacy of parish churches – more than 9000 – and in some parts of England, in this age of somewhat lukewarm piety, the supply considerably exceeded the demand, for as late as 1750 the

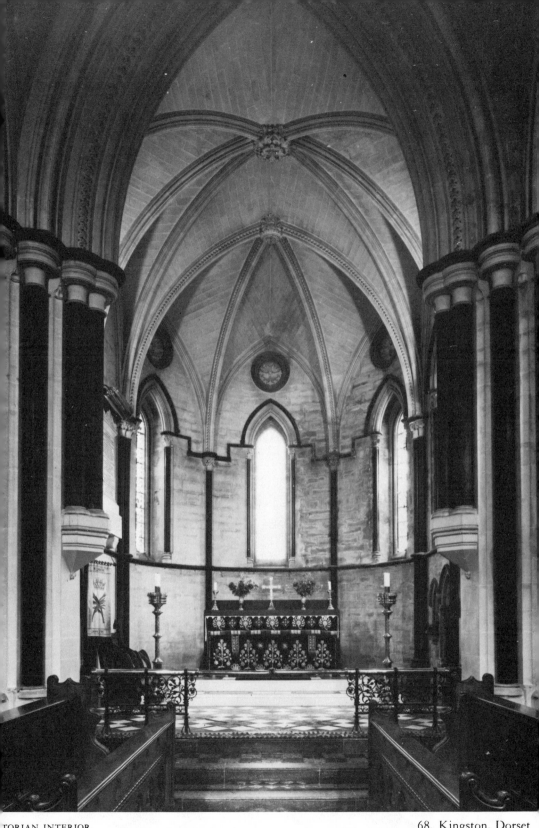

68. Kingston, Dorset

69. Shobdon, Herefordshire

GEORGIAN INTERIORS

70. Worcester, St Swithun

population still only numbered a little over seven millions.

In London, however, owing to the Great Fire, there was a pressing need for new churches. But people wanted something quite different from their medieval forebears. With Protestantism, ritual was at a discount. What was required were good straightforward preaching places, as light as possible inside, not lacking in dignity, but not over-decorated.

It was never the intention to replace all the eighty-six London churches burnt in the Fire. It was decided to rebuild fifty-one. Work had already been started on seventeen of them by 1670. To pay for them, a coal duty was imposed, which produced ample funds to finance them all. As many as thirty-two survived until 1940. But when the bombing ended in 1945 only fifteen of the City churches were more or less intact.

There can be no doubt that Wren personally designed the whole fifty-one. It was a most difficult undertaking, because he had to fit each church on to the site of its predecessor, and some of the sites were very oddly shaped. Sometimes he was even expected to utilise the foundations of the old church, although quite a different kind of building was now wanted. So great ingenuity was necessary.

Except on the skyline, there was, as we noted earlier, not much scope for external effects. At a lower level almost every one of these churches was so hemmed in that Wren could do very little about the outside walls. Within, much had to be left to the masons, the carpenters and the plasterers, often working under the active supervision of the parish vestries, and responsible to one or other of the three Surveyors. Wren did not and could not exercise the firm control over detail which he showed at St Paul's. So the churches, when finished, varied considerably in quality and importance. Most of the interiors were structurally fairly plain. Some of the detail was rather coarse. The plasterwork, for instance, though effective enough if not examined too carefully, was mostly not of very high quality. The woodwork reached a better standard, but it is significant that, with the single exception of the reredos of St Mary Abchurch, Grinling Gibbons did not work for Wren in any of the City of London churches. He did more at St James, Piccadilly, but this church is in Westminster.

Moreover, the Victorians did appalling damage to these interiors. Nearly all of them were repewed. Sometimes shiny tiles were introduced, and hopelessly unsuitable glass, and inappropriate memorials. Only St Mildred, Bread Street, preserved until 1941 all its original fittings – reredos, altar rails, pulpit with a grand tester, and so on; the destruction of this little church by German bombs was therefore a great loss. So was the burning of the richly carved vestry of St Lawrence Jewry.

The bombing did, however, also remove some of the Victorian anomalies, and remnants of their former rich furnishings do still adorn some of the City churches. Otherwise what is notable about them, apart from their steeples already discussed, is their planning. It is sad to realise that some of the best examples of Wren's wonderfully resourceful and ingenious planning are among the churches long since demolished. One such was St Antholin, close to Cannon Street station, which was an elongated octagon roofed by a lightly constructed elliptical dome. This went in 1875. St Benet Fink, another attractive example of a plan of the centralised type, was pulled down as long ago as 1844. But the little church of St Anne and St Agnes in Gresham Street has happily been restored, for here is a beautiful plan (and one with a long ancestry): a square within a square, with a lofty groined vault in the centre, four internal domelets over the corners, and in the four adjacent bays short tunnel vaults. Thereby a basically dull shape has been effectively articulated.

The most generally admired, and deservedly, of all Wren's church plans is that of St Stephen, Walbrook, badly sited just behind the Mansion House. The building was completed in 1687. Here again, an essentially uninteresting shape, a plain rectangle, was given internal articulation. But instead of the groined vault of St Anne and St Agnes there is a dome at the centre, yet there is also a short nave, suggesting a Latin cross. So, we ask ourselves on entering, are we in a long-nave church or one of the centralised type? And the charming answer is that we are in both. Standing under the dome, we have a remarkable sense of space and of airy lightness. The arches at the four compass points rise high to meet the dome. The other four, that is to say the four on the diagonals, have been given triangular groined vaults (of plaster over brick), with lunette-shaped windows facing in both directions. It is all extraordinarily ingenious: a sort of intellectual tight-rope walking. It has not, I believe, one tithe of the emotional appeal of some of the no less brilliant vaulting achievements of the Middle Ages; but intellectually it is admirable.

The dome of St Stephen is only of wood, plastered, and therefore exerts very little thrust; this is just as well, for its only supports are eight comparatively thin columns. But it is a dome of satisfying proportions, very carefully restored after the last war in accordance with Wren's original design.

But alas, the bases of the columns now seem meaningless and even ugly. This is because the high box-pews have been removed. In all these churches, when the original box-pews were still *in situ*, the bases of the columns were the proper height. Now all too often they look uncomfortably 'leggy'.

Classical churches left unraped by the Victorians are unfortunately not very common. But there are some in every mood. As a model of what a large and stately town church in the classical style should be, one of the best examples is All Saints, Northampton, which was altered but mercifully not Gothicized in the nineteenth century. This building was completed in 1680, its predecessor having been destroyed in the great Northampton fire five years earlier. It has ugly windows but, as usual in the time of Charles II, bold plaster ceilings, a handsome pulpit and mayor's chair, and a fine spaciousness; the plan of the main part of the church is square, with a domed ceiling at the centre. In this solemn vein there are a number of early Georgian town interiors: St Philip, Birmingham (the Cathedral), Blandford and Gainsborough are among the best. Hawksmoor's interiors are *sui generis*, while Wren's cover the whole gamut of emotions from solemnity to light-heartedness.

Most blithe of all are the 'drawing rooms of the Lord'. Of these the gem is undoubtedly Shobdon in Herefordshire (*69*), built in 1752–56. This delightful Rococo–Gothick interior, restored with skill and taste, is marred by two anomalies: the Norman font and the east window. The font, from the twelfth-century church, is a likeable bumpkin which no longer belongs here, as was recognised in 1756, when it was removed to do long service as a garden ornament. Its return to this church was a mistake: it looks very ill at ease in its present surroundings. Shobdon has its own Gothick font, and its Norman predecessor should go to some other church in Herefordshire. There must be several which would be happy to have it. The horrible greenery-yallery east window of 1907 commemorates the second Baron Bateman; as the title has been extinct for more than fifty years and Shobdon Court has been pulled down, there seems no good reason for not extinguishing the window too. Berkley, near Frome, built in 1751 by the landowner, probably to his own design, was ruined by the Victorians up to dado level and contains another wretched east window, but the upper walls and ceiling, with an octagonal 'dome', are adorned with very pretty, mildly Rococo plasterwork. The motifs are conventional plant forms, arabesques, shells, and so on: not ecclesiastical. The colour is pale blue-green on white. Binley, now within the city confines of Coventry, is half a generation later (1771–73) and less playful. This little church was built by an Earl of Craven (Combe Abbey, once the home of the Cravens, is close by) in a somewhat Adamish manner. The plasterwork is restrained but very elegant; the colour-scheme is now Wedgwood blue and white, and perhaps always was. Though the pews are wrong, this is in every other respect a charming little church, now fully used.

Worcestershire has three much larger churches notable for the elegance of their Georgian interiors. In Worcester itself, since its restoration in 1959, St Swithun has again become a model of urbanity and good manners. It dates from 1736. The main front, with a Venetian window, a pediment and a nice clock, faces east (see p. 132). Within (*70*) are most

St Swithun, in the eighteenth century

of the original furnishings, including an elegant three-decker pulpit with a wonderful tester surmounted by a gilded pelican. There is a little baluster font and a small organ with gilded pipes in the correct place: the west gallery. There is no west window, and clear glass with leaded lights everywhere else except at the east end: an ideal scheme of lighting. Croome d'Abitot was referred to externally in Chapter 2. Its interior was due to Robert Adam himself, and he created a Gothick–Classic hybrid; but this spacious, light building (luckily with no stained glass) gives great pleasure, especially for its pulpit, font and lively plasterwork. Far more remarkable is another estate church, Great Witley, standing beside the grand if gaunt burnt-out shell of Witley Court. Although very mild by comparison with the prodigious and enchanting fantasies of the Rococo churches of Bavaria, this is an interior of surprising exuberance for England. The building dates from 1735, but the decoration, from Canons, Edgware, is fifteen years earlier and Baroque therefore rather than Rococo. The ten painted windows have nothing to do with the traditional art of stained glass but look very well here, in a building in which mystery does not and cannot figure. A long and expensive restoration some years ago has happily assured the preservation for posterity of this unique church.

When in due course these excursions into 'paganism' gave place to works of more obviously pious inspiration, an individual character again emerged. Despite the doctrinaire instructions of the Camden Society and others, the best Victorian churches have a distinctive personality which is unmistakable. The interiors may sometimes have the richness, and the darkness, of a Christmas pudding, which would not be most people's choice for an everyday diet, but they are a positive, not just an imitative, contribution to art.

One of the most original and prodigious of the Victorian churches, however, is a brick building with nothing whatever of the Christmas pudding about it. St Bartholomew, in a back street of Brighton, was never finished: the nave alone was built. Nor was it vaulted; it has only a wagon roof, strengthened at intervals by tie-beams. But it soars up to a greater height than any other English parish church: 135 feet from floor to ridge. The architecture is stark, but overwhelmingly impressive. It is perhaps the only church in England which looks as if it might have been built by Imperial Rome. It was the work of a local man, Edmund Scott, about whom almost nothing is recorded. His church was opened in 1874.

The most perfect Victorian church, using that adjective in its precise sense, is in my opinion Kingston in the Isle of Purbeck. The architect was Street. It was built, quite unnecessarily, for Kingston had an adequate though uninteresting village church only forty years old, at the behest of the 3rd Earl of Eldon, who at the time was young, pious and very rich. But most of the world's best architecture is, and always has been, 'unnecessary', judged by the mean standards of utility! Indeed, I would say that one can never hope to have even a good, let alone a great, building unless one is able and willing to spend considerably more than the basic minimum. Lord Eldon was prepared to spend the then very large sum of £70 000 on his church, and for this Street gave him (1873–80) a cathedral in miniature, with splended materials and superb masoncraft. Situated in this part of Dorset the building is, of course, of grey Purbeck limestone throughout, including the roofs; but in addition this stone in its polished form, known as Purbeck marble, is used profusely and with great skill to outline with its almost black lines the principal shapes. Only the unattractive tiled floors and the insignificant though harmless stained glass fall short of these high standards. There is a lofty but austere central tower which is visible for miles from its hill-top site. Within, every part of the cruciform church except the nave is vaulted. The east end (*68*) is apsidal and is a composition of cool classical beauty without parallel in an English Gothic parish church. It has been said that Kingston is a bookish design which shows little originality, and also that it is cold and unlovable. Both these comments are in some measure justified here, but they are no less applicable to a great deal of classical art. Kingston is Gothic church architecture at its most classical and least quirky; if it is chilly, it is the chillness of perfection.

The early years of the present century saw the construction of two churches of remarkable but not wilful originality, carried through with strength and conviction. All Saints at Brockhampton-by-Ross in Herefordshire was built in 1901–02 by W. R. Lethaby. The rather dark interior is not at all seductive. The idiom is uncompromising. The arches, for instance, have very little curve in them and die into the walls without the help of capitals. The windows also eschew curves. The vaults are of limewashed concrete. But outside, crowning the pink and blue-grey sandstone walls, the roofs are of reed-thatch. St Andrew, Roker, by E. S. Prior and dating from 1906–07, is a finer achievement, both in its architecture and in its furnishings. It is built of Magnesian limestone from the Marsden quarry, a few miles to the north of Sunderland, of which Roker is a suburb. The bold internal arches are parabolic, and luckily in stone, not concrete. Both these churches were paid for by well-to-do private donors. Roker cost about £10 000. Today it could hardly be built for thirty times that sum.

What nearly all these churches have in common is that they are of the long nave type. Centralised plans have of course always made more appeal to Classical and Baroque architects than to Romanesque or Gothic. Wren liked them and produced a number of interesting variants on the theme, some ingeniously combined with longitudinal elements. Three of his churches were of the filled-in Greek cross type, and so is All Saints, Northampton, referred to earlier, which may be by Henry Bell of King's Lynn. Hawksmoor planned two of his London churches centrally: St Mary Woolnoth and St George, Bloomsbury. Half a century or so later, a few variants were tried; St Mary, Birmingham, destroyed in 1925, was octagonal; All Saints, Newcastle-upon-Tyne, is elliptical, with two shallow apses on the longer axis (a charming plan, of 1786); and at St Chad, Shrewsbury (1790–92), by George Steuart, a big church, the nave is completely circular. Artistically, such plans as these are very satisfying, but the clergy disliked them, both because they were not Gothic and because it was held that they made the conduct of services more difficult.

Longitudinal planning is therefore the rule, and even when a church is cruciform, it will still have a markedly longer east–west axis. The problem facing churches which have a tightly enclosed chancel is certainly a very real one, but the installation of a nave altar as a permanent feature is always disfiguring. The reasons why the nave is so often much more imposing than the chancel were explained in the preceding chapter. Where there is a fine chancel, it will quite often be found that the foundation, if not originally monastic, was collegiate, a term which is worth a short explanation, because if our guide-book tells us that 'the church was collegiate', it is likely to merit a visit. For it will probably be found to have not only a larger and more impressive chancel than usual, but often some old stalls (and, if we are lucky, misericords), and perhaps some other interesting buildings serving as an almshouse or as part of a school.

The constitutions of the original collegiate foundations varied considerably, but after the middle of the fourteenth century the great majority of these priestly colleges, including almost all those associated with parish churches, were what are known as chantry foundations. A chantry, to quote G. H. Cook, who devoted a whole book to the collegiate churches, 'was the name given to an intercessory mass that was recited at an altar in a church for the well-being of the founder during his life-time and for the repose of his soul after his death. Gradually there sprang up an array of unbeneficed priests whose prime duty was the singing of soul-masses, and whose stipends issued from chantry endowments'. It must be admitted that the chantry foundations throw a somewhat unedifying light upon our ancestors. They reveal a people scared and superstitious; they were another (and somewhat morbid) manifestation of 'keeping up with the Joneses' ('my endowment will provide for eight priests: he only has six'), and also of rich men currying favour with the Almighty. At Fotheringhay, for example, where the grandly proportioned church is still dramatic and remarkable, despite the destruction of the chancel after the Dissolution, the college kept open house, within set limits, to the poor wayfarer, but otherwise its thirty-four members (a master, twelve fellows, eight clerks and thirteen choristers) seem to have had virtually nothing to do but to pray, in this case, 'for the good estate of Henry IV and his Queen, the Prince of Wales, the Duke of York and all the royal family, and for their souls after death'. They were clearly on to a good thing, and by 1547 there were many thousands of these people, mostly performing no useful work. Beverley at the suppression had seventy-seven people on the foundation, who were promptly reduced to a sensible number, namely four. Detestable as Henry VIII was in many ways, one cannot feel very indignant about the Crown's confiscation of the chantry endowments. The confiscation was not in fact carried out until just after Henry had died, but the inane practice of continually reciting masses for the dead had been proscribed since 1529 wherever a stipend was involved.

The credit side of the chantry system is best seen in the spread of education and in the creation of architecture. It was to chantry endowments that we owe the foundation not only of famous educational institutions such as Winchester and New College, Eton and King's, but also of many small schools, where buildings still occasionally survive from the fifteenth century to enhance the beauty of little country towns like, for instance, Higham Ferrers in Northamptonshire. When a parish church was raised to collegiate rank, there might be little to show for it; at Cobham in Kent, for example, where a college was founded in 1362, a grand chancel had already been built a century earlier. On the other hand, not merely the chancel but the entire church might be rebuilt on a more imposing scale, as happened at Howden. At Stoke-by-Clare in 1535 Matthew Parker (who was to become Archbishop of Canterbury under Elizabeth 1) rebuilt the nave for the use of the parishioners.[25]

Time to go in. This in itself will nowadays often pose a problem. The numbers of locked churches increase every year on account of the appalling growth of vandalism. It is to the great credit of the Church of England that, even so, only about 30% of all its churches are at present kept permanently locked. Whether a church will be found to be open depends very much on its location. In cities, except at their very centre, most churches have to be kept locked: in Merseyside, more than four out of five. About half the surburban churches are also locked, but these are often of no special architectural interest, and if a church is graded A there is decidedly better chance of finding it open, and under supervision. Village churches away from industrial centres are also much more likely to be accessible; in Cornwall as many as 93% are not kept locked. Frustrating though it is to find a church locked, it would be unreasonable, in the climate of today, to be reproachful on that score. What can be regarded as discourteous and inconsiderate is when there is no notice on the church door to indicate where the key can be obtained, and unfortunately this is by no means rare.

The key itself may be worth looking at, and so may the hinges and, here and there, ornamental ironwork on the door. The key to the south door at Overbury in Worcestershire is a giant. Hascombe in Surrey has another grand old key, very large, for which the Victorians had a new lock made. The standard of artistry revealed even in the making of a handle, as in the fourteenth-century example at Adderbury (91), is a continual source of pleasure and wonder to those who allow themselves time for looking. Staplehurst in Kent has wrought ironwork dating from the twelfth century, expressing a sense of life though not of order. Although this place is nowhere near the coast, the motifs are for some reason all marine. Morville in Shropshire has a more complete scheme, purely ornamental in character, which is partly of a similar date. The blacksmiths of the thirteen century wrought some magnificent ironwork for church doors, the entire surface of which might be covered with scrolly arabesques springing from the hinges. Fine examples are at Uffington and Faringdon in Berkshire, the latter incorporating several dragons' heads, and at three churches in Bedfordshire: Leighton Buzzard, Turvey and Eaton Bay (90), all no doubt from the workshop which also produced the famous Thomas de Leghtone, if indeed these were not his own work. Another notable example of ironwork on a church door, quite different in style, is at Dartmouth in South Devon. This incorporates large leaves and two prancing leopards. Although later, it is also cruder, but decorative.

Sometimes, placed so trustingly on a table near the door, there will be a descriptive booklet. Here is one of the bastions of absolutely free enterprise. We never know what we are going to find. Some of these booklets are well-written, scholarly and good. Others are frankly embarrassing. Their most common faults are verbosity, sentimentality, and a tendency to make excessive claims for buildings or features of only medium quality. 'Cathedral-like proportions' is a phrase all too likely to crop up when any large village church is being described, regardless of the fact that the proportions do not resemble those of a cathedral in any way whatsoever. Moreover, I am just a visitor, and I do not care to be apostrophised as 'Brother', 'Pilgrim' or 'Wayfarer'. The general standard is certainly improving, but some of these booklets are still much too generously supplied with platitudes, heart-throbs ('this ancient fane', and so on) and touches of facetiousness. On the other hand, one can usually sympathise with the cries of pain. Several in my collection say quite candidly that their Victorian glass is dreadful, and recommend its removal. My favourite is Wrington, where in the typewritten notes by a former vicar there is – or used to be – a section headed 'Points not to be noticed'. These include some egregious Victorian glass, as well as uninteresting and far too numerous pews. Some of these booklets are the repositories of queer little pieces of history and gossip. At Sompting one of the eighteenth-century vicars is recorded as having written a poem with the title 'Laugh and Lye down ; or, a pleasant but sure remedy for the Gout'. At Westham, adjoining Pevensey, 'owls sometimes find their way into the church and are difficult to dislodge'. On one occasion it is recorded that half a dozen of them sat in a row upon the rafters and listened, with unwavering attention, and not a hint of dissent, to a reading of the Thiry-Nine Articles.

In the production of guides an outstanding contribution has been made by the Diocese of Chichester. Starting in 1933, and with the active encouragement of that good friend of the arts the late Bishop Bell, this diocese, in collaboration with the Sussex Archaeological Society, planned to produce a guidebook for every one of its old churches. Forty-eight have so far appeared. Until shortly before his death in 1961 the editor, and writer of many of them, was Walter H. Godfrey. Each one has a plan, a few photographs and complete freedom from heart-throbs. Godfrey had a fixed tariff to cover all costs of production, and the parish, or some other benefactor, had to raise this sum first. Nowadays a Parochial Church Council which wants a guide but cannot afford to pay for the printing will generally be financed by the Sussex Historic Churches Trust, which is reimbursed by the parish from the proceeds of sales. When all expenses have been met, the profits go to the funds of the church concerned. After Godfrey died Francis Steer became editor, and personally wrote twenty-seven more of these guides; but on his death in 1978 the project unhappily lapsed. It is a pity that this admirable venture has not yet been much emulated elsewhere; one would like to see every diocese in the country following suit. There is a real need for competent editorship and a certain measure of uniformity in the presentation. Some guides make the mistake of including too much, and of having as a result to be too highly priced.

Before looking at the booklet, however, or at Pevsner or any other book, one takes stock. Every church has its own personality and its own atmosphere, even sometimes its own smell, and some communicate a sensation of pleasure, or of repulsion, immediately upon entering. Some too have a pleasant atmosphere but not much else: the 'pleasantly dull' category touched on earlier. In these buildings nothing is as good as the first *coup d'oeil*. And plenty of people nowadays are more responsive to the atmosphere than to the aumbry. Some churches are externally charming and a great ornament to their villages, yet devoid of interest inside. Others, like Stow, Swaton or Stone, convey externally no hint of the extraordinary impact of the interior.

Stow is a large cruciform church with a handsome Perpendicular central tower and very rubbly walls, situated in a remote part of Lincolnshire. The moment of stepping inside is unforgettable. This is a Norman church, strong and simple in nave and transepts, much richer in the chancel (*112*). Now the surprising fact is that the chancel as it is seen today is largely the outcome of Pearson's restoration of 1863–65. It was he who gave it the vault which, although certainly intended, it may never before have had. As Victorian restorations go, this one, apart from the wretched tiled floor, was outstandingly good. Swaton is another Lincolnshire church, but this time in the Early English and Decorated styles, with window tracery that, at the east end in particular, is pure poetry in stone. This is a cruciform church with a central tower; the chancel and transepts are normal. But when about 1323 the nave was reached, an entirely new design was produced, of great audacity; the central space and aisles are all under one roof; the arcades sweep up until they almost touch it, and the Reticulated west window is enormous. For a village church the proportions of this short nave are extraordinarily big and bold and the sense of space altogether remarkable. Stone in Kent stands strikingly on a hill above the Thames in a situation that must once have been a delight. Today the tall chimneys of the adjacent cement works dwarf the church and bespatter it with dust. The building has undergone formidable restoration outside and in, and, what with the deplorable nave glass, the pitch-pine pews and the quite unsatisfactory raftered roofs, there is no question of any 'whoop of joy' when one steps inside this church. Yet architecturally, as I indicated earlier, it is astonishing. As at

Swaton the nave arcades, here Early English, rise to roof level. The scale is venturesome and the details exquisite, while the resemblance to Westminster Abbey is so strong that we can be sure that when the masons had finished there, it was to Stone that they came. Some of the windows have bar tracery which is exactly as at the Abbey. The chancel, as at Stow, is largely the result of a good Victorian restoration, in this case by G. E. Street, in 1859–60. He too replaced the missing vault. The surface decoration in this chancel, again as at Stow, is profuse; and what is not original is fairly well authenticated. To find here such a church as this is extraordinary.

It is matter of constant observation that churches in villages are more enjoyable than those in towns. There are of course village churches that are poverty stricken and utterly without interest, but, looking at England as a whole, the number of these is remarkably small. There are also plenty of very handsome town churches, including some of the grandest of all. But in general my feeling is that town churches are more difficult to like; this particularly applies to counties such as Surrey in which there was abundant money in the Victorian period. One is put off by the pews, almost always too many: by the Victorian stained glass, almost always too much: by the restoration, almost always excessive. These are the kind of buildings which get the Church of England a bad name, especially among the young, and one only has to enter them to understand why. Such interiors convey sensations neither of vitality nor of beauty; only at night, with the help of imaginative lighting, can they sometimes be greatly improved.

I therefore believe that, in making our aesthetic assessments, we are sometimes unfair to town churches. The oppressive, often smug atmosphere is liable to mask genuine excellencies, the frequent darkness to hide them. Let us give more detailed attention now to the chief enemies of our pleasure, in the parish churches. These I would rank, on a descending scale of dislike, in the following order: bad glass, bad seating, bad floors, bad organs, stripped walls, ugly pulpits, fonts, and monuments. A formidable list.

The wholesale destruction of medieval stained glass was the greatest calamity that has ever befallen English art. When it is realised that most of our large and many smaller churches had every window filled with richly coloured or at least finely painted *grisaille* glass, and that today more than half of our cathedrals and nearly all our parish churches possess virtually no old glass at all, some idea may be gained of the extent of the destruction. Not all this glass, of course, was first-class; one can see some rather second-rate examples of medieval glass at Fairford, where, because this is the only parish church in England to have retained a complete set of pre-Reformation windows, twenty-eight in all, critical standards are commonly thrown to the winds. There is in fact a good deal of late-Gothic glass in France which is much superior to that at Fairford: the twenty-one early sixteenth-century windows at Conches-en-Ouche in Normandy, for example, or the eleven huge windows and a rose in the Sainte Chapelle at Champigny-sur-Veude near Chinon, dating from 1528–60. Nevertheless Fairford is a sumptuous church.

The diabolical smashing of our church windows is usually associated with the Puritans of Cromwell's time, and it is certainly true that they did the most grievous damage; but there had been serious losses at the time of the Dissolution and during the first wave of Puritanism under Edward VI. As mentioned earlier, much of what was left disappeared in the Georgian period. David Verey described what happened at Cirencester:

> 'From documentary evidence and from the fragments which survive in the tracery of many windows, it is clear that at the Reformation all forty-two windows were filled with stained glass. In 1639 there were complaints that the glass was not looked after as well as at Fairford, and in 1642 some windows were broken by relatives trying to introduce food to Prince Rupert's prisoners inside; but in 1712 Atkyns could still report the remains of very fine glass in 'most of the windows'. However, by the end of the eighteenth century the glass had become so fragmentary that it was decided to collect it all into the great E. and W. windows, which was done by the antiquary Samuel Lysons. What was not re-used was packed into crates and forgotten, till it was unluckily tipped into a ditch at the foot of the Cirencester–Kemble railway line about the year 1890. One case escaped and in 1929 the contents were set by F. C. Eden in the small two-light window in the south sanctuary wall'.

This shocking story of neglect and waste is probably all too typical. In a good many places, however, a principal reason for this loss of medieval stained glass was the decay of the lead cames. Since clear glass suited the later seventeenth and eighteenth centuries, and Gothic art was not normally regarded as possessing either antiquarian interest or artistic merit, there was no incentive to undertake releading. So the old coloured glass was just cleared away. It was only with the revived interest in ritual during the early part of Queen Victoria's reign, and the ardour for everything medieval which accompanied it, that there was a renewed concern with stained glass. By the end of the nineteenth century it is probably correct to say that no town church had not acquired several large memorial windows and that many village churches were afflicted with at least one. 'Afflicted' is not always the just word; there is quite a lot of Victorian glass that is innocuous, some that is good, and a very little that is excellent. To this we will return. Nevertheless, the general standard of these windows is frankly appalling.

Here are some examples. St John, Devizes, so handsome and interesting outside, is darkened and drearified within by detestable glass. Sleaford is entirely filled with Victorian glass which, with one partial exception (a pale window by Morris and Co., 1900) is all indifferent or worse. Maidstone has quite a good west window; otherwise, wherever one looks, there are disagreeable windows obfuscating the church unnecessarily. Thame is full of glass that illustrates, as the booklet there rightly remarks, 'the deplorable taste of the third quarter of the nineteenth century'. At Totnes the impressive screens are difficult to see because of the profusion of dull glass. At Westbury, Cuckfield, Halesowen, Shifnal, Cottingham, Mansfield and St Mary, Nottingham, it is the same story: potentially pleasing churches darkened and spoiled by commonplace glass. At St Mary, Bury St Edmunds, in addition to poor figurative glass, there is horrible dirty-green glass in the clerestory windows. Gayton in Northamptonshire is obscured by opaque white glass with patterns and borders and Elm in Cambridgeshire by green glass which in both churches serves no conceivable purpose. Chipping Norton has pink as well as green glass in its clerestory. Necton in Norfolk has a dozen windows ranging from the unworthy to the execrable. At Stoke-by-Nayland in Suffolk the glass can only be described as an insult to the church. At Morton in Lincolnshire, as at Highnam in Gloucestershire, lights have to be kept on even on a sunny summer morning. Grantchester has its lovely Decorated chancel marred and its nave darkened by feeble Victorian glass. Clipsham has bad glass in every window, the only merit of which is that it renders a little less visible the horrible tiled floor. Weston in Lincolnshire would be dark anyway, as it is an early Gothic church with very small clerestory windows; nevertheless they are all filled with vexatious glass. At Evercreech (with that marvellous tower), at Chaddesley Corbett in Worcestershire, Dorrington in Lincolnshire and Isleham in Cambridgeshire, it is the glass of the east window which is such a tragedy, for of course this is the most conspicuous in the church; at Chaddesley Corbett, in particular, the Decorated tracery is superb, but the glass is cruel, and the window can therefore only be enjoyed from outside. At Honiley in Warwickshire even a nice little Georgian church was presented with three excruciatingly unsuitable windows (one is the east) in the apse; all the other windows here have nasty frosted glass.

One naturally wonders why, with so much enthusiasm for the Middle Ages, the Victorians usually failed, and often dismally, to produce stained glass which can hold a candle to the medieval glass in quality or artistic significance. There seem to be three answers: in the Victorian age the technique was different, the material was different, and above all the artistic impulse was very different.

Until about the middle of the fourteenth century many church interiors must have been dark, but the coloured glass glowed through the darkness with intense emotional effect, as it still does, superbly, at Chartres, Troyes, León and elsewhere. This was partly because the colours were glorious, as can still be seen to best advantage in England at Canterbury and in a few windows at Lincoln and Wells: in smaller quantities also at a good many other places, of which perhaps the most notable are Tewkesbury Abbey, Stanford-on-Avon in Northamptonshire, Madley and Eaton Bishop in Herefordshire and Deerhurst and Arlingham in Gloucestershire. (It must, however, be added that the most beautiful glass in any village church in England is at none of these; it fills the east window of the otherwise undistinguished little church at Twycross in Leicestershire, and though marred at present by inept borders – it needs re-setting – it is French glass of resplendent quality, partly from the Sainte Chapelle. At the Revolution it came into the possession of George III. His son William IV gave it to Earl Howe, who lived nearby. It was presented to the church in 1840.) Technically the early glass was somewhat rough and ready, for it was uneven in thickness and not always free from air-bubbles, sometimes quite big ones. The colour variations resulting from the uneven thickness are altogether delightful; the colours seem to glow all the more because of their varying translucency.

At this time the colours were used simply to suit the design, not to reproduce nature. The figures were often deliberately distorted – elongated, for example – to enhance the expressive effect. There was no attempt to portray depth nor perspective; a little conventional tree would be enough to suggest open country, a single arch to indicate a house. The leads themselves define the main outline of the figures and of the composition. The painting of details on the surface of the glass is reduced to the minimum, and there is practically no shading.

Between the fourteenth and the nineteenth centuries drawing became steadily more naturalistic, which implied more and more surface painting. So the colours were no longer able to glow, in Ruskin's fine phrase 'like flaming jewellery', in the dim light of the churches. In the Georgian period this did not matter. There was no place in their churches for flaming jewellery: no place indeed for stained, as opposed to painted, glass at all. To the Victorians, however, this spelt disaster. For them too, with rare exceptions, only naturalistic drawing was acceptable. Yet there was now a revived taste for densely coloured windows. But if the glass is covered with painted details, it can no longer admit light, so cannot glow. Of the medieval combination of beauty and darkness, the Victorians were usually able to recapture only the latter. And, as I have indicated, there are few places more depressing than a church darkened with indifferent glass.

Technically, for reasons of economy, what was aimed at in the nineteenth century, and all too successfully realised, was the production of thin glass, dead flat, free from colour variations within the piece, and devoid of all texture. In coloured glass in fact, as in the Academy pictures of the same period, a quasi-mechanical finish was the ideal. So few things are more distressing about the typical Victorian window than the complete absence of 'quality' in the glass itself.

The methods by which the great majority of these windows were produced had little or no connection with art. Every studio had a big collection of post cards and Alinari and Anderson photographs of Italian pictures, especially of the Umbrian school; in addition to Raphael and Perugino, an old stained glass worker told me that Francia, more naturalistic and more sentimental than either, was a great favourite. These photographs were in continual use; an arm was copied from this one, a piece of drapery from that, and sometimes an entire angel. The cartoons were therefore compilations produced by a process analogous to the 'scissors and paste' method of writing, by people who had nothing of their own that they wanted to express; they were just the paid employees of commercial stained glass firms. Add to this the taste for pink flesh-tints and the exceptionally crude colouring of much of the glass of the 'sixties and 'seventies (towards the end of the century there was some improvement in this respect), and it is no wonder that the trumpery products of these methods had no more artistic value than, say, an illustrated magazine today.

The concern with naturalistic details was nothing new. Even in the fifteenth century, as for instance at Great Malvern Priory, we sometimes find architectural and landscape backgrounds. The sixteenth, seventeenth and eighteenth centuries went much further in this direction: the aim then was often simply to imitate oil paintings and Georgian windows are nothing more, as a rule, than pictures painted in coloured enamels on large pieces of white glass. This technique the Victorians rightly abandoned, but none the less most of them continued to design pictorially. That is to say, they still tried to get their effects by the accumulation of detail – facial expressions intended to look saint-like, and so on – and not through stylisation, simplification, and the imaginative use of colour. Ruskin himself was fully aware of this; in the appendix to the second volume of *The Stones of Venice* he wrote that 'glass, considered as a material for a picture, is exactly as bad as oil paint is good', and 'therefore the attempt to turn painted windows into pretty pictures is one of the most gross and ridiculous barbarisms of this pre-eminently barbarous century'. That was very much to the point, but his good advice, alas, was not followed.

The difference in artistic impulse between the Gothic age and the Gothic revival will be too familiar to need much stressing. This, in my judgment, was the most important factor of all in accounting for the so flaccid, so mawkish character of most Victorian glass – in explaining its utter lack of intensity and conviction. In the Middle Ages the glazier was generally required to do one of two things: either he had to glorify Christ or the Virgin Mary, the prophets or the saints, in creating tall figures of more than human majesty and nobility, or he was expected to tell a story as simply and vividly as possible to people who had no books and who could not have read them if they had. Therefore, the windows were for them a kind of illustrated substitute for the Bible and the lives of the saints.

In the nineteenth century this second motive was naturally entirely absent; and as to the first, it will be noted that most Victorian windows are of a commemorative character. Anyone who could afford to do so was free to present a memorial window to the church, and many did. These windows bore no aesthetic relationship to one another; indeed, more often than not they were in competition. They were often quite inappropriate to their setting. Usually the Church authorities, one suspects, could not easily refuse these gifts without giving offence, even had they wanted to, which was not always so. The platitudinous results are there for all to see. In 1901 the rector of Church Iccomb in Gloucestershire chose to commemorate his wife not with a window but by installing a purely functional heating apparatus. Would that many more had done likewise.

It has been necessary to write harshly about most Victorian glass because, more than any other single factor, it has spoiled for me, as for many others, a large part of the pleasure to be had from churches in all parts of the country. The clergy will often be found to be in complete agreement about this. Not so long ago one vicar remarked to me, turning towards the east window, 'If the village boys were to throw some stones at that thing "by mistake", I shouldn't mind a bit'. The implied criticism was fully justified; the window was tasteless and commonplace. What should be done about this stuff? There can only be one answer. Remove it. In the forties bombs did the job at Southwold (leaving only the west window, which is bearable), and also, though not completely, at Aldeburgh, and in Cheshire a land-mine performed the task at Bunbury, in all cases to the great benefit of the church in this respect, however regrettable the other damage. It is a pity that the post-war east window at Bunbury is such a feeble replacement.

Since then a few churches have had the courage to remove their bad glass. A shining example is St Mary Magdalene at Bridgnorth, now the parish church. Here in 1978, at a cost of £10 000, six very large windows filled with the most deplorable Victorian glass gave place to clear glass in rectangular panes, as Telford, the architect, intended. At Hartland in Devon, a few years earlier, twelve obfuscating Victorian windows were replaced by six of nearly clear glass with small figures and heraldry, and six others entirely clear. At Steeple Ashton in Wiltshire the appeal of a sumptuous interior has been immeasurably enhanced since the removal, about 1977 (in the face, I was told, of lively controversy in the village) of a quite outrageous Victorian window. The eclipse of unworthy nineteenth-century glass has also greatly benefitted, among other churches, Dennington in Suffolk, Felmersham in Bedfordshire, Elkstone in Gloucestershire, Whitchurch in Shropshire, Willen in Buckinghamshire, and Tynemouth in Northumberland. When the church is in a classical style, it is safe to say that the removal of Victorian glass will never fail to be an improvement. At Euston in Suffolk, where the theft of lead from the roof, for some time undiscovered, had such dire consequences that only by the most strenuous efforts was the church saved from destruction, the full-scale restoration provided an excellent opportunity for the removal of poor Victorian glass, with results that only those who knew the church before 1971 can wholly appreciate. The insertion of much clear glass at Farnham, together with internal whitening, has effected a great improvement there too. But far, far more needs to be done. Sometimes this will require the goodwill and co-operation of the descendants of the people commemorated. But let the Church at least make the attempt. Some years ago I talked in a church with a young man who remarked, 'My father's memorial to my grandfather was to insert that window', indicating a feeble effort in the north aisle. 'My memorial to him, I hope, will be to take it out again!' I trust that it will, but he may encounter difficulties. What could be removed at no great cost and without the slightest embarrassment nor risk of offending the descendants of any past donors are the acres of opaque and tinted non-figurative glass which render church after church dim and depressing for no purpose whatsoever. It is indeed a great mystery that this senseless glazing has managed to survive for so long.

If there were to be a wholesale removal of bad Victorian glass all over the country, not only would the churches be immensely improved but so would the reputation of Victorian glass. For much would remain, and the best might then be properly seen for what it is: very good glass indeed. In addition to the often quite acceptable work by firms such as Hardman, Clayton and Bell, James Powell and Morris, all windows by recognised glass artists such as Willement, Hedgeland, O'Connor, Wailes, Gibbs, William Morris, Burne-Jones, Kempe and Whall would usually have to be retained, even though, in my opinion, not all their work is good and some has lately been much over-praised.[26] What would, I hope, receive more appreciation than at present are windows of really good quality by glass artists whose very names are not always known. Maids Moreton in Buckinghamshire, Houghton Conquest in Bedfordshire and St Wendreda at March in Cambridgeshire all have Victorian east windows which are worthy embellishments of lovely churches. At Thursford in central Norfolk the east window is still better. This, like those at Brant Broughton referred to earlier (p. 27), was designed by the incumbent, the Rev. Arthur Moore, in 1862, and is an astonishing achievement for its date. The triple lancets contain robust figures (no simpering attitudes here), plain backgrounds and fine rich colour. The sun, moon and stars are treated almost as an abstract artist might have handled them. Pevsner called this window 'one of the most beautiful of its time in England, or indeed Europe', and one can easily agree.

Writers on Victorian glass generally seem to enthuse a little indiscriminately over the windows of Burne-Jones and Morris, but in truth their quality varies considerably. In a good many of them Burne-Jones's figures look languid and epicene, characteristics that are not wholly absent from his 'Last Judgment' at Easthampstead in Berkshire, a well-composed and pleasingly coloured window of c. 1875. Of about the same date, but better, is the east window at Rotherfield in Sussex, for which Burne-Jones designed the figures and Morris the attractive pattern of foliage. It is too bad that the base of this excellent window should be cut off by a wretched reredos. In the tradition of Morris and Burne-Jones, yet superior to either Easthampstead or Rotherfield, is the east window at Roker (see p. 134) by H. A. Payne of Birmingham. This lovely work, dated 1907, has the quality of a rich tapestry, and glows like jewellery.

It would be good to be able to say that in the present century there has been a revival of the art of stained glass: good but, alas, untrue. In recent years there has been a swing towards 'more light', which is no doubt a reaction from the lack-lustre dimness of innumerable Victorian interiors. But aesthetically the results have been very unsatisfactory. The practice of setting pieces of coloured glass on a ground of absolutely clear glass is entirely wrong: it effectively drains the colours of much of their richness – or would do if they had any. In fact, a predilection for pale colours has been very common since 1945, especially for thin, brassy yellows, wishy-washy pinks and mauves, and a particularly nasty green. The use of these colours, for instance in the windows of Hugh Easton and Christopher Webb *passim*, may have been governed by their cheapness (they certainly look poverty-stricken), but whatever the cause these pasty-faced windows have nothing to offer. Easton is reported as having said, 'In glass the important thing is to get the drawing right. The colours can take care of themselves' – which is very revealing.

It is significant that in the Perpendicular period, when the aim was also to introduce colour into large, light areas, the colours were glowing and the 'white' areas were never clear glass: they were translucent but not transparent, and transmitted a silvery light quite different from today's glare. Despite many patchings, the effect can be well appreciated at Great Malvern Priory or in the antechapel of New College, Oxford, and on a vast scale in the east window of Gloucester Cathedral. The big east window at East Harling in Norfolk is another notable example of this type, while at Kidlington in Oxfordshire the east window is like a patchwork quilt of old glass, a reconstruction of great sensibility. Another such east window is at Greystoke in Cumberland. It is strange that with such examples as these, and many more – for instance, at York – available for study, the work of today's practitioners is mostly so mediocre.

In 1928–33 Douglas Strachan almost filled the church at Winchelsea in Sussex with a series of windows of very distinctive character, which created something of a sensation at the time. He had 'streaky' glass specially made for him, and employed 'new' aniline-dye colours, and very close leading. It was a courageous undertaking, and the church certainly benefits from having all its windows except the three in the chancel by the same artist. But the windows do not stand up well to detailed study. The drawing is not sensitive; the sense of composition is defective; there is far too much paint on the glass; and the overall effect is 'busy', also, as Pevsner said, decidedly sentimental. The most satisfying parish church windows of the last generation have been individual works, like Evie Hone's 'Last Supper' at St Michael, Highgate. Some of the best windows of the present century are not widely known. At St Luke, Wallsend-on-Tyne, an ambitious Crucifixion, spread over five graded lancets, is an early work (1922) by Evie Hone, skilfully planned, splendid in colour, and, as always with her, completely free from sentimentality. Downe in Kent has a smaller and much later Crucifixion by the same artist (1950); another window of fine quality. St Andrew, Plymouth, has six windows by John Piper and Patrick Reyntiens, of which the big one at the west end, a memorial to the second Viscount Astor, is specially successful. The church, gutted by German bombs and rebuilt in the 1950s, is still flooded with light through windows of clear glass, and all the better for it; it is therefore very fortunate that this window could be placed in the shadow provided by the underside of the west tower. Viewed from the east end it is a gorgeous sight. Nettlebed in Oxfordshire, a poor little brick church, has an exquisite three-light east window also by John Piper, installed as recently as 1970. The butterflies, symbols of the Resurrection, on a jade green ground are pendant to fishes, on a red ground, with the Tree of Life in the central light. These artists can be seen near their best at All Hallows, Wellingborough, as also in Eton College Chapel, where the east window is Evie Hone's masterpiece. In a very different vein are Brian Thomas's thoughtful, highly accomplished windows at St Vedast; although when they were built, plain glass was usually preferred, many of the Wren churches have received new stained glass since the last war, but of them all only Thomas's, in my opinion, are really right for the church.

This leads on to the delicate question of the qualifications of the donors and of the attitude of the clergy towards well-to-do and perhaps influential benefactors. There can be little doubt that a principal reason for the indifferent quality of so much contemporary glass is that most donors have never studied the art and know little or nothing about it. Paradoxically enough, the situation is worse in the cathedrals and in the royal 'peculiars' than in the parish churches, because projects for windows in the latter have at least to clear the hurdle of the Diocesan Advisory Committee, which offers a protection which is very welcome to many incumbents. Shocking designs of the most sentimental religiosity, and sometimes introducing, at the request of prospective donors, portraits of their late spouses and pictorial details of quite inappropriately photographic realism, are continually being submitted and, sometimes, rejected. Deans and Chapters are, in my view quite improperly, under no such obligation; and while it would be both ungracious and unjust not to recognise the devotion shown by many to the famous buildings under their care, devotion is unfortunately no substitute for artistic perception. There is, it is true, now a Cathedral Advisory Committee, but its advice does not have to be accepted. Windows have been inserted since 1945, in a number of our great churches and cathedrals, whose level of taste is embarrassing, and as bad as anything perpetrated by the Victorians. It is perfectly understandable that one of the windows in Westminster Abbey (by Easton) should have been nicknamed by the vergers, 'Bath night, darling!' The parish churches do at least enjoy *some* measure of protection, although sometimes, one has to conclude, very little. At Badingham in Suffolk the ghastly east window, again by Easton, is already overdue for removal. At St Michael, Southampton, the post-war glass is unsigned, and one can understand why. At North Thoresby in Lincolnshire there is an east window of *c.* 1947 which can only be described as painful, surpassing Easton and Webb at their feeblest. Of these two latter, and of Comper at his most anaemic, visits to Chesterfield and to Holy Trinity, Coventry, will provide very enervating experiences.

With the art in such a generally sick state, my belief is that the right course for Diocesan Advisory Committees should usually be to turn down any proposal for more stained glass in a church. There are certainly churches which cry out for some colour in the windows: in particular those late-Perpendicular edifices which are 'more glass than wall'. Fotheringhay is an example of one with no stained glass at all, in which some good glass of the right kind would be welcome (and also, in its enormous windows, formidably expensive). At Tattershall in Lincoln-shire the windows are also large, and, in the nave and transept, for the reason explained earlier (page 21), again entirely without colour; and one misses it. So also in one of the best Gothick churches in England, King's Norton in Leicestershire, completed in 1775, the most notable of those which took King's College chapel, Cambridge, as their model (and added, here, a good tower). This is a lofty, aisleless hall, devoid of internal adornments, and the introduction of colour would have to be done with great care; but at present the interior is undeniably cold.

Often, however, the absence of stained glass is a great aesthetic advantage. Where the glass is not positively good, it is an irrelevance, if not an embarrassment. One of Suffolk's stateliest churches, Blythburgh, has no Victorian nor modern glass at all, and as a result is flooded with light and, sometimes, sunshine, falling with splendid effect on to the white walls and pinkish brick floor. Among other churches which benefit very much from having no, or almost no, coloured glass are Navestock in Essex, South Acre, Wickmere and Great Ellingham in Norfolk, Brooke and Great Casterton in Rutland, Haltham-on-Bain in Lincolnshire, Wym-ington in Bedfordshire, Sampford Courtenay in Devon and Launcells in Cornwall. (At Brooke, in the floor of the north choir aisle, a stone com-memorates a man who died in 1742 aged 70, by which time he had buried four wives and married a fifth, and also lost both his sons by his first wife. In a church filled with Victorian glass this touching record would have been invisible.)

From this general dictum, however, it is necessary to make one important reservation. Churches like Hawling in Gloucestershire, Morcott in Rutland and Tilty in Essex must be very uncomfortable buildings in which to attend a service, for as there is no stained glass in the east window one sits facing a blaze of light. Short of the common Georgian solution, a blank wall at the east end with a tall reredos of Commandments boards and the like, there are only two acceptable alternatives: stained glass in the east window(s) even if nowhere else, as at St Swithun, Worcester (pp. 131–132), or trees. Several of the churches mentioned above have high, dense trees outside to mask the bright light in summer, and so have Warlingworth, Charsfield and Little Waldingfield in Suffolk, West Walton in Norfolk, Buckden in Huntingdonshire, Stapleford in Leicestershire, Acton Burnell in Shropshire, Fownhope in Herefordshire, Edington in Wiltshire and Warnford in Hampshire. Luckiest of all are Horne in Surrey, Ile Abbots in Somerset and South Luffenham in Rutland, which have yews: the perfect foil to excessive light from the east. South Luffenham, it should be added, is fortunate in this respect only, for here is a once attractive church which has been savaged (there is no other word) by the Victorian restorers.

After the acres of bad commercial glass, the most serious damage that the Victorians wreaked on our hapless churches was through their pews. Nearly all those in towns and a good many village churches had during the Victorian period to submit to the installation of pews, which were usually made of one of the hardest of the so-called soft woods, known as pitch-pine. Many interiors are half stifled by their pews; at Hemel Hempstead, for example, none of the bases of the massive circular Norman piers is visible from the central aisle, which from the architectural standpoint is deplorable.

Until the fifteenth century seats were seldom provided in churches for the congregation. Occasionally there might be stone seats against the side walls, as at Rickinghall Superior in Suffolk and Chipstead in Surrey (in the chancel); or stone seats might encircle one or more piers, as at Baumber, Moulton and Skirbeck, all in Lincolnshire. At Snettisham and South Creake in Norfolk all the piers are surrounded by stone seats; that was most unusual. Some churches in Italy and other countries of the Mediterranean region, especially those adhering to the Greek Orthodox faith, are still without seats, to their great visual advantage. The demand for seating, however, cannot be regarded as unreasonable, most of all when the sermon might continue for a full hour!

Benches began to appear in English churches towards the end of the thirteenth century; the earliest survivors would seem to be those at Dunsfold in Surrey, which are believed to date from 1270. Beautiful in its chaste simplicity is the comparable set at Icklingham All Saints in Suffolk (*71*), a miraculously unspoiled old church which also houses a very fine early-fourteenth-century ironbound chest. They did not become general until the fifteenth century, and even then did not necessarily fill the church. The large churches of East Anglia, such as Blythburgh or Salle, never had seats in the western part of the nave, which is occupied only by the font; often admirably placed upon a stepped base along the central axis of the church, this benefits greatly from the empty space surrounding it. For the many churches which are half-choked today with pews that are seldom or never used there is a salutary lesson to be learned here.

The oak seating which was made in large quantities in the fifteenth and early sixteenth centuries is all very uncomfortable, but visually can be a wonderful addition to the church. A great deal of the original work has survived in East Anglia and in the South-West. Norfolk and Suffolk churches each preserve over a thousand of their late-medieval bench-ends; in Norfolk no fewer than 117 churches retain portions at least. Sometimes the benches were formed into a continuous curb that surrounded the entire block; the purpose of this high and often moulded curb was probably to contain rushes or straw, strewn on the floor below the seats in order to help people to keep their feet a trifle warmer in the unheated churches. In the best East Anglian collections, not only the ends of the benches but the whole length of the backs were moulded and carved in a variety of different patterns, such as a vine trail with leaves and shields, or pierced tracery. The most imposing set is at Wiggenhall St Mary the Virgin (R)[27] in the Norfolk Marshland, where the effect is exceedingly harmonious (74), although the oak here has been stained and is now too dark. Unnecessary staining and oiling have done untold harm in a good many churches. At Fressingfield in Suffolk, on the other hand, the oak is a seductive silver-brown, and this church certainly has one of the half dozen most elegant collections in England (72).

Barningham is another Suffolk church which is transformed by the cumulative effect of its richly carved benches. They impart to a simple building a sumptuousness which it would otherwise entirely lack, and of which the exterior gives not the slighest indication. A number of Norfolk churches besides Wiggenhall St Mary are also much enriched by complete, or nearly complete, sets of benches. Among them may be mentioned Wilton, St Mary at Feltwell and Gooderstone, which has also kept its painted screen. From the Tudor period date a collection of 25 benches at Wiggenhall St Germans, in much the same handsome style as at St Mary the Virgin across the Ouse, and a set at Bressingham dated 1572, which are in a semi-Renaissance style, more clumsily designed but none the less a great enhancement to the beauty of the church. For their lively and interesting figurative carvings most of these collections of benches are worth examining in detail.

The East Anglian bench-end often has only tracery on its face but terminates, almost invariably, in a handsome finial known as a poppy-head. The name has nothing to do with poppies; it derives, through old French, from the Latin *puppis*, meaning the curved poop, or sometimes figurehead, of a ship. The usual poppy-head, based on a kind of conventionalised fleur-de-lis, was replaced here and there by a figure; at Blythburgh, for example, some of the poppies illustrate the seven deadly sins, with Sloth in bed, Drunkenness in the stocks, Avarice seated on a chest of money, and so on. More figures occupy the arm-rests, some of them humorous, like the pensive unicorn at Stowlangtoft, apparently engaged in scratching his back-side with his horn.

The bench-ends were cut from oak planks three or four inches thick, sawn vertically from sections of the trunk to the length required, and known as butts. Thousands of them have now survived for five centuries; and in the restoration of bench-ends, and sometimes in the provision of additional ones of similar pattern, the work of the Victorian craftsmen could be extremely good.

Great numbers of original bench-ends are to be found in the South-West: the churches of Somerset and Devon, like those of Norfolk and

Suffolk, have over a thousand each, and Cornwall several hundred. Compared with East Anglia the general level of accomplishment in the South-West is not quite as high, but, with the aid of judicious Victorian restoration and additions, the number of churches completely filled by collections of benches with carved ends is really surprising. In Devon, East Budleigh and High Bickington each have about seventy ends, and Braunton only a few less. Just across the Cornish border Altarnun, dedicated to St Nonna, has seventy-nine, all dating from c. 1525–30 and including a man playing the bagpipes (75)! At Broomfield in the Quantocks there is a specially charming Somerset collection, delicious alike in colour and in texture. In Dorset Trent has a lively set, rudely carved but entertaining.

A famous set at Brent Knoll in Somerset exposes to ridicule a mitred Abbot. He is seen as a fox, preaching to a congregation consisting of three pigs in cowls, assumed to be monks, and a number of geese, the parishioners (73). Successive bench-ends show the fox-abbot in the stocks and then hanging from the gallows; the carver was clearly no lover of monks! This is only rough 'peasant' carving, but full of vitality, and in this instance there are poppy-head finials. Usually, however, in the South-West the benches are lower, and square-topped. They tend also to be a little later in date than in East Anglia, and in a good many of them the details are of a decidedly Renaissance character, as at Lansallos near Polperro (76). This church, with its dedication to another of those obscure and purely local Cornish worthies, St Ildierna, has thirty-four bench-ends *temp.* Henry VIII. A fine set at Mullion, in the Lizard peninsula, dating from not earlier than 1535, includes portrait-busts of a man and his wife, possibly the original holders of that particular sitting. At Sandford in central Devon the benches, which date only from about 1600, continue this same style; one, a most decorative design, and entirely appropriate to wood, has the head of an old man, reminiscent of Bacchus, surrounded by conventional foliage.

Entire books have been devoted to our late-medieval and early-Renaissance bench-ends; the penance is to have to sit on the benches, which in an unheated church in winter must have been almost intolerable. Georgian box-pews are in this respect only a little better, and, although acceptable in a church designed to receive them, they generally make a poor impression in a Gothic church. The Victorians therefore had an opportunity to devise seating which would be at once more comely and more comfortable.

Occasionally one comes upon pleasing Victorian pews. Clipsham in Rutland, a church which has been cited several times in this book for its deficiencies, is in this respect unusually good. The pews have backs pierced with quatrefoils and the like, treated uniformly throughout the

church, and the resultant effect – if only the glass would allow us to see it
– is rather rich. Marsh Chapel in Lincolnshire has a profusion of
Victorian woodwork in excellent taste. But many sets of pews,
commonplace in design and carried out not in oak but in pitch-pine
smothered with yellow varnish, are visually repellent. When, as so often
in town churches, they fill the entire nave and aisles, the effect is
suffocating. At Aldeburgh, for instance, the church guide (by Ronald
Blythe) records that 'the Victorian pew-seating is far too cumbersome and
lends an unduly heavy effect to what is actually a very graceful building'.
And although churchgoers did at last have the benefit of sloping backs, by
no stretch of the imagination could the usual pew be described as
comfortable.

In recent years churches all over the country, from Gedney in
Lincolnshire to Madley in Herefordshire, from Tredington in Warwickshire to Creed in Cornwall, have turned out their pews (or most of them)
and substituted chairs. Not everyone approves. It is said that chairs have a
temporary look and the pews are more dignified. Where the pews are
really handsome, I would agree; but how seldom is this so. The large
majority of pews are without artistic merit, and many are encumbrances.
Psychologically they are also wrong today; they look 'stuffy' and
unfriendly.

Moreover, if, in order that churches may survive, their naves (as I
suggested earlier) must be made available in the future for a range of
activities comparable with those of the Middle Ages, there can be no
choice; the pews will have to be cleared away. On aesthetic grounds this
will often be entirely welcome.

The churches which in these conditions will have a real problem are
those that possess fine sets of benches or handsome pews. These will be
difficult or impossible to remove, which may well rule out the chance of
alternative uses. All one can say at the moment about such buildings as
these is that each case will need to be judged on its merits when a decision
is required. A great many large churches could make a start, and improve
their appearance enormously, by clearing away a proportion of their pews
– those hardly ever used. The chairs that are introduced to replace pews
when there is a complete clearance must of course be well designed.

One of the most unaccountable aberrations of Victorian taste was
its addiction to machine-made encaustic tiles, largely a Staffordshire
product, for covering floors, and sometimes even glazed tile dadoes for
walls as well, as at North Tuddingham in Norfolk and Kentisbeare in
Devon. All over the country the Victorians inherited floors of good stone,
or, as at Navestock, of red tiles, large and square, unglazed and mellow,
many of them incorporating inscribed slabs known as ledgers. These were

often a delightful addition to a floor. Many materials were employed,
Black 'marble' (in fact a Carboniferous limestone known here as 'touch')
from Belgium was a favourite (*124*), but limestone, sandstone, slate,
granite and even cast iron were all used in the areas in which they were
local or the most easily accessible products. In Kent alone there are 160
ledgers distributed over fifty churches.[28] At Staple Fitzpaine in Somerset
the sanctuary floor consists entirely of handsome ledgers. Nearly all the
best belong to the eighteenth century; the incised lettering is usually
excellent, and some of these ledgers are enriched with grand heraldry,
which may be quite deeply cut.

I do not know that the Victorians cleared away any of these Georgian
ledgers, although it is possible. But where they had a free hand with the
floor, they seldom failed to introduce small, shiny tiles, usually coloured
earth-red, pasty yellow or black. Most are plain but some have designs,
allegedly modelled on the floor tiles of the medieval period, specially
associated with the thirteenth century with Chertsey Abbey and in the
fifteenth with Great Malvern Priory. Here and there numbers of these old
tiles survive, as at West Hendred in Berkshire. The resemblances of the
nineteenth-century tiles to the old ones are in fact slight, at least in their
general effect, for the Victorian products are characterised by a hard
efficiency and a relentless precision intended to resist into eternity the
wear and tear of boots and shoes. And this indeed, so far, they have done;
even the foolish fashion, a few years back, for stiletto heels, which ruined
so many parquet and other wooden floors all over the country, left these
tiled floors quite unaffected.

In that charming book, *Small Talk at Wreyland*, Cecil Torr, writing in
1918 about Lustleigh church in South Devon, says: 'The church has high
pews and a three-decker pulpit, and until it was removed in 1871,
everything was whitewashed. Nearly all the windows had plain glass so
that one could see the trees and the sky. Now these are hidden by glass that
is exasperating in its colour and design. Lavatory tiles replace the granite
paving of the chancel, and there is marble of the sort that one sees on
washstands.' All this in a Devon country church...

The removal of these horrible shiny tiles would not be a very costly
matter, and it should be done all over the country. A beginning has been
made. At Great Coggeshall in Essex a bomb which in 1940 destroyed
the nave and part of the tower forced the authorities into action. The
new interior, opened in 1957, is delightful, except for four Victorian
windows and two heavy parclose screens, which unfortunately survived.
There are no pews, but only chairs, which leaves the western third of the
nave unencumbered; the walls are entirely lime-washed (and not dead
white, which is right, for white is too cold); and all the floors are of
stone.

The largest piece of furniture in many of our churches, and often the most difficult to accommodate pleasingly, is the organ. On this subject there is one indispensable book, *The British Organ*, by Cecil Clutton and Austin Niland (1963), to which I am indebted for much of the factual information in the next few pages.

As early as the middle of the tenth century Winchester Cathedral had a 400-pipe organ, of which a description survives in a poem by Wulstan. 'Seventy strong men, labouring with their arms, covered with perspiration' were required to supply wind. This prodigious, if highly inefficient, instrument emitted so much noise that 'everyone stops with his hands to his gaping ears, being in no wise able to bear the sound which so many combinations produce. The music is heard throughout the town, and the flying fame thereof is gone out over the whole country'. But, perhaps fortunately, this instrument was unique in England. Although references to organs occur not infrequently in medieval churchwardens' accounts, it is evident that they were all small, often indeed so small as to be easily portable. Thus they were not only moved about in the church itself, but lent to neighbouring parishes as occasions required.

With the advent of the Tudors a few organs became larger, in parish churches as well as in cathedrals. The earliest surviving cases belong to this period. The oldest organ case in Britain is just across the Welsh border at Old Radnor. Although it looks much reconstructed, it dates from the reign of Henry VIII. It is Renaissance rather than Gothic in spirit despite the profusion of linenfold panelling. 'Even allowing for the living having been in the royal gift from 1502 to 1534', Clutton and Niland observe, 'and for the then flourishing school of woodcarving at Llananno, it is difficult enough to account for the presence of this sumptuous case, standing 18 feet high, in this small and remote Welsh village.'

Only nine other organ cases of British manufacture earlier than 1660 have been identified, and of these only four are in parish churches. None of the four was in its present home as early as the Restoration, at which time the Appleby organ was still in Carlisle Cathedral, the Stanford-on-Avon organ was probably in the Chapel Royal, Whitehall, the Framlingham organ was at Pembroke College, Cambridge, whilst that at Old Bilton, Warwickshire, was at St John's College, Cambridge. Of these the most enjoyable today, visually, is that at Stanford-on-Avon, on the Leicestershire border of Northamptonshire (*86*), whither it was removed about 1663. This is not only an early Renaissance-style case of grace and charm; it is excellent in scale in relation to the fourteeenth-century church, and is in the best possible place for an organ, a western gallery.

That so few pre-1660 organs have survived was due to the Puritans. In pre-Reformation days the loft that stretched out east and west, often so gracefully, from the top of the chancel screen accommodated not only, permanently, the rood but also, when required, a preacher, a group of singers, and a small organ. Anti-Popish objections to roods, combined with puritanical dislike of the allegedly sensuous pleasure of church music, prompted the Orders of 1547 and 1561 decreeing the complete removal of all lofts. So down came the organs too, and in an age when organ music was no longer demanded nor appreciated many were left to decay or were dismantled. This phase culminated in the Ordinance of 1644 in which organs were grouped with 'images and all matters of superstitious ornaments' as objects 'illegal in the worship of God' and therefore to be demolished with all speed.

With the Restoration, therefore, and the removal of the ban on organs as on so much else, the way was open for what was virtually a clean start, and the following fifty years saw the creation of nearly all the most beautiful organ-cases ever made in England. The great names are Bernard ('Father') Smith (c. 1629–1708) and his rival Renatus Harris (c. 1652–1724). Both of them designed in a manner which was at once architectural and mildly Baroque: strong, assured, self-confident and zestful. The Victorians, needless to say, were to disapprove. Sir John Sutton, in his *Short Account of Organs*, published in 1847, complained primly of the 'wreaths of flowers and indelicate fat cupids, by way of angels, with drapery used for every purpose but to cover the nakedness, ... very much out of place in a Church, and offensive to the feelings of right-minded persons'. Smith and Harris worked mostly for Wren, and a fine case by the former can be seen at St Katherine Cree, Leadenhall Street. For rich examples of Harris's work one should go to St James, Piccadilly, where the carvings are by Grinling Gibbons, and to Twickenham, where in 1938–40 all the finest furniture from All Hallows, Lombard Street, was rehoused in a new building attached to the rebuilt tower of the original church. Outside London Father Smith worked principally at Cambridge, where his best parish church organ can be seen in Great St Mary (*87*). It should be noted that every one of these Restoration organs was placed, as a matter of course, in a west gallery.

Yet even at this time a church organ in England was the exception rather than the rule. Of the fifty-three churches erected in London by Wren, only twelve are known to have had an organ installed at the time of building, and these did not include such important examples as St Mary-le-Bow and St Stephen, Walbrook. The average English parish church could not afford an organ and would seem to have managed perfectly happily without one. Some years ago I visited a church near Ravenna a few minutes before the celebration of a simple country wedding. Suddenly, from behind the high altar, a small chamber orchestra struck up. The 'cellist played beautifully and the big uncluttered church accorded a wonderful resonance to the music. Such was the way in which

Icklingham All Saints, Suffolk

MEDIEVAL BENCHES

Fressingfield, Suffolk

73. Brent Knoll, Somerset

BENCH-ENDS

74. Wiggenhall St Mary Virgin, Norfolk

75. Altarnun, Cornwall

76. Lansallos, Cornwall

music was made in many of our churches too, until about the middle of the last century; and very agreeable it must often have been, not least for the players. Many will recall Hardy's description of the Mellstock Quire, in *Under the Greenwood Tree*, and the despondency with which they viewed Parson Maybold's unwanted new organ. Here and there, usually now in a glass case, old instruments have been preserved. Old Alresford in Hampshire and Rumburgh in Suffolk have a 'clarionet': Battisford, also in Suffolk, a 'serpent' (now in Christchurch Mansion, Ipswich): Shermanbury in Sussex recorders and a viol: Easby in Yorkshire a pitch-pipe, used to give the congregation the starting note for hymns. At Great Milton, Oxfordshire, the orchestra comprised a 'cello, an English concertina, a key bugle and an ophicleide (a large bass trumpet); the two latter are still in the church. At Redmire, near Leyburn, in Wensleydale, the band, still functioning in 1879, comprised fiddles, cornets, woodwind and an euphonium. At Scar Top Chapel, west of Haworth, in the Brontë country, there were two clarinets, a trombone, an ophicleide and a double bass. Ridlington in Rutland still keeps its compete set of instruments which were in use until about 1860: a violin, a flute, two clarinets and a bassoon 4 feet 7½ inches long, made about 1793. In those days it is evident that each church had its own tradition, its own ideas on the particular form that its music should take. It may originally have been dependent upon what musical skills it could command. And in earlier times, if there were no skills there was no music. Later, there were barrel organs! Bressingham in Norfolk still has one which plays a few hymn-tunes remarkably well. There are others at Shelland in Suffolk and at Farnham in the West Riding, the latter made in 1831.

A few fine organ-cases followed in the wake of Father Smith and the Harris family. Tiverton has a beauty by Christian Smith, Bernard's nephew, and Finedon in Northamptonshire a very handsome instrument by Christopher Shrider, his son-in-law, dating from 1717. The notable organ, with exquisite carvings, at Great Packington, Warwickshire, originally at Gopsall Hall, was the work of Richard Bridge, who was almost certainly a pupil of John Harris, the son of Renatus. This specimen, which dates from 1750, is said on good authority to have been designed by Handel, whose name is attached to a number of other mid-eighteenth-century organs in England. In the third quarter of the century some very distinguished organs were made by Johann Snetzler, an immigrant from Germany. He not only built the large one in Beverley Minster but a number of chamber-size organs, of which one was brought from the Assembly Rooms at York to Sculthorpe in Norfolk. Mildly neo-Classical in spirit, it presents, as Mr Clutton says, a perfect blend of richness and simplicity (see p. 160).

In general, however, English organs under the four Georges are of no

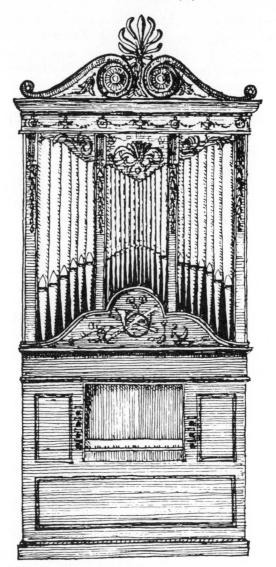

Organ by Snetzler at Sculthorpe, Norfolk, 1756

great aesthetic interest, especially towards the end of the period. They did possess one great negative virtue: they were nearly all small, sometimes, it must be said, to the point of insignificance. But the fact is that until well into the nineteenth century large organs were not wanted in England, even in cathedrals where there was ample room for them. And, as Clutton and Niland also point out, most of our medieval churches have always been, because of their comprative lowness, quite unsuited to the housing of big organs.

It was the High Church movement of early Victorian days which was responsible for the change. Large surpliced choirs now made their appearance in the bigger churches; chancels were extended, partly to allow the choir to be placed between the high altar and the congregation, and the organ and organist migrated eastwards to be near to it. The population was also increasing fast and often the churches were not short of money. British organs suddenly grew enormous. For a short period, through the fifties and early sixties of the nineteenth century, they were tonally the best in the world. The cases, which were at best designed in Puginesque Gothic, are usually deplorable. And since the architects of the churches did not provide any suitable positions for these huge instruments, resort had to be made to a number of expedients which were all unsatisfactory, such as filling a triforlium, a transept or a chapel, or, still worse, by adding, generally on the north side of the chancel, an ugly box known as an organ chamber, as inimical to musical artistry as to architectural propriety.

Tetbury church in Gloucestershire offers a prize instance of the folly of moving the organ eastwards from the west gallery, for there is no west window here, and the gallery now has a blank recess aching to be filled, whereas the organ is a gross-looking lump at the end of the south aisle, an eyesore in an otherwise rather distinguished and unusual church (built in 1781). At Blandford in 1970 the *faux pas* of 1896 was happily corrected, when the organ, a real ornament to the church, was very properly returned to the west gallery. But sometimes the pleasure of an English church interior is marred more by an obtrusive, ugly organ even than by bad glass. Stoke Golding in Leicestershire has a richly moulded Decorated arcade and some notably fine window tracery, but enjoyment of all this is half-ruined by the organ case, an uncouth pitch-pine monster, very prominently sited near the east end of the south (here the only) aisle. Northorpe in Lincolnshire is, as observed earlier (p. 36), an almost perfect English village church, with but one jarring note, the obtrusive organ. At another village church, Ingham in Norfolk, the organ fills two whole bays of an aisle.

The outcome of the Victorian legacy is that many parish churches now contain organs that are musically far too large for their needs and architecturally impossible to site pleasingly. A big organ cannot even be placed in a west gallery when, as often in England, the building depends for some of its light on a large west window; moreover, in a long Gothic church, with the small congregations that are usual nowadays, it has to be accepted that an organ and choir in a west gallery are too far away. Not many parish churches are as fortunate as Great Malvern Priory, which had the perfect place for an organ under the arch that once led into the demolished south transept. The handsome case of 1932, designed by W. D.

Caröe, is of light oak with plenty of carving and, for once, a real asset to the church. The usual solution must surely be to substitute a small modern instrument of good design whenever the opportunity offers. Uncased organs, preferably having pipes of tin or with a high tin content so that their colour is silver, are visually acceptable* in the context of contemporary architecture, but not in medieval nor in classically designed churches. Here the organ, in its case, ought to be, as occasionally it is, an object of dignified decorative enrichment.

I have suggested that the other principal enemies of pleasure in our churches are stripped walls and ugly pulpits, fonts and monuments. Stripped, scraped and skinned walls have already been discussed (p. 25). A church which provides an object lesson in contrasted wall surfaces is Lyddington in Rutland, a handsome Perpendicular building, spacious, lofty and light. (The only stained glass is a lamentable east window of 1870). The nave and aisle walls are entirely rendered, and the plaster is now rather blotchy and shabby; nevertheless it looks right. The chancel has been skinned, and the hardstone very assiduously repointed with a darkish grey mortar; and it could not look more wrong. This removal of plaster was certainly one of the worst practices of the Victorian church restorers. The rougher the wall and the darker the stone, the worse it looks. Counties which seem to have been specially unfortunate in this respect include Northumberland, Lincolnshire, Rutland, Derbyshire, Warwickshire, Devon and Cornwall, but none has escaped. Poor Cotterstock in Northamptonshire, which should offer a very rewarding experience, for it has a noble chancel provided for a collegiate foundation, is in fact distressing, for in addition to skinned and ribbon-pointed walls, it has a horrible tiled floor, an ugly, obtrusive organ and green-tinted opaque glass. With a benefaction of a few thousand pounds, an architect equipped with both knowledge and taste would be able to give back to this church much of its former grace and distinction.

Pulpits and fonts offered a rich field for Victorian tastelessness. There are about 60 pre-Reformation stone pulpits still in use, ten of which are in Devon, but the great majority are wood. Some go back to the fifteenth century; one at Burnham Norton in Norfolk, no longer used, has a wine-glass stem base and six painted panels showing the four Latin doctors (Augustine, Ambrose, Jerome and Gregory) and two donors with scrolls. This enchanting object dates from about 1450. Edlesborough in Buckinghamshire even has its tester, with four tiers of crocketed

---

* I am told that musically such organs are always unsatisfactory, because the case performs a definite function, which is to help to project the sound in the desired direction.

pinnacles. These two little pulpits are hexagonal, but the majority are octagonal. Under Elizabeth I, for political reasons, a licence was needed in order to preach, and from many of the clergy this was withheld. It was only under her successor that it was deemed safe to relax the regulations. The sermon then became important, which is why so many pulpits, including some elaboratory carved examples, are Jacobean. But the richest pulpits are late Stuart (*89*) or Georgian. If one wants to see what the Victorians could do to an old church, Sudbourne in Suffolk is a truly shocking example. The east window gives one the creeps, and the pitch-pine roof is a brute. But even the Victorian 'restorer' did not touch the early eighteenth-century pulpit, an object that combines dignity with charm. These pulpits are always amply proportioned and sometimes have very fine carving. They may also have gracefully curved staircases and large testers, or they may be double or triple deckers. (They may also preserve their hour glasses; at Earl Stonham in Suffolk there are three, registering respectively a quarter of an hour, a half-hour and a whole hour!)

With all these precedents, the Victorians produced some of the ugliest pulpits to be seen anywhere. The profusion of the carving could be enjoyable if it were less sentimentally executed, but what is unpardonable is the choice of material. Whereas the cheap ones are usually pitch-pine, the expensive pulpits are always of shiny stone, usually with variegated colour-markings. Favourites were 'streaky bacon' alabaster with a soapy texture and the so-called Devon marbles (carboniferous limestone hard enough to take a polish) quarried at a number of places between Plymouth and Newton Abbot. In themselves these are handsome stones; they polish brilliantly and often have the veining and figuring associated with true marble, and in a wide range of colours, from shell pink through deep red to dark green, grey and black. Employed with discretion, these rather dressy 'marbles' can be an embellishment, but in a Gothic church they always look wrong, and are indeed often an eyesore.

These materials were also sought after in the Victorian period for reredoses and fonts, for which they are equally unsuitable. Other Victorian fonts were produced in large numbers in the local limestones and sandstones. Some are harmless enough, but a good many are coarse-looking and ugly. Yet, despite mutilation, many hundreds of earlier fonts survive. The three most notable groups are the urbane late Stuart and Georgian fonts, the bowl if not the whole generally of marble, often rather small, and on a baluster-type stem:[29] the Seven Sacraments fonts of the fifteenth century, of limestone, octagonal, not of a high sculptural standard but accorded much dignity, as mentioned earlier, by being raised aloft on stepped pedestals (all but two of these fonts, of which some 29 survive, are in Norfolk and Suffolk); and the Norman fonts.

Some of the most vigorous and enjoyable Romanesque sculpture in England is to be found on fonts, especially in the counties of the west, already cited (p. 115) for the interest of their twelfth-century tympana. Three of these fonts, at Castle Frome (77) and at Eardisley (79) in Herefordshire and at Stottesdon in southern Shropshire, are truly magnificent objects, with very large bowls on short stems: the whole outer surface of both bowl and stem is lavishly adorned with carving of a distinctly 'wiry' kind, which like the doorway at Kilpeck shows Viking influence as well as French. All three are noble embellishments to what are now, thanks to the restorers, decidedly dull churches. Another font belonging to the same group is at Chaddesley Corbett in Worcestershire; the proportions here are better but the carving, though powerful, is more coarsely executed.

Memorable fonts of this period survive in isolation elsewhere. The most remotely situated, at Bridekirk in Cumberland, is of particular interest, as on one face the sculptor has added a representation of himself at work. This font is also unique for its date in having a runic inscription. It is not a graceful object, but the carving has great vitality. So has that at East Keal in Lincolnshire, where the carvings include what must surely be the most Rabelaisian detail on any English font: a real piece of rude!

Besides those in the west, there are two other very notable concentrations of Norman fonts. One is in the district around Aylesbury, where there are seven or eight fonts which must be the work of the same man. They are not as vigorous as the West Country group and have no figures, but they are more refined and better proportioned. The fonts are bowl-shaped and stand on what look rather like inverted scalloped capitals. Bledlow has one of the best (78). The other, a less homogeneous but more remarkable group, is in western Norfolk. As works of art the two finest are Toftrees and Shernborne (80), both grandly proportioned and very richly decorated. Both are the sole objects of interest in sadly undistinguished little churches. The survival of these splendid Norman fonts, 'hallowed by use in one of the great sacraments of the church', makes the nineteenth-century products look doubly insignificant.

Some fonts have covers, and in a few cases canopies, of great elaboration. The function of these covers was to protect, against dust and dirt and the risk of profanation, the specially sanctified water associated with the sacrament of Baptism. For this consecrated water was sometimes stolen by those who practised black magic. So from 1236 covers were compulsory. The most amazing of all the covers is at Ufford in Suffolk, a wooden spire eighteen feet high, but alas, in a somewhat sorry state. All the larger statues with which it was once encircled in three tiers were long ago destroyed, and there has been other damage too. The smaller spired canopy at St Gregory, Sudbury, looks very elegant after restoration, with

Castle Frome, Herefordshire

78. Bledlow, Buckinghamshire

Eardisley, Herefordshire

80. Shernborne, Norfolk

81. Attleborough, Norfolk

SCREENS

82. Aymestrey, Herefordshire

Plymtree, Devon

84. Hughley, Shropshire

SCREENS

St Margarets, Herefordshire

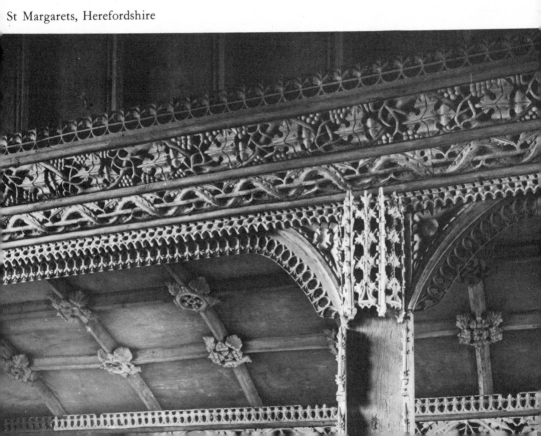

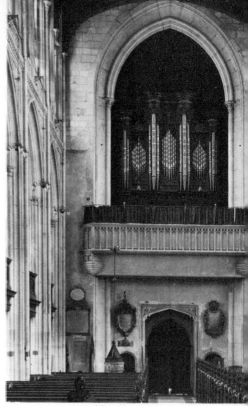

86. Stanford-on-Avon,
Northamptonshire

ORGANS

87. Cambridge: Great St Ma

88. Brancepeth, County Durham

PULPITS

89. London: St Mary Abchu

discreet recolouring in blue and red and regilding. These fantastic canopies cannot of course be lifted off: in order to get at the font each has an ingenious contraption by which the lowest stage can be telescoped up over the one above it, such as that at Swinbridge in Devon.

Only four English churches have fonts protected not merely by covers resting on the upper surface of the bowl but by elaborate canopies supported independently. These are Luton, Trunch, St Peter Mancroft at Norwich and Durham Cathedral. The two Norfolk examples have certain resemblances; otherwise these font canopies differ widely in date and in style, and are not even all of the same material. For the earliest, at Luton, is of limestone, a typical product of the late Decorated style. It is 20 feet high and the dominant feature of the church. The others are of oak and must have been lovely, but both the Norfolk canopies were desecrated by the Puritans and largely spoilt. The one at Trunch, the smaller and later (*c.* 1500) of the two, is today markedly the finer work of art; although the paintings and the carved figures have all gone, the topmost stage, culminating with a flourish in a huge pumpkin-shaped finial, is a grand example of Tudor opulence.

Victorian church monuments are generally poor, but have the negative virtue of being usually not very conspicuous. Apart from the sad decline in the quality of the lettering, the principal lapse of taste was in the employment of inappropriate materials, with again a predilection for shiny surfaces and for polychromy. Unfortunately a good deal of brass was used, which can appear decidedly vulgar, but wherever, as often nowadays, this is neither cleaned nor polished, it just looks drab.

If the parish churches, like life itself, are an amalgam of splendours and miseries, it has seemed necessary, in the latter part of this chapter, to devote some attention to the miseries, although even here the splendours have kept on breaking in. Now, in the final chapter, we shall be free to concern ourselves very largely with the delights of the English church interior.

SIX

The Interior (2)

IN MY ESTIMATION, the six best counties for parish churches are Somerset, Lincolnshire, Norfolk, Suffolk, Yorkshire and Gloucestershire. It is impossible to establish an exact order of merit. For towers we have seen that Somerset is *facile princeps*, and the Somerset churches have many other beauties besides. For sheer architectural brilliance and wonderful richness of sculptural detail the supreme areas would seem to be the Kesteven and Holland divisions of Lincolnshire, the Cotswold part of Gloucestershire and the East Riding of Yorkshire. Norfolk – except in the great Marshland area – and Suffolk labour under the great disadvantage of having only flint for the fabric of most of their churches, an inferior material indeed, compared with limestone. Where the East Anglian churches surpass all others is in the glory of their woodwork, and especially their roofs.

And apart from the architecture, what does the amateur of churches expect most often to find? In Italy it will generally be paintings and sculpture. In France, again plenty of sculpture, and, if he is lucky, some good glass too. (Contemporary stained glass in France can also be excellent. The general level is much higher than here.) In England the greatest glories of the church interiors are, nine times out of ten, their woodwork. We were very fortunate in possessing in the Middle Ages limitless supplies of one of the finest of all hardwoods, oak. Until the second half of the seventeenth century practically all our church woodwork was oak; with such a wonderful wood at our disposal what incentive could there have been to look for alternatives? Oak was used in our parish churches in numerous ways, and it is to some of these that we will now turn.

The grandest effects are to be found where complete sets of furnishings have survived from a single date. As was noted in the last chapter, a number of churches both in East Anglia and the South-West preserve entire sets of pre-Reformation benches; Fressingfield is fortunate in having its original hammer-beam roof as well. Lakenheath and Tostock are other Suffolk churches which have kept their fine fifteenth-century roofs in addition to lovely sets of benches with pierced traceried backs, brattishing mouldings along the top rail and poppy-heads; they make a splendid display. In the South-West too, the churches with old benches often have their original screens and wagon roofs as well.

Church furnishings of the seventeenth century offer exuberant displays at a number of places. At Croscombe in Somerset, in Jacobean times a prosperous little clothing town, all the woodwork except the chancel roof dates from 1616. In black oak, it may not be to everyone's taste, but it is worth a visit. The weird and wonderful screen rises in tiers to a great height and to a forest of strapwork and obelisks. The heavy pulpit and tester are *en suite*, and so is the pair of readers' desks. Some of the box-pews are also Jacobean.

From the next reign there is one spectacular church: St John, Leeds. Built in 1632–34, it is not architecturally of much interest, but the original donor's endowment was sufficient to pay for a fine display of woodwork and plasterwork. The woodwork includes a lavish screen with carved frieze and delicate tracery, a magnificent pulpit and tester, and a big collection of benches (which here might be termed pews) with a profusion of turned knobs. Miraculously, all this survived both Victorian restoration (fortunately the architect for the restoration was Norman Shaw, then only thirty-seven) and the bombing of 1940–41. The church is very well maintained; gilding has been applied to the woodwork with taste and discretion, most successfully.

Leaving aside Staunton Harold, built in 1653, because, as observed earlier, it is not a parish church, there are two other memorable assemblages of seventeenth-century furnishings, both in County Durham. Both stemmed from the initiative of that remarkable man John Cosin, who after thirteen years in exile during the Commonwealth was Bishop of Durham from 1662 until his death ten years later. He was a High Churchman with a nice sense of the value of fine display. His furnishings were to enrich the Cathedral (with a resplendent font canopy) and his private chapels in the Castle and at Bishop Auckland as well as a number of churches in the diocese, of which Brancepeth and Sedgefield are much the most notable. Some of this joinery belongs to the 1630s, some to the 1660s. At Brancepeth, Cosin was rector in the early years of Charles I, and the fittings are extraordinarily complete, even to the inclusion of a pair of family pews, one in each transept. The style of the earlier pieces, dated 1638, of which the best is the two-decker pulpit (*88*), is still essentially Jacobean, with an abundance of little obelisks and the usual strap-work decoration. The screen, a later work, is more elaborate, but not as original nor as exciting as the one at Sedgefield, even though it will be evident to anyone familiar with the great stone screen in Durham Cathedral, the fourteenth-century Neville screen, that for Sedgefield this was the source of inspiration. All this Cosin woodwork is stylistically something of a hotchpotch, and not exactly beautiful, but none the less it is a great enrichment to the churches that possess it.

Reference was made earlier to the furnishing of the Wren churches in the City of London, which, despite serious losses, can still endow plain structures with a welcome sumptuousness. At St Mary Abchurch (*89*) one can see how the enormous tester, in addition to serving as a sounding-board, helped to enhance the *persona* of the preacher. This pulpit, carved by William Grey, is not the artistic equal of Grinling Gibbons's reredos in the same church, but is a work of glorious exuberance, and unusual in preserving its original curving staircase with twisted balusters. Some of the most lavish pieces, like the screen and pulpit-tester at St Margaret, Lothbury, and the pulpit at St James, Garlickhythe, were originally in other churches, long ago destroyed. Of Georgian fittings something has already been said. A church entirely furnished in the Georgian style, like St Swithun, Worcester, is always enjoyable.

The three major items of parish church woodwork are the screens, the stalls and the roofs. In all three, both the carpenters and the carvers from time to time excelled.

The origin and function of the screen were utilitarian: to protect the chancel, with the altar, from the ordinary layman, and to secure for the parishioners the free use of the nave, which was often required for secular purposes. The notion of erecting a loft on the screen followed, but the association of the two was not inevitable. The screen, which was an invariable part of the furnishing of a church until the Reformation, was sometimes placed not exactly under the chancel arch but slightly to the west of it, so that it could be extended along the east walls of the two nave aisles to embrace altars, which is visually a very satisfying arrangement. The early church screens were sometimes, as at Westwell in Kent, of stone, and so are a few late ones, notably at Totnes; in the design of the typical wooden screen it is evident that part of the original inspiration came from lithic forms.

The two principal areas in which to see the best screens are exactly the same as for bench-ends: East Anglia and the South-West. The two types differ radically. East Anglia in the late Middle Ages was much the richer of the two areas. The churches are therefore bigger and, in particular, loftier; so in Norfolk and Suffolk the typical screen also rises much higher than in the South-West, has tall, narrow openings, very slender posts between the bays, and a general air of lightness and elegance. The removal of most of the lofts, as a result of the Orders of 1547 and 1561, has had a very adverse effect upon their appearance; East Anglian lofts were comparatively narrow, but aesthetically the screen needs this solid section at the top, just as classical columns require to support an adequate entablature. A happy exception is the screen at Attleborough in Norfolk

(*81*), quaint, venerable, and not exactly masterly, yet immensely likeable for its frail delicacy and soft original colouring. It stretches 52 feet across nave and aisles, and incorporates former altars in the manner described above. Most unusual, however, is the high parapet to the loft, with paintings of the coats of arms of the episcopal sees. The finest screen in Suffolk is at Bramfield. Here too, happily, the loft has survived, coved underneath on both sides with 'vaulting' of lierne type. Between the liernes, painted on the webs, is a flutter of tiny angels, an enchanting detail. Although as usual there has been much damage and restoration, a surprising quantity of the original colouring still remains here; the principal colours are grey-white, pinkish red, lapis lazuli and gold. It can be seen that the colours were applied on a gesso ground. Of medieval screens Bramfield is certainly one of the most enjoyable.

All these screens were originally a blaze of colours, and for the painters the most important area was the solid panelling below the openings. The tall narrow panels were usually filled with single figures of apostles and other saints, and in recent years much careful restoration of these paintings has been undertaken, grant-aided and under expert supervision. The quality it should be added, varies greatly; some are lifeless dolls which would not be worth restoring. But there is something different at St Gregory, Sudbury. Only one panel has survived here; the subject of the painting is a physician curing gout by conjuring a devil out of a boot*. The best of all are at Ranworth in Norfolk, where the figures include St George and St Michael, on projecting wings separating the side altars from the central archway. Although some are damaged, at Barton Turf in Norfolk there are saints, Sillia and Apollonia especially, of exceptional artistic quality, and rather Flemish in feeling; the top of this screen, with a good cove, is better than at Ranworth. At Cawston in Norfolk and at Southwold in Suffolk are screens on a much larger scale, for these are big churches, but unhappily both suffer greatly from having lost their loft and the weighting at the top which this gave them. Nor is their figure painting so good. At Southwold, however, the backgrounds to the figures are a joy. Behind each figure is a richly diapered pattern in faultless taste, with tiny flowers, leaf-sprays and so on, executed in combination with low-relief gesso. The figure of St James has a diaper of tiny shells (his emblem) in gesso, of exquisite delicacy. For these painted and gesso decorative backgrounds, the Southwold screen has no rival.

Very different from the East Anglian screens are those of Devon and West Somerset. Here in place of the predominantly vertical emphasis of the East Anglian screens, the accent is on the horizontal. The openings

* This panel is now on view at Gainsborough's House, Sudbury.

are lower and wider, and filled with tracery that was closely modelled on Perpendicular windows in stone. More striking is the development above the openings. Although almost all their parapets were removed, a great many lofts managed to survive, and in this part of the country the lofts are much wider than in the East. As well as the ribbed coves, which often have a profusion of carved bosses, there is the bressummer, the broad beam which runs along the top of the screen and is adorned with what are called trails. A trail is a long strip of wood carved in a fretwork technique to produce a waving stem, in between the loops of which are all kinds of motifs drawn from nature. The favourite is the vine, both leaves and grapes, but oak-leaves and acorns are not unusual, and little animals, birds and heraldic badges are entwined within the foliage. To improve the effect, the large beam behind was hollowed out, so that all this carving could be seen in relief against quite dark shadows visible through the pierced openings. The carving of these trails was rather a mass-produced affair, and one's pleasure is not usually enhanced by a close scrutiny of the details, but on first entering the church the effect of a screen of this type is sometimes sensational, and a splendid asset to the interior.

Within the present century many of the Devon screens have been repainted and gilded, in an attempt, no doubt, to recapture something of the original effect – for when they were first set up they were all gay with colour. There is, it must be admitted, a touch of the fairground about some of this festive repainting, at least when the paint is fresh. But after a while it settles down nicely. This is what happened at Plymtree. When I first saw it after repainting, it looked a little garish. Now this screen (*83*) is as beguiling as the name of its village. It is the show-piece of a charming church which also has a complete set of traceried bench-ends and good seventeenth-century woodwork. The loft has three trails. On the panels below are an Annunciation, a Visitation, an Adoration of the Magi and a row of saints: village work, but enjoyable. Not far away, at Kentisbeare, a church that suffered much from the Victorian restorers, there is another beautiful painted screen; the colours, dull red, dull gold and silver-grey, are soft and mellow and not in the least garish. As this screen is unusually lofty for Devon, it is a treasure.

The Devon type of screen is seen equally well in West Somerset. A specially fine one, dated 1499, stretches for over 50 feet across the former Priory church at Dunster. There are also a few screens of this kind in Cornwall, of which perhaps the most beautiful is at St Buryan, extensively but sensitively restored in the last century. The two trails here are mainly original, and one of them is unusual, for peeping out through thick foliage is a strange assemblage of little heads, some with horns, some with ass's ears. Were they an expression, one wonders, of the haunting fears which beset life in the Middle Ages?

Apart from East Anglia and the South-West, the distribution of church screens is less concentrated, but nearly every English county (and several in Wales too) has something good to show. Where the oak has been stained very dark, as at Sleaford, it would be much improved by discreet gilding. The Welsh border counties have screens of both the types just described. The remote Herefordshire church of St Margarets, four miles from Abbey Dore, has a lovely example of the 'horizontal' kind, exceptionally well preserved, even to the retention of the parapet of the loft, which is most unusual. The trail at the base of the coving has acorns and oak-leaves (*85*). There is a great profusion of brattishing. At Aymestrey in the north of the county, by contrast, the proportions of the screen recall East Anglia (*82*); the base is simple but the head and the loft are rich. Below the bressummer, as at Attleborough, there are charming pendant arches. Shropshire has a little gem at Hughley, near Much Wenlock; here the decorative ribs of the cove are arranged in stellar patterns (*84*). Hughley church is tiny and isolated, and has nothing else to show but its screen. It is enough.

Stalls, sometimes canopied and often with misericord seats, were another of the greatest contributions of the wood-carvers to the beauty of our churches; yet the majority of these buildings never had them. If one enters a church and finds stalls in the chancel, the likelihood is that this will once have been a collegiate foundation. The supreme instance is Beverley Minster, where the famous stalls, sixty-eight of them, were carved about 1520, the work of a family whose surname, appropriately enough, was Carver. All have their misericords, which are therefore one of the largest sets in the country. Sets of stalls, not always with canopies, will be found at most of the other formerly collegiate churches listed in footnote 25 on page 243. Usually they were paid for out of the funds provided by the founder.

A good many sets of stalls found their way from monastic into parish churches at the Dissolution. Lancashire has two notable examples. At Whalley, St Mary's church has a graceful canopied set with two exquisite stall-ends and an interesting set of misericords which were brought from the nearby Abbey, and therefore never left the little town. The magnificent stalls at Lancaster probably came from Cockersand, a Premonstratensian abbey of which now only the chapter house survives, on the seashore a few miles to the southwest. Did a set of stalls ever incorporate so many portrait heads as these? Even some of the cusps are in the form of heads. These stalls are so lavish that some people hold that they must have come from a much grander abbey, such as Furness, which by 1340, when they were carved, may be assumed to have departed from Cistercian austerity. At Swinbrook, in the valley of the Windrush in west

Oxfordshire, an unprepossessing little village church will be found to have five stalls with elbow pieces and misericords (*94*), all extremely well carved. These came from the fine but historically complicated church at Burford, not far away.

If a parish church, not formerly monastic nor collegiate, has stalls, it is probably because a private donor was generous enough to provide them. Canopied stalls under these conditions were uncommon, but there are a few. Probably the finest are at Nantwich; it seems likely that these were inspired by the example of Chester – then a Benedictine abbey: not yet a cathedral – which has what is arguably the finest set of stalls and misericords in the country. It is a pity that the oak of the Nantwich stalls has been stained nearly black.

There are also canopied stalls with misericords in the parish church of All Saints at Hereford (*95*), and they may have been provided in emulation of the cathedral. All these sets belong to the fourteenth century. At Cartmel Priory in Lancashire the modest stalls and misericords of the Augustinian canons date from about 1400. After the Dissolution this church fell into a state of decay, from which it was rescued about 1620 by the rich and generous owner of Holker Hall near-by. Some ten years later he provided the stalls with lofty backs, forming on the west side of the choir a screen in an exuberant mixture of Gothic and Classic, a most unexpected embellishment to what was by then just a large and fairly plain parish church in a remote country area.

Exquisite as some of these stall canopies are, with their elaborate gables and profusion of crockets, finials and cusps, it is impossible not to think of them as woodcarving imitating decorative forms first evolved in stone. Technically the achievement is remarkable, and it can, I feel, be held that the motifs are as well suited to realisation in wood as in stone; nevertheless some may find the less ambitious, more 'woody' work easier to enjoy. The English parish church with the largest number of uncanopied stalls is St Mary, Beverley, which has twenty-eight, all but five with their original misericords of very high quality, dating from *c.* 1450. The great wool church at Boston has stalls that are sixty years older than these, with another very notable set of misericords; here there are canopies too, but only since 1860.

There have been many studies of English misericords, those little seats shaped and carved like corbels, which were fitted under the tip-up seats of stalls to provide some support for monks and priests condemned to long periods of standing during services. Since they were often hidden from view, misericords gave the carvers a chance really to enjoy themselves, and of this they did not fail to take full advantage. Several thousand survive, mainly from the fourteenth and fifteenth centuries. Aesthetically they vary greatly. The best, mostly, as one would expect, in the cathedrals, are

Eaton Bray, Bedfordshire

WROUGHT IRON AND BRASS

Bristol: St Mary Redcliffe

93. Ashburton, Devon

94. Swinbrook, Oxfordshire
95. Hereford; All Saints
96–98. Ripple, Worcestershire
99–101. Ludlow, Shropshire

MISERICORDS

little masterpieces of design and of craftsmanship; the worst are clumsy and crude. Many, particularly the later ones, are overcrowded and too anecdotal. But even these are often of much interest for other reasons; they tell us a great deal about medieval life and customs, and about such subjects as sports and costumes.

The misericord was usually designed symmetrically, with the main subject in the centre under the little seat, and to either side, perhaps linked to it by entwining stems, two 'supporters', or 'ears' as they were often called. The sources of the subjects were immensely wide. Only a very few can be mentioned here. One of the most enjoyable sets known to me is in a village church, at Ripple in Worcestershire. The sixteen misericords here include the Sun, symbolising Day (96) and the Moon, Night (97); there are also, on twelve others, the Occupations of the Months, the only complete representation of this subject on misericords in the country. Plate 98 shows two men kneeling beside piles of grain with bins and half-filled sacks; the removal of the corn for malting was the occupation for September. Another village church, at Enville in Staffordshire, has only four stalls and misericords, but they are of quite exceptional quality and interest. One of them has a man and woman in a pew praying, with a splendid winged devil looming above them, a design at once decorative and original. Two of the others have musicians and bear-baiting. The fourth is a brilliant and unique piece of story-telling. We are shown a horseman transfixed by a falling portcullis, and a little head peeping out between the battlements of the castle tower above, just as in a painting by, say, Sassetta.

A fascinating misericord at Minster-in-Thanet has, in the centre, a woman wearing a huge head-dress, between the horns of which is seated – the devil. The supporters are a pair of lions' heads with long protruding tongues. Animals and birds provide some of the most rewarding subjects. Owls, partly because of a reference to them in the Book of Isaiah (xiii, 21) but also, I like to think, because they are so decorative, appear quite often on misericords. There is a lovely one with a grave, pensive, introverted face at Edlesborough in Buckinghamshire. This church, which is in the Vale of Aylesbury just below Whipsnade, also has a bat: no more than humble village carving, but full of expression. Another bat, observed frontally, makes possible an absolutely symmetrical design. A pair of dolphins at Etchingham in Sussex could hardly be more modest, but the carver has expressed very successfully a sensation of swift movement through the strength and vigour of their curving bodies. This church also has a particularly successful representation of the fox and geese theme; on a misericord there is no room for accessories of any kind, but, without any loss of vigour, the carver has achieved a work of truly decorative beauty.

As works of art one of the best parochial sets of misericords, although not all of one date, is in the church of St Laurence at Ludlow. All but eight of the thirty date from 1447. Compared with most, they are small, but compact in design and executed in an admirably crisp style. The subjects include fashionable feminine headgear and hairstyles (*99*), another owl, with bird supporters (*100*), and, perhaps the most lively of all, a mermaid with her mirror, between two fishes (*101*).

Even now it is not perhaps as widely known as it should be that the English parish churches possess some of the most beautiful roofs ever made. Certain of the grand monastic and collegiate buildings serving today as parish churches have their stone vaults, some of great beauty, and there are a few spectacular vaults covering parts only of parish churches, of which there will be more to say later; but even among the cathedrals there are about a dozen which to this day are roofed partly if not entirely with wood, although in some cases for reasons of economy rather than from choice, as is evident from their resemblance to stone vaults in form. These, however, are not the type with which we are here concerned.

Most English timber roofs owe nothing to stone construction. They could only have been conceived and carried out in wood. It is in no way surprising that master-carpenters ranked second only to master-masons in the organisation of the medieval building trade. The best are remarkable alike for their carpentry (construction) and for their carving (ornamentation). They are widely, but by no means evenly, distributed over the country. The most numerous, and many of the finest, are in Suffolk and Norfolk. That they are not more familiar is mainly, no doubt, because the large majority are in village churches off the main roads. A tour, or indeed a series of tours, planned around the churches possessing fine roofs, would be an excellent way of seeing some of England's loveliest churches in the context of a specific theme of study.

Although in some districts, notably the South-West, a single type of roof, as also of screen, was repeated in a large number of churches with only very limited variations, one is impressed, in considering England as a whole, by the wide variety of designs evolved, both structurally and ornamentally. Nevertheless, nearly all the best English church roofs belong to one or other of three basic types, tie-beam, arch-braced or hammer-beam. Sometimes two kinds of structure are combined in the same roof, as at Walsham-le-Willows in Suffolk (*103*: tie- and hammer-beams in alternation), and occasionally all three, as at Mildenhall in Suffolk, where the roof is dated 1507.

The tie-beams are the great beams which stretch across the church at intervals and rest upon the side-walls. This type of roof construction is at once the oldest, the simplest and the strongest. But in the later Gothic period the structural members were enriched, not only with carving but often also with painting and gilding. Tie-beam roofs can be seen at their best in Somerset: Martock, Weston Zoyland (*106*), High Ham and East Pennard are all admirable examples, and among those of flatter pitch Somerton (*c.* 1520) is outstanding. The Weston Zoyland roof is of light-coloured oak. Both the tie-beams and the bold cornices are decorated with rosettes and crowned by a moulding of pierced quatrefoils, and the whole space above the tie-beams is filled with tracery. In the centre of each, facing both east and west, and along the cornices, there are half-length figures of angels holding shields, on which were probably once painted the instruments of the Passion.

In roofs of this type, the tie-beams are often slightly cambered: that is to say, each beam falls away from the centre towards both sides. The original reason for this was to counteract the tendency of these heavy timbers to sag at the centre. To obtain these cambered beams, the most economical method was to find a tree with a natural bend, but usually it was necessary to hew or saw somewhat extravagantly from very big trees. This form of beam became very popular in the late-Perpendicular period, when lead-covered roofs of low pitch replaced the steeper slopes, as at Burwell in Cambridgeshire (*104*), a fine example, where the cambered tie-beams are supported by complete arched-bracing.

The most spectacular camber-beam roofs are those divided on their undersurface into square panels filled with decorative tracery. Of this type the *tour de force* is the roof of the south porch at Kersey in Suffolk, which has sixteen compartments all differently enriched. Somerset has three striking examples, at Brent Knoll, at Mark in the Isle of Athelney (*108*), and at Keynsham. In each case these are aisle roofs of the early Tudor period. At Mark, the ridge-piece is as massive as the tie-beam, which produces a most imposing effect. Every structural member is carefully moulded, and this roof strikes a perfect balance between robust construction and exuberant decoration.

In the next type, the arch-braced roof, the cross-beams have disappeared, and instead the principal rafters are supported by gently curving braces which meet at a shallow point either close to the apex of the roof or, more frequently, at a short cross-beam a little way below the ridge, known as a collar. The resultant effect is altogether lighter and more airy than with the tie-beam, and there is a good deal less weight of wood to be carried on the walls. In the later Gothic age the favourite variant on this type was the wagon or cradle roof.

The name 'wagon roof' derives from the canvas awning over the old-fashioned country cart, which was habitually of this arched form, and here and there still is among the gypsies and in the west of Ireland. A good fourteenth-century example can be seen in one of the marginal drawings of the Luttrell Psalter in the British Museum. Innumerable roofs of this kind occur in West Somerset, Devon and Cornwall, and quite often there are three parallel roofs of this type, one over nave and chancel and two more over the flanking aisles. The keynote here is not strength but delicacy.

Sometimes, as at Ashburton (*93*), the wagon roofs were left open, and it is always a pleasure to look up into the shadows between the rafters. But a good many of these south-western roofs, either at the time or later, were filled in with plaster between the principal rafters, probably for greater warmth. This would, however, add several tons to the weight of the roof, which is probably the reason why it is much less common in Norfolk and Suffolk, where the churches are loftier and the walls often only of flint rubble. Some of these roofs in the South-West, St Decuman, Watchet (*105*), for example, have pretty cornices with vine-trails and angels, and 'four-leaved flower' bosses.

The great precursor of the hammer-beam type of roof can still be seen in Westminster Hall, where it was finished not later than 1402. No church roof is as vast as this one, nor as early. But although for its carpentry this roof was a masterpiece some of its successors in churches far surpass it in richness of carving. Hammer-beam roofs occur occasionally in various parts of England (there are several, for instance, in Shropshire) but far the largest number, and all the finest, are in East Anglia. The hammer-beam roofs of Norfolk and Suffolk are indeed the greatest glory of English medieval woodwork.

The structural justification for this type of roof rested on the desire for wider spans. This was achieved by supporting the curved braces on brackets which might project several feet from the wall on either side, as at Cawston in central Norfolk. These are the hammer-beams. But the fact is that the late medieval carpenters were, understandably, so well pleased with the effect that before long they started introducing hammer-beams where structurally they were quite unnecessary: that is to say, for purely aesthetic reasons.

The rafter construction at Cawston, as usual in East Anglia, is completely visible, and is carried through with unerring assurance. The decorative enrichment is beautiful. The colour of the oak is silver-brown. There are half-length angels on the cornice, six to every bay: tracery in the spandrels; floral bosses to mask the joins: and above all there are angels standing on the ends of the hammer-beams. Although no longer coloured, these, from the aspect of design, with their feathered bodies and outstretched wings, are all that one could wish. The hammer-beam in the easternmost bay has not an angel but the Virgin Mary, a figure which is said to have been moved from the rood loft.

Not far away, over the nave of the old priory church at Wymondham, there is a superb hammer-beam roof, set up about 1450 (*102*). As at

Cawston, there are long wall-posts between the clerestory windows, which are a great asset aesthetically. In both roofs, these appear to rest on corbels, but this is an illusion. I have seen roofs in which, owing to the shrinkage of the wall-posts, as much as an inch or more will separate the base of the post from the corbel, while in other cases there are no corbels. They were therefore introduced for purely ornamental reasons, to satisfy the eye, which they assuredly do. The function of the long wall-post was not to transmit a downward thrust, but to grip the wall and so prevent the roof from spreading outwards. The point of springing of the braces at Wymondham is so far back along the hammer-beams that these cannot be deemed to serve any really essential structural purpose either, but decoratively they are grand, the entire beams being carved into the semblance of great angels. The enormous conventional foliage bosses are of an uncommon and exquisite design.

The most spectacular achievement of all was the double hammer-beam roof, of which, with the exception of the very lovely and often photographed one in the church of St Wendreda at March in Cambridgeshire, Suffolk and Norfolk have all the leading examples. The one selected for illustration here is at Woolpit in Suffolk (*107*), where as can been seen there are two tiers of hammer-beams. The impulse was now purely aesthetic, for it will be evident that the upper tier of hammer-beams cannot rest on the wall, and is structurally therefore of no consequence. Decoratively, however, this roof of silver-brown oak, not unrestored but with over 100 angels, is a glorious sight.

Yet even these lovely roofs did not escape the destructive urges of the Puritan iconoclasts in the seventeenth century. They specially sought to destroy the angels. Finding these inconveniently inaccessible, they fired at them with shot-guns. Restorers have found several of the finest roofs, Mildenhall and Shepton Mallet among them, smothered with buckshot. But at Blythburgh (*109*) the damage occurred later. This church has a low-pitched cambered tie-beam roof which preserves a good deal of its medieval colouring: earth-red, *terre verte* and black, on a whitish ground, with the sacred monogram repeated along the rafters. It has lately been established that the buckshot here is not of the kind used in the seventeenth century, and it almost certainly reflects the concern of the Georgian churchwardens to rid the building of jackdaws, sheltering behind the angelic wings.[30] Hence, again, many amputations.

Many of these roofs were originally coloured. Extensive use – if some-times crude rather than subtle – was made of colour and gilding in the church interiors of the Middle Ages, and here and there these have been renewed. How far this practice is to be encouraged is questionable. Reference has already been made to the repainting and gilding of some screens, notably in the West Country. Nor can it be doubted that many

English roofs have suffered greatly from the misguided application in the past of dark brown stain or varnish, so that today attractive carved details can hardly be identified from 30 or 40 feet below. Thus at Bacton in Suffolk the recolouring of the chancel roof and of the celure at the east end of the lovely double hammer-beam roof over the nave was very welcome. On the other hand the glorious nave roof at Walsham-le-Willows near-by (*103*) preserves, in addition to its overall and very beautiful silver-brown hue, enough of its original colour (chiefly red) and gilding (on the suns) for it to be said that this one must on no account be re-coloured. In short, each church must be considered *ad hoc*.

After the Reformation the coloured church interior was no longer approved of, and for a while almost the only permissible decorative motif was the Biblical text, perhaps on a painted scroll. The Georgians did not eschew the use of colour, but architects like Adam and Wyatt handled it in an entirely different fashion from that current in the Middle Ages. It was the Arts and Crafts Movement towards the end of the nineteenth century which was largely responsible for the revival of a more traditional style, followed as recently as 1963 at Flore in Northamptonshire, when the whole chancel roof was decoratively painted under the supervision of Stephen Dykes Bower. Some of the more successful examples of decorative painting, and by no means confined to roofs, are associated with the names of G. F. Bodley and Sir Ninian Comper. Bodley's colours are always pleasing, but, especially when he used tempera, they have faded badly. At St John the Baptist, Tue Brook, a north-eastern suburb of Liverpool, his church of 1868–71 would hardly be noticed if it were not for the resplendent fittings, as Pevsner justly remarks. These 'make' the church, but far more so since the colours were comprehensively restored in 1970–71. Comper's most resplendent interior is St Mary, Welling-borough, begun in 1908 and continued lovingly for over fifty years. (Horace Walpole, had he been able to see it, would surely have called it Comperissimo! The garden at Rousham, it will be recalled, he termed Kentissimo.) It is basically derivative, a stylistic farrago and not a building of much creative imagination, yet the interior, the plaster pendant-lierne 'vault' especially, makes a great impression, and colour here plays a dominant part.

It is difficult now for us to realise how extensively colour was employed in the Middle Ages. No medieval church would have been regarded as finished until it had been painted internally, over a groundwork of plaster. Even finely-jointed ashlar masonry, before the Perpendicular period, received an overcoat of limewash. On this were painted many figure-subjects, but a great deal of the surface was just diapered or treated with other ornamental motifs. For example, at Cliffe in Kent, John Newman tells us that the piers of the nave were boldly painted with thick

NOBLE HAMMER-BEAM ROOF

103. Walsham-le-Willows,
Suffolk

ROOFS

104. Burwell, Cambridgeshire

105. Watchet, Somerse
St Decuman: North A

. Weston Zoyland, Somerset

107. Woolpit, Suffolk

ROOFS

. Mark, Somerset: South Aisle

109. Blythburgh, Suffolk

ELEGANT PLASTERWORK

red zigzags; there were masonry lines in the spandrels and a repeating fleur-de-lis motif round the arches. Attempts were made in the last century in France to restore such painted schemes, for example at Issoire and at Notre-Dame-la-Grande at Poitiers, and they fill one with dismay.

Over large areas, in the twelfth, thirteenth and early fourteenth centuries, there were just red lines intended to simulate mortar courses: the practice known as 'stoning'. This too can be seen, renewed, in a number of French churches: at Chauvigny in Poitou for instance. The effect is deplorable. The notion of covering even ashlar masonry with limewash and then of ruling thin red lines all over the surface is really extraordinary, and a reminder that those who suppose that everything in the medieval garden was lovely have something to learn.

What of the figure-subjects? Very little has yet been said in this book about wall-painting, for the reason that, for most amateurs of churches, this is the most disappointing field imaginable. My best course would really be to refer the reader to Clive Rouse's excellent little pocket guide, *Wall Paintings* (1980), and leave it at that. For the intention of the figure paintings was not artistic but didactic, or just devotional, as with stained glass, but in an incomparably inferior medium. With rare exceptions English wall paintings were not even true frescoes, but only *freschi secchi*: paintings, that is, done on a dry plaster wall. The only readily available pigments were red ochre and yellow ochre (both oxides of iron), lime white, lamp or charcoal black, and sometimes green (from copper). As Rouse points out, they were not intended to last indefinitely. Sometimes, therefore, at a later date other paintings were spread on top of the old ones, as can be seen at Stoke Orchard in Gloucestershire.

Had these paintings survived, good work would have been found here and there, and a great deal that was incompetent and artistically more or less worthless. As it is, the loss of our wall paintings has been even more complete than that of our stained glass. By no means as much as one per cent has been preserved. And most of what has survived, after having been hidden for centuries under whitewash (the Order in Council of 1547 decreed the 'obliteration and destruction of popish and superstitious images, so that the memory of them shall not remain in the churches ...'), is in a very fragmentary condition and largely incomprehensible except to the expert, or has been much repainted or touched up.

Artistically I do not believe that the disappearance of nearly all our medieval wall paintings is much to be regretted. Many good churches must have been considerably spoiled by being smothered with these often very indifferent paintings. They were applied to the walls without, as a rule, any regard for the architecture, as can be seen at Pickering in Yorkshire. There was much repainting here in the 1880s, but enough survives to give a good idea of the general effect. Some of the paintings, particularly the scene showing John the Baptist with Herod and Salome, are quite enjoyable in themselves, but whereas good stained glass will also greatly enhance a building through the glory of colour, these paintings, which nearly all have narrative subjects unconnected with decoration, usually do nothing for the building; and it is not too much to say that in dozens of churches where what survives is, after restoration, fragmentary and only just decipherable, the paintings are artistically a liability rather than an asset, as their presence inhibits redecoration. Such a view will, I am sure, be regarded as shockingly heretical among students of our wall paintings, and I recognise that, once they have been rediscovered, the church that has them must tolerate their presence however little pleasure they give; but let us at least not delude ourselves that those we are preserving, sometimes with generous help from bodies such as the Pilgrim and Dulverton Trusts, are usually of much account as works of art. Since the first edition of this book, much work and thought, it is fair to say, has been devoted to their evaluation.

And of course there are exceptions. No parish church has paintings to equal the best in Canterbury and Winchester cathedrals, but, widely distributed over the country, there are a certain number of wall paintings of real value. Unquestionably the most worthy of a visit are those that nearly fill the little Norman chancel of St Mary at Kempley, in Gloucestershire. They date from the second quarter of the twelfth century and are exceptional in England in having been executed in *buon fresco*: that is to say, in having been painted on to the wet plaster, thereby becoming incorporated in it as it dried, which was the almost invariable method in Italy. This has been a great help to their preservation. They cover the tunnel vault and all the walls above 5 feet. Hidden by limewash at the Reformation, they were rediscovered in 1872, when they were most unwisely coated with a resinous varnish, in the mistaken idea that this would help to preserve them. It did the opposite; but in a skilful restoration in 1955–56 Eve Baker was able to remove the varnish, and now, for England, where damp walls have been responsible for more damage then all the fury of fanatical Protestants and Puritans, they are unusually complete. On the vault are Christ in Majesty – unfortunately the least intact figure of any – with the sun, the moon, the seven golden candlesticks, the Evangelistic symbols and some of the heavenly hierarchy; on the walls are the Apostles and other figures, including, next to the east window, a specially imposing bishop. The style is not aristocratic, but not crude either, and the scheme is exceptional in bearing a real relationship to the architecture.

The only other scheme of paintings comparable to these, and of much the same date, is at Copford in Essex, but these are not true frescoes and are either in a bad state of preservation or much spoiled by repainting.

Four churches in Sussex, Coombes, Hardham, Clayton and West Chiltington, also have the remains of paintings done in the first half of the twelfth century; not many years ago they were little more than ghosts, but in recent years some very good restoration has been undertaken here, and they may now be regarded as perhaps the best surviving examples of English primitive painting, of which no equivalents exist in our museums and galleries. West Chiltington also has, in the nave, mid-thirteenth-century paintings which still communicate faint echoes of their original charm. 'Doom' paintings range from that on the west wall at Chaldon in Surrey, of the late twelfth century, to the early Tudor one over the chancel arch of the church of St Thomas of Canterbury, Salisbury. Both are on a large scale. The Chaldon painting should more properly be called the Ladder of Salvation, up which little naked souls are endeavouring to ascend to heaven. As works of art both these paintings are of minimal value, but they are interesting and, thanks to touching up at Chaldon and extensive repainting at Salisbury, they can at least be seen, which in the field of English wall painting is a welcome change.

Several schemes of post-Reformation painting are completely visible. The most distinguished, no doubt, are the prophets and evangelists at Passenham in Northamptonshire. These were later covered with whitewash and were in poor condition before the thorough and highly skilful restoration in 1957 by Clive Rouse. The figures are fully life-size and stand in shell-headed niches within an architectural framework (all *trompe l'oeil*). The style is provincial *Cinquecento* Venetian. There is nothing else at all like them in an English church, and as Passenham also has beautiful oak furnishings presented by the squire at the same time – 1626 – it is exceptionally worth visiting. A few years earlier the wagon roof at Muchelney in Somerset had been decorated with a host of angels,[31] endearing but not a little hilarious, exhorting those below to 'come up hither'! Seated on puddingy clouds, these are very much the village girls and boys decked out in feathers for the occasion. The chancel ceiling at Bromfield Priory in Shropshire, painted a generation later, has a somewhat similar subject, more competently carried out. This ceiling is enjoyable. The clouds are again puddings, but there is quite a good overall design. The sky is alive with angels grasping very long scrolls with texts, and on the east wall a pair of them hold open a big book. The painter was one Thomas Francis from Aston-by-Sutton in Cheshire: the date 1672.

Another field for the post-Reformation painter was the Royal Arms. These first appeared in churches soon after 1534, the year in which Parliament confirmed the assumption by Henry VIII of the title of 'supreme head on earth of the Church of England'. Mostly removed under Mary, they reappeared under her successor, but it was not until 1660 that it became compulsory to display the Royal Arms in every church, as a reminder to clergy and congregation that the monarch was the head. After the beginning of the nineteenth century the practice began gradually to fall into desuetude, although there has recently been some revival. The very large majority, therefore, are late Stuart or Hanoverian. Many different methods were adopted to represent them, and they also vary greatly in size. Some were painted direct on to walls, or on to boards or canvas. Others were modelled in plaster on the walls: some of these were exuberant. Marwood in Devon has a beauty, George III, about 7 feet wide. But all the best examples were carved, generally in wood. A grand one, Charles II, in nearly black oak is at Norham in Northumberland. A much smaller one, but of very fine quality, George I, is above the south door at Long Melford in Suffolk. An outside situation is rare, but in London at St Martin-in-the-Fields there are the arms of George I over the chancel arch and another fine coat of the same monarch in the Portland stone of the west pediment.

Coats of arms of local families also figure prominently in some churches, painted on lozenge-shaped wooden panels known as hatchments. These are usually Georgian, and the traditional practice was to display the hatchment on the front of the deceased person's house for several months before transferring it to the church. The background was always black except where one partner of a married couple survived; it was then half black and half white. Some hatchments display excellent heraldic painting and can be a real embellishment. But they should not be allowed to impinge upon the architecture.

Anyone interested in finding out how a medieval church was furnished may still come across a number of pre-Reformation altars and reredoses. But, in many more instances, only the evidence of a piscina (a stone basin with a drain set into the church wall) will show that there had been one or more side chapels as well as the main altar in the chancel. A few pre-Reformation stone altar slabs in chancel or chapels have survived in use (e.g. New Shoreham, Sussex: Lady Chapel, Christchurch, Hampshire: Forthampton, Gloucestershire: Peterchurch, Herefordshire: Porlock, Somerset). Elsewhere, they were relegated to the chancel floor.

In the parish churches the reredos, in the chancel or one of the side chapels, was generally long and low – the purpose of its imagery being to edify the priest celebrating mass, not to be a focus for the congregation. Youlgreave, Derbyshire has an example in alabaster with a central figure of the Madonna flanked by the donor's family: Bampton, Oxfordshire dwarf-like figures of Christ and the twelve Apostles under crocketed canopies: Somerton in the same county five figures under canopies (these Oxfordshire examples are classed in Pevsner as 'rustic C14 work'): Ottery St Mary, Devon an interesting example with four buttresses enclosing figure niches (restored in 1833): Harlton, Cambridgeshire (13 small niches filled with a good modern carving) and Drayton, Berkshire (six panels of a sixteenth-century alabaster altar, one showing the Entombment – discovered buried in the churchyard). In other instances, only the stone frame remains to tell of what was once there as at Castor, Huntingdonshire, Barnwell, Northamptonshire: Patrington, East Riding, Yorkshire and Eaton Bray, Bedfordshire.

In the greater churches, the reredos was more ambitious with two or more tiers of figures (a richly-sculptured stone screen of c. 1350 at Christchurch Priory and a painted wooden reredos of c. 1525 at Romsey Abbey, both in Hampshire). All these must once have been coloured and gilded.

Of wooden examples, Elham, Kent has a fifteenth-century polyptych painted in 1907 but the most enjoyable one is the retable at Thornham Parva, Suffolk probably dating from c. 1300 and likely to be the work of royal masons. It has panels of the Crucifixion and eight saints including two Dominicans and St Edmund, King and Martyr, whom one might call the Patron Saint of East Anglia. The figures are slim and graceful. This retable may have been painted for an East Anglian Dominican Priory and has only recently been discovered.

After the Reformation, when the use of colour in liturgical furnishings and on church walls and roofs became unacceptable, colour was largely restricted to monuments and enrichment of church furnishings restricted to fine carved work with some gilding. But all over the country very good altar tables in wood, equal to the best to be found in houses of well-to-do yeomen and nobility, were supplied to replace the stone altars now generally destroyed. With them went fine wooden reredoses; the earliest generally included tables of the Commandments, often the Lord's Prayer and sometimes the Creed, flanked not infrequently by rather naïve portrayals of Moses and Aaron. But the finest and some of the most sophisticated reredoses are to be found in the post-Reformation churches built in the City of London by Sir Christopher Wren after the Great Fire of 1666. St Magnus the Martyr is notable but the top, surmounted by a Martin Travers rood of 1924–5, is modern. A fine example is to be seen at St Mary at Hill, much gilded according to custom in Wren's time. St Margaret, Lothbury's reredos with Corinthian columns carrying two segmental pediments and openwork foliage volutes at the sides is a splendid furnishing but the *pièce de resistance* is the magnificent example at St Mary Abchurch, known to have been executed by Grinling Gibbons himself. As late as 1946, a letter signed by him addressed to the churchwardens of St Lawrence Pountney, requesting their share of the cost of the 'Olter Pees' was discovered. The parish of St Lawrence Pountney, not rebuilt after the Fire, was linked with that of St Mary

Abchurch until the latter was made a Guild Church and its parish transferred to St Stephen's, Walbrook.

Outside London, attractive eighteenth century reredoses are to be seen in St Michael-le-Belfry, St Martin cum Gregory and a simple example at Holy Trinity, Goodramgate of 1721, all in York. The first is a beautiful furnishing with large Corinthian columns. In Suffolk, there is a fine one of c. 1700–10 at Framlingham and another of c. 1745 at Shotley; in Norwich, there is a late eighteenth-century altarpiece at St George, Colegate and, in Lincolnshire, one with fluted Corinthian columns and segmental pediment at Langton-by-Spilsby.

Some country churches were magnificently refurnished during this period, for example King's Norton, Leicestershire, Mildenhall, Wiltshire, and Chislehampton, Oxfordshire, where reredos, altar and rails, pulpit and pews were all designed en suite.

With the introduction of the Gothic Revival, taste changed; some architects like Sir Gilbert Scott virtually standardised the fittings supplied to the clients for whom they built new churches; the Cambridge Camden Society laid down certain norms which many people considered 'correct' and, if the parishes could not afford to employ the leading architects, church furnishing firms, which had recently sprung up, supplied somewhat more prosaic versions of the masterpieces of Butterfield, Carpenter, G. E. Street and others. Instances where the architect's influence on the furnishings is evident are St Peter, Vauxhall, London (J. L. Pearson), St John, Torquay (G. E. Street) and St Clement, Bournemouth (J. D. Sedding).

The turn of the century saw interest rekindled in English Gothic and English liturgical tradition by a new generation of scholars, reacting against the Continental artistic and ecclesiastical formulae adopted and adapted by nineteenth-century ecclesiologists. G. F. Bodley and Sir Ninian Comper, with F.C.Eden, were the leading church architects of this period. Holy Trinity, Prince Consort Road, Kensington, London: St Augustine, Pendlebury near Manchester, Lancashire and Hoar Cross, Staffordshire, all by G. F. Bodley: St Cyprian, Clarence Gate, London and All Saints, Wellingborough, Northamptonshire by Sir Ninian Comper are notable examples. The work of these architects brought a new refinement and a richer use of colour without their predecessors' inhibitions regarding the intermixing of Gothic and Renaissance detail.

An exciting and finely executed example of a painted reredos is the work executed by David Shepherd at St George's Garrison Church at Bordon in Hampshire, showing Christ – as Guardian of the British Army – towering over various war scenes going back to the Boer War. It is a memorable experience to enter the church and be confronted with this huge painting.

Sedilia (from the Latin sedile – a seat) are seats which, from the late 12th century onwards, were usually provided in this country – although less so on the Continent – on the south side of the chancel for the priest and his assistants (deacon and sub-deacon) when celebrating mass. They were normally of stone recessed into the wall near the altar. Very occasionally they were of wood, a notable example being the much restored fifteenth-century ones at Rodmersham, Kent, set under a canopy and integrated into a parclose screen. It is possible that there may have been more wooden examples which have not survived in churches where there are no sedilia. A very simple form was obtained by lowering the sill of a window and widening it for a bench.

The arches are usually ornamented and the seats divided by detached shafts or masonry divisions which might be pierced. Often, the seats are graduated in height to relate with the status of the clergy using them, the priest using the higher (highest) seat to the east near the altar. Piscinas were often incorporated into the design (e.g. Old Coulsdon in Surrey and Swavesey in Cambridgeshire) so that all four recesses could be united under ornamental arches and, as at Nantwich in Cheshire, embellished with a canopy and tracery. Cases occur of four sedilia with the fourth seat reserved for the clerk, two only, and even one (sedile) as at Up Waltham in Sussex and Lenham in Kent – the latter having stone elbows resembling those of an arm-chair.

Two notable Norman examples are to be seen at Earls Barton in Northamptonshire – stepped and with rich zigzag ornamentation – and an especially fine one at St Mary-de-Castro, Leicester with beautifully decorated capitals and rich zigzag in the arches. But the most unforgettable examples are the fourteenth century sedilia at Hawton in Nottinghamshire and Heckington in Lincolnshire, in the most exuberant, even flamboyant style of the full flower of the Decorated period.

It has long been customary to provide a chair in the sanctuary for visiting bishops, some beautifully carved. Many are Elizabethan or Jacobean. Teversal in Nottinghamshire has two Georgian ones and, at St Mary's Rotherhithe in London, the seats are made of timbers from 'The Fighting Temeraire'.

In earlier times, however, they were in fact seats of sanctuary or frith-stools, thought to have been used by the officer investigating pleas for sanctuary. Beverley in the East Riding of Yorkshire has a stone seat in which the arms and back are of the same height. This is pre-Conquest as is Wilfrid's Throne in Hexham, Northumberland, also with arms and back of the same height. This tub-shaped chair is thought to be quite probably of the seventh or eighth century.

Little Dunmow in Essex has a chair made up of part of a thirteenth-century stall and is referred to as the Dunmow Flitch Chair whilst, at Bishops Canning in Wiltshire there is a 'Penitential Seat' with a huge hand painted on the wall behind it with inscriptions referring to sin and death. Sir Nikolaus Pevsner estimates it to be seventeenth-century work.

Decorative plasterwork was not a medieval material, but appears almost as a matter of course in the interiors of classical churches. The usual place for it is the ceiling. Much of the ornamental plasterwork in Wren's churches was unhappily lost in the last war. A good ceiling of the years 1678–80 which survives intact is at the church of King Charles the Martyr, Tunbridge Wells. One of the two plasterers responsible, Henry Doogood, did a great deal for Wren in London. Some of the relief is shallow, some bold: the latter includes some of those wreaths of luscious fruit which were a favourite motif at this time. At Euston in Suffolk the very pretty ceiling over the former Arlington pew of 1676 (*110*) strikes a more playful note. The larger late-Stuart ceilings, as at Ingestre, are always clearly separated into compartments. Later, with the arrival in England of Artari and Bagutti, a more Rococo style developed; but compared with the plasterers' carnival in the churches of Bavaria and elsewhere their work here might almost be termed sedate.

The contribution of the metals to the interest and beauty of the English church interior has taken various forms. From the Middle Ages there are a few lead fonts, which are aesthetically nothing, perhaps, to get excited about, and a very large number of brasses, more indeed than in the whole of the rest of Europe. (There are about 1000 dating from earlier than 1485, and 2100 from between then and 1650. The two dozen or so later than 1650 are without artistic merit.) The metal, known as latten, was, like brass (the two are virtually identical), an alloy of copper and zinc, hammered into thin sheets. At all periods there are great variations in quality. Some, like the half-length portrait of Walter Frilende at Ockham in Surrey (1376) – he was the Rector – are works of lively characterisation, while others, such as the life-size brass to Sir John de Creke and his lady at Westley Waterless in Cambridgeshire (1325) or the incomplete but famous one to Sir Hugh Hastings (*ob.* 1347) at Elsing in Norfolk, are metal engravings of the highest distinction. Aesthetically the most direct statements are usually the most effective, as in the little one at Wheathampstead dated 1436, commemorating Mrs Hugh Bostock (*122*). A good many brasses, however, seem poorly designed and mechanical in execution. The activities of the rubbers render the study of brasses increasingly difficult, for if one seeks out a well-known example nowadays, the likelihood is that it will be hidden under a sheet of paper or that one will have to take one's place in a queue. Rubbing within reason is a pleasant hobby, but now that very high prices can be obtained for good rubbings, especially in the United States, it has become a largely commercial activity. The often impoverished churches cannot be expected to resist the opportunity of fees, and probably ought to charge a good deal more than they do. Some churches, however – whether intentionally or not – have countered the activities of the rubbers by lifting their brasses on to the walls. This is a proceeding which meets with strong disapproval in certain quarters. But there are churches like Euston, or Felbrigg in Norfolk, in which it is impossible to walk along the nave without treading on them, so narrow is the passage between the pews. For good preservation, in fact, they could hardly be worse placed. In such cases the obviously sensible course is to remove the brasses to the walls, where they are also much better seen as well as being a little more difficult to rub. It is of course necessary for such a church to have a dry and well-lit area of available wall-space.

Ornamental wrought ironwork, especially the beautiful scrolled hinges on the outer faces of doors associated with the name of Thomas of Leghtone (90) has already been touched on (Cf. p. 136). Interior delights in wrought iron mostly belong to the early years of the eighteenth century, and unfortunately they are scarce. St Mary Redcliffe has very fine work of 1710 by the Bristol smith, William Edney, including the gates of the former chancel screen, now under the tower (92). All this ironwork is today resplendent in black and gold. The screens, gates and sword-rests which he made for two other Bristol churches were destroyed in the last war. When the mayor went to church at the beginning of the eighteenth century he was very prone to inconvenience himself by carrying a sword, so a number of lovely sword-rests were made in wrought iron. St Swithun, Worcester, has a pleasantly decorative example, and All Saints in the same city a very handsome piece; there are others in Norwich and elsewhere.

Grandest of all the wrought ironwork, however, are the screens of c. 1730 in All Saints, Derby (now a cathedral, but a parish church until 1927). They run right across the church, with two parclose screens of simpler design at right angles, and are a great embellishment to an otherwise rather dull building. Their maker was Robert Bakewell, the king of English smiths. The very fine communion rails of c. 1700 at Lydiard Tregoze in Wiltshire, with swags, wreaths, cupids and the rest, partly gilt, are believed to be the work of an Italian. Mention must be made of the brass chandeliers, all of seventeenth- or eighteenth-century date, with which many of our churches are adorned. These were generally gifts from private donors, and carry inscriptions. Some were of Dutch origin. They may hang from elegant wrought iron suspension rods, which never fail to give pleasure. Some, like that at Walpole St Peter in Norfolk, or the two at Waltham-on-the-Wolds in Leicestershire, or the handsome one dated 1748 at Congleton in Cheshire, or the fine one of about 1775 at Ashburton (*93*), are beautifully kept; others, alas, are not. In odd contrast with all of them, however, are some of the Victorian appurtenances of church lighting. A specially egregious example is the gasolier in the centre of the nave of the charming little Georgian interior at Glynde in Sussex: in this church an incomprehensible monstrosity. It must regretfully be added that modern light-fittings are also all too liable to be eyesores.

For centuries, church bells have sounded throughout England to summon people to worship. Bells made of bronze for hanging in church towers were being cast in this country in the seventh century. There are, however, few bells in existence dating from before AD 1200. The early ones were of small diameter (18/18½ inches), long-waisted and almost straight-sided with metal of uniform thickness except on the sound bow, the base upon which the clapper strikes. The earliest inscribed bell, dating from between 1207 and 1219, is at Caversfield, Oxfordshire.

Many of these early bells were probably moulded on a horizontal lathe, as illustrated at York Minster in the Richard Tunnoc bellfounder's window of *c.* 1330, but this method imposed limitations on the diameter. These were overcome in the thirteenth century by moulding in an upright position, enabling the founder to adjust the height and diameter to produce the required note and the more shapely contours of the present bell.

Until the fourteenth century, bells were chimed by a rope hung on a simple spindle. This method was then elaborated when ringers began to experiment with new ways of hanging the bells. Eventually, a design was evolved for mounting the bell so that it could rotate full circle rather than just swing back and forth. To support the great weight, the main loop at the top, called the argent, was buttressed by smaller loops called canons and these were all firmly secured to a massive elm headstock. A stay and sliders steadied the bells and ringing was by means of ropes turning large wooden wheels, the ropes passing through the floor of the bell-chamber to the ringers below. Where, however, the foundations were not firm, the considerable pull on the walls of the towers led to these being completely detached from the church as at West Walton and Terrington St Clement in Norfolk. At East Bergholt in Suffolk the bells are rung from a frame laying on the ground; this used also to be the practice at Cape Town Cathedral until a special bell-tower was built.

Bells were often recast and those at St Mary-le-Bow in the City of London – one of the best-known of all rings – were tuned a semitone lower after they had crashed to the ground when the church was bombed during the 1939–45 War. Such work, however, is carefully controlled by diocesan authorities and no bell cast prior to AD 1600 may be recast.

New methods of ringing were developed in the seventeenth century. The mounting of the bells on a wheel made it possible to change the order in which they were rung and mathematical precision was brought to this so-called change-ringing by a Cambridge printer, Fabian Stedman, some changes without repetition taking three hours or more to complete, as on the occasion of the Queen Mother's 85th birthday (4th August 1985), when the bells of St Paul's Cathedral in London were rung for four hours.

Early inscriptions on bells were often names of saints amongst which St Katherine, patron saint of the Guild of Bellfounders, was popular and dedications to the name of the Virgin Mary were of common occurrence. After the Reformation, these changed to glorification of God and general religious sentiments such as *'Our Hope is in The Lord'*. Many later inscriptions carried the name of the donor or of the maker.

Change-ringing is a peculiarly English custom for, whilst this country has 5189 towers with bells, there are only 170 in Wales, 35 in Ireland and 67 overseas. Even so, it is confined to Established churches; for over 300 years, Roman Catholic churches were forbidden to have any bells at all. One of the latest rings – at Guildford Cathedral – has ten bells ranging from the tenor of $30\frac{1}{2}$ cwt to the treble of $5\frac{3}{4}$ cwt.

Apart from summoning people to church, bells peal joyfully for a wedding and toll sorrowfully for a funeral. And, well into the nineteenth century, they rang the curfew in many parishes, as is still done every night on the fifth of Chertsey in Surrey's eight bells from Michaelmas to Lady Day. They also peal out on occasions of national rejoicing.

Ringers used to be paid for their services and, by the early 1700s, change-ringing was being performed mainly for money by local people who had little to do with the church and who then repaired to the local pub (hence the frequency of the sign 'The Six Bells' on public houses). The most remunerative ringing, however, was tolling for a funeral. Various rings were employed to denote the sex and age of the deceased, and even whether it was a child who had died. Throughout the last century, a special ringing took place in Dorking, Surrey on Shrove Tuesday when the so-called pancake bell was rung between 11.00 and 12.00 a.m.

The Victorians put an end to financial inducements and, today bell-ringing is a favoured pastime among people from many sections of society. Little excuse is sought by ringers to practise their art. From national events such as the birth of Prince William to purely local events (such as the marriage of two fellow bellringers), the ringers are only too ready – as Evelyn Cox so aptly puts it – to 'take to their towers'. Perhaps this modern enthusiasm for campanology has led others, who live near churches, to feel that one can have too much of a good thing but this very English sound is still welcomed at the right time and was sorely missed during the dark days of the 1939–45 War.

Whatever the reason for bellringing, the inscription on the former bell at Oxted in Surrey, cast by the London founder R. Phelps in 1729 sums it all up very well:

> *Good Folks with one accord*
> *We call to hear God's word,*
> *We honour to the King*
> *And joy to brides do sing,*
> *We triumphs loudly tell,*
> *And ring your last farewell.*

Carillons are sets of usually small bells tuned to the chromatic scale through at least two octaves, and containing no fewer than 23 bells. They are bolted firmly to a framework of steel beams and are struck by hammers, controlled by a player on a keyboard. They are a feature of Belgium, the Netherlands and French Flanders, where almost every village had its fine carillon. Recitals still arouse widespread interest. The most famous carillon is the one of 43 bells at Malines in Belgium where there is a famous school of carillon playing. This was the training ground of many of the best carilloneurs of the U.S.A. where there are some 50 carillons, the largest being in New York with a bourdon bell ten feet in diameter and weighing $20\frac{1}{2}$ tons. At the other end of the scale, the smallest bell of many carillons is only six inches across and weighs about eleven pounds.

Carillons are not unknown in England for, in addition to its ring of eight bells, St Peter's Church in Chertsey, Surrey has a carillon dating from 1892 which plays, four times a day, two hymns; 'We love the place, O God' and 'Now the day is over', and two songs; 'Home Sweet Home' and 'Sicilian Mariners'.

Hand bells, rung manually, are an interesting feature of church music.*

One never knows what surprises the parish church may have in store for the visitor who is not in a hurry. The old musical instruments have been mentioned earlier. Wimborne Minster has an orrery clock in which the sun moves round the dial once a day and the moon once a month. At Ashby-de-la-Zouch there is a finger-pillory, the only one known to me. At Walpole St Peter in Norfolk, Wingfield in Suffolk, Brookland and Ivychurch in Kent (there are probably others) are preserved, inside the churches, quaint early-nineteenth-century 'sentry-boxes' called 'Hudds' or 'Hoods', which were formerly used by officiating priests before the

---

*A debt is acknowledged for much of the above to the section on 'Bells' by Peter Came in *A Guide to Essex Churches*, edited by Christoper Starr and published in 1980 by The Essex Churches Support Trust.

invention of umbrellas to shelter themselves from wet weather at funerals. (The clergy could at least claim that they had vestments – not to mention wigs – that needed protection.)

At Newport in Essex, there is a unique thirteenth-century example of what might be called a travelling altar. It is in the form of a chest, the lid of which is painted to provide a retable. The paintings (of the Crucifixion and saints) are the oldest oil paintings on wood in the country, the predominating colours being red and green. The chest has a false bottom with a secret sliding panel which concealed the altar stone.

Portable altars were, at one time, common in Cornwall, and the Cornish saints took their altars with them on their evangelizing missions. 'Altarnun' means the altar of St Nonna, the mother of St David.

Chests or coffers normally, however, were used only for the storage of the church's valuables, although Henry II (1154–89) ordered – this was confirmed later by Pope Innocent III – that they should be installed to collect 'Saladin Tithe' to enable poor knights to go on Crusade.

Originally just a square baulk of timber with the top sawn off and attached separately to form a lid, and the bottom part crudely hollowed out (as at Betchworth, Surrey and many churches in Warwickshire), these chests – known as dugouts – developed a structure consisting of four planks of oak bound together with ironwork and clamped. Fourteenth and fifteenth century practice was to make them of four stiles, prolonged below the chest to raise it off the ground, and to carve roundels of geometric design on the front for decoration. Stedham Sussex has one such and Climping in the same county has a delightful late C13 example with arcading decoration also. These embellishments developed into elaborate patterns with even a tilting scene at Harty in Kent.

Later, chests were panelled and often provided with three locks, the keys of which were held by different functionaries of the church. Locks, bolts and hinges were frequently of most ingenious construction. Jacobean chests were solid and heavy, often nearly black in colour; a dated example (1622) is to be seen at Thursley, Surrey. Eventually, chests fell out of use with the employment of chests of drawers, which were of little use in churches. The most usual timber employed was oak but examples of elm chests exist and, at Cheveley in Cambridgeshire, there is one of cypress, doubtless used as a deterrent to moths.

Saxon chests survive at Wimborne Minster in Dorset and at West Grinstead in Sussex. However, the oddest of all is Wickham in Berkshire, which in its north aisle has on the ends of hammer-beams not angels but elephants' heads, in *papier-mâché*! Four of the eight were shown at the Paris exhibition of 1862 and acquired for the rectory. Found to be too large even for that big house, they were transferred to the church, for which four more were made to match. And why not? A nice change from the usual angels, which here, on the nave roof, are also *papier-mâché*, but less richly coloured.

And so we return to stone: to the supreme material, the one to which our churches owe more than to any other, more even than to wood. Stone does not claim so great a part of our attention inside the church as outside, but none the less its contribution to our artistic pleasure is of paramount importance. Admittedly, many of the finest 'stone effects' occur in the former abbey and priory churches which are not really the subject of this book, for these buildings were designed on a more lavish scale and with much greater expenditure, especially in the Norman and early Gothic periods. But even if one leaves out of account such glories as the vaults of Tewkesbury, Sherborne or Bath, the bosses of Pershore or the wall arcades of Beverley, there is still enough fine designing in stone in the parish churches to merit another book.

The triple ordonnance of arcade, tribune and clerestory is certainly rare in a parish church, but can be seen at St John, Chester and at New Shoreham, both close to 1200. There are, however, any number of very robust two-storey Norman naves, sometimes with lofty chancel arches, as at Stow. In the Anglo-Saxon period the chancel arch could be the dominant feature of the church, as at Wittering in the Soke of Peterborough (*111*), where Nikolaus Pevsner's phrase, 'cyclopean without equal', is the perfect description. Even arches as simple and strong as the Saxon one at Bosham[32] or the Norman one at Studland pale beside this. At Stow (*112*), (cf. p. 138) there is some confusion at the crossing because the present Perpendicular tower was built inside a Norman one no longer surviving; but in dissonance there is still grandeur. Elsewhere, the Normans sometimes liked to make the chancel arch a feature of tremendous richness, even in quite small churches like Kilpeck in Herefordshire, Iffley in Oxfordshire (*113*), Barfreston in Kent or, above all, Tickencote in Rutland (*114*), where there are no fewer than six orders, and the weight of the masonry is such that the sagging arch is now seriously out of true. Apart from Kilpeck, with its six memorable apostles attached to the shafts flanking the jambs (*115*), not much of this chancel arch carving is figurative, except here and there on capitals.

No Norman parish church has capitals comparable in quality with the dozen or so best in the crypt of Canterbury Cathedral, but there is a good set of *c.* 1150 at St Peter, Northampton, of the large, cushion type, with lively animals and birds in among the conventionalised foliage on some of them. Compared, however, with the continent of Europe, and especially France, English Romanesque capitals must be accounted a disappointment; very few of them have figure-carving. At least two churches have brought their Norman tympana inside: Fownhope in Herefordshire and

Charney Bassett in Berkshire (55), where the subject is Alexander the Great's legendary journey to heaven, borne aloft by two winged griffins. No tympanum in the country is more decorative. From the Saxon period Barnack and Castor both possess very fine sculpture. Barnack has a late Saxon Christ in Majesty in high relief which is the essence of nobility and dignity. Castor has a smaller, earlier relief representing a man under an arcade, a precious little piece of the greatest refinement. There is also a notable collection of still earlier sculpture, believed to date from the latter part of the eighth century, at Breedon-on-the-Hill in Leicestershire; unfortunately not all of it is easy to see. Enville in Staffordshire has a relief, perhaps pre-Conquest, of very primitive character, but with an engaging subject; standing on a big, grotesque head is a figure with hands raised, holding a flabellum or fan for whisking flies off the consecrated elements.

Compared with the church art of the preceding century, that of the thirteenth was much more sunny. In the first half of Henry III's reign, the stimulus was provided by a group of remarkable bishops, motivated by a confident and optimistic attitude to the world. The three chief non-monastic churches were Lincoln and Salisbury cathedrals and St John, Beverley, which if it had been located elsewhere would also without doubt be a cathedral today. The application of blind arcading, trefoil-headed and, in the later work, ogee-crested as well, to the walls of Beverley is but one example of the sumptuous enrichment of that superb building. Needless to say, this kind of embellishment was beyond the resources of the normal parish church, but it can be seen in the chancel of Stone in Kent, with exquisite leaf decoration in the spandrels, restored by Street. Another Kentish parish church, St Leonard, Hythe, has a beautiful chancel of c. 1235 with a three-storey elevation, so unexpected in this type of building. (This chancel was not finished until Pearson vaulted it in 1886. Much of its beauty was destroyed when a truly shameful east window was inserted in 1951.)

The stiff-leaf motif was adopted well nigh universally in the first half of the thirteenth century, but of course the quality of execution varies greatly. In the village churches no capitals of this type are more crisply carved than those at Eaton Bray (116), all slightly different. The set at West Walton in the Norfolk Marshland is also deservedly famous. At Slimbridge in Gloucestershire, where there is another well-known set, the absence of annulets is to be regretted, but the undercutting is bold and the treatment unconventional; no two are the same and some are most original. At Ivinghoe in Buckinghamshire the effect is slightly windswept. In other sculptural features, such as sedilia, the popularity of Purbeck marble in the Early English period only served to emphasise the sharp crisp lines and precise clarity of intention which are so characteristic of this phase, and for which the dog-tooth was an ideally appropriate invention in the ornamentation of mouldings.

The Early Decorated period corresponds almost exactly with the reign of Edward I, and now a more wordly attitude can sometimes be detected. The King himself would appear to have preferred castles to churches, and it has even been suggested that Harlech, Conway and Caernarvon were built on an unnecessarily imposing scale for the sheer love of the thing. Here and there too, as at Wells and Durham, a bishop of this period would devote his principal resources to the enlargement and embellishment of his palace. Into the parish churches the actual world now entered with confidence and often with a smile. The profusion of portrait heads in some churches is remarkable; they are to be found on capitals, on corbels, as headstops, almost everywhere. Oxfordshire has a specially large collection, at Woodstock, Bloxham, Adderbury, Hampton Poyle and elsewhere. Foliage is sometimes wholly naturalistic now, although of course always subjected to the discipline of architectural form. Few indeed are the travellers along the Great North Road who find time to digress, just short of Newark if travelling north, to see Claypole, the handsome spire of which is easily visible from the road. Yet this fine limestone church has, among other delights, foliage capitals only slightly inferior to the famous leaves of Southwell (*117*).

The losses of large-scale sculpture from this period have been grievous. Very often one sees image brackets and canopies, but, sadly, no figures; sometimes the small sculptures, corbels for example, have managed to survive, as in the nave at Cley-next-the-Sea in Norfolk, which has a delightful series, or at Whatton in Nottinghamshire, which has only two, but the undamaged one, showing David playing the harp, is a work of art of much charm and refinement. Nottinghamshire has far more famous examples of Decorated sculpture than these, notably, apart from Southwell Minster, in the church of Hawton, where the very rich but also, alas, badly smashed Easter Sepulchre and sedilia, though *tours de force* of ornamental carving, are perhaps prodigious rather than beautiful. For all their brilliance, it is possible to feel that here and there the sculptors of the Decorated period did overreach themselves as artists.

In general, however, as is evidenced by the capitals at Patrington (*118*), there is much less undercutting and much less crispness now than in the Early English phase. Profiles indeed tend to exhibit a 'middle-aged-spread'. Arcades and piers have much less light and shade. The supplanting of the pointed dog-tooth by the rounded ball-flower as the standard ornamental form for mouldings is a significant tell-tale. In my view the supreme achievement of this period, apart from towers and spires, was in the infinite inventiveness and, sometimes, beauty of the window tracery, of which fortunately a great deal has survived intact, especially in the north-east Midlands and Lincolnshire. But, as stated earlier, this is almost always better appreciated from outside, not only because of the frequency of indifferent glass but also because externally the windows are more impressively 'framed', with ball-flower mouldings, good dripstones and sometimes ogee-shaped canopies.

It is customary to think of the Perpendicular style as marking, at any rate at its inception, a reaction from the luxuriance of later Decorated in the direction of greater sobriety, even austerity. In some respects this was certainly the truth; capitals now become smaller and except in Devon and Cornwall much less often floriated; mouldings, after the abandonment of the ball-flowers, become plainer and still more shallow; most significant of all, sinuosity is abandoned in favour of rectilinear patterns. Aesthetically it can be held that these were all changes for the worse; as noted earlier, the window tracery is the least enjoyable feature of Perpendicular Gothic. The gradual lowering of the roof-pitch is another characteristic of the style which is often no artistic asset. Nevertheless, in so far as Perpendicular can be regarded as the outcome of one of those puritanical swings of the pendulum that occur periodically throughout the history of art, and not only in England, it must be said that it was not a very big swing, nor one that lasted long. Two of the masterpieces of the style, the new nave at Canterbury and the restructured Norman nave at Winchester, were both begun before the end of the fourteenth century, and puritanical is the last word which could be applied to either. Anyone who has persevered thus far with this book will, I hope, be in no doubt by now that, despite the uninteresting, even ugly, window traceries, despite the hard, mechanical, mass-produced appearance of some of the poorer examples of the style, despite the loss of charm as compared with the Decorated, and the decline in spirituality as compared with earlier medieval churches, Perpendicular at its best rates for me as the high-water mark of our parish church architecture. Most of the finest towers, all the great timber roofs, almost all the other pre-Reformation church woodwork and many of the vaults were the products of this long, last, magnificent phase of English Gothic.

Among village churches it would not be easy to find a more beautiful example of the style than Walpole St Peter in Norfolk. This is almost entirely an early Perpendicular creation, for of the earlier church on the site only the lower part of the tower survived a disastrous flood in 1337. That is perhaps why the tower, though dignified, is somewhat plain and a little too small for the rest. All else is parish church Perpendicular at its most stately. It stands in an open situation, with the east end in the rectory garden. If the exterior, in its beautifully kept churchyard, is richly satisfying, the interior is still better. One steps into a church bathed in light; the nave windows are clear, and have lovely Crown glass over 200 years old. The stained glass in the chancel is innocuous. Everywhere the floors are paved with stone, while walls show a wholly satisfying combination of light grey Barnack freestone and colourwash to tone with it. The tie-beam roof, though plain, is of a good colour and sensitive in quality. The east end of the long, aisleless chancel with the altar, is raised ten steps above the nave. It was built in this way so that a vaulted passage could be carried beneath it, not as at Hythe in Kent, to allow processions to make the tour of the building without quitting consecrated ground, but simply to preserve an old right of way. If, however, the raising of the east end was fortuitous, it was a very lucky accident, for architecturally it provides a fine point of climax. The woodwork includes good fifteenth-century doors, an exquisite parclose screen of similar date across the south aisle, some nice old benches, stalls with delightful heraldic animals and tiny bosses in the form of heads, and, stretching right across the church near its west end, a Jacobean screen. Memorable too is the handsome two-tiered Dutch chandelier in the nave, bought in 1701 for £33. This and the six smaller modern ones in the chancel all have graceful wrought-iron suspensions rods. There are no doubt many village churches, including at least one, West Walton, in the Marshland, which have individual features that are still more memorable. It is the ensemble at Walpole St Peter which offers such a wonderful and, once seen, unforgettable aesthetic experience.

Townspeople could sometimes afford to be still more lavish, as can be seen at St Mary Redcliffe, Bristol. Some parts of this church belong to the early fourteenth century, including the south aisle and, in particular, the hexagonal, lierne-vaulted north porch, an astonishing creation, suggesting the Manueline architecture of Portugal two centuries before that style had been evolved. But the interior (28) is now to all intents and purposes an early Perpendicular church of exceptional splendour. When I first saw it there was, especially in the Lady Chapel, Victorian glass so appalling that it was quite painful to linger. Mercifully the bombs cleared it all away, and this chapel now has five large windows (1959–65) by H. J. Stammers which are decidedly better than today's average. The interior is now very nearly faultless. Even the pulpit, of 1856, with small carved figures, is unusually good for its date.

St Mary Redcliffe is cruciform; the transepts are lofty and appear more so because they are very narrow, but they have aisles – an opulent addition. Still more remarkable is the fact that the entire building is vaulted, which for an English parish church is very rare indeed. These vaults date from the middle of the fifteenth century. They are of the lierne type with the webs plastered and tinted to the same colour as the pale buff Dundry oolite with which the whole church is faced. The thin fillets on the surface of the moulded ribs have been gilded. Admittedly the ribs do not benefit from having sprouting thorn-like projections at intervals; the pretty star vaults in the nave aisles are the best. There are said to be over a thousand bosses. The lovely wrought ironwork was referred to a few pages back. St Mary Redcliffe is maintained in a manner worthy of it, which is to say, magnificently. It is one of the great sights of England.

Because it is so often absent from parish churches, very little has been said in this book about vaulting. Nearly all the most beautiful stone vaults, lierne at Tewkesbury, tierceron and lierne at Pershore, lierne and fan at Sherborne, fan at Bath (the nave a good nineteenth-century copy of the original choir vault), are in former abbey churches designed on much grander lines than those built solely for parochial use. The Normans might vault a small structure, or at least the sanctuary and apse, and now and again a larger chancel, as at Hemel Hempstead, which still preserves its very heavy ribbed vault planned over two square bays. By the middle of the fourteenth century Beverley Minster, apart from its west front, was complete and wholly vaulted; the webs of the nave vault, as mentioned earlier are of brick, which was unique in England at that time. In the second quarter of the fourteenth century a tierceron vault of the kind seen to perfection in Exeter Cathedral was erected over St Michael's Chapel in the north chancel of St Mary, Beverley. A few years later Ottery St Mary was given lierne vaults throughout, but they are not very engaging; another example from this period is the chancel at Nantwich.

Perpendicular vaulting in a village church is best seen at Steeple Ashton, where with a fine prodigality they seem to have contemplated covering the whole building. In fact the chancel and the nave aisles have excellent lierne vaults in stone; the nave has only a very good imitation in wood. Usually, however, the later Gothic vaults in parish churches are confined to limited, generally square, spaces, such as towers and porches. The stellar vault of Boston Stump, 137 feet above the floor, is a specially attractive example. Woolpit has a very pretty star vault inside the porch. But the majority of these late vaults, some of which are extremely decorative, occur towards the South-West: in Gloucestershire, Wiltshire, Somerset and Devon. At Sevenhampton in Gloucestershire, about 1500, a lantern tower over the crossing was ingeniously inserted, with a lovely little tierceron vault: a fascinating sight. Cricklade in Wiltshire has an elaborate lierne vault under its elephantine tower. Most of these lierne vaults are enriched with bosses, usually floral or heraldic. The Tudor period also brought with it a few fan vaults. A delicate example, created in 1508, spans the chantry chapel of St Catherine and St Nicholas in the church at Cirencester. The Dorset aisle at Ottery St Mary has a fan vault, though with unpleasing pendants. But another Devon example, that over the lofty Lane aisle at Cullompton (119), which was erected only in 1526, is very enjoyable, and masterly in its assurance.

Should the reluctance to build vaults and the strong preference for wooden roofs be regarded as an indication of English architectural inferiority? It is undeniable that the vault is a more logical and a better integrated kind of roof for a stone building. By comparison a wooden roof is more like a lid, resting on top of the walls. A major church, and especially a cathedral, which has no vaults would seem to lack something essential. Nevertheless, many church vaults on the continent of Europe are no more than utility structures, completely plain and devoid of aesthetic interest; whereas some of our roofs, no one would deny, are works of art of a high order. Is it therefore right to argue that a roof, however fine, is architecturally not a satisfactory substitute for a stone vault? My own view is that it all depends upon the scale and importance of the church. For major churches, yes; for the average English parish church, on the other hand, the wooden roof would seem aesthetically to be perfectly acceptable.

Surely the weakest architectural features of the English parish churches are the frequently unworthy proportions of the chancel, caused by the divided legal responsibility for nave and chancel described on page 91, and the almost invariable preference for a flat east end. How incomparably finer is the French *chevet*, the apse surrounded at a lower level by an ambulatory, and often by chapels as well. This endows the French interior with a worthy point of climax as one moves eastwards, whereas in England the effect is all too often one of anti-climax. Speaking of cathedrals, Nikolaus Pevsner says: 'Rheims seems vigorously pulled together, Lincoln comfortably spread out. ... The preference for the "additive" plan must be accepted as a national peculiarity.' Of the parish churches this is unfortunately no less the truth.

We come finally, in our consideration of the parish church interior, to the great number of works in stone associated with death: chantry chapels, family burial chapels and all kinds of funerary monuments. As we noted in Chapter 2, there are not a few English churches in which the monuments are the principal, or even the sole, source of interest.

Chantry chapels, and the parrot-recital of masses with which they were associated, needed several resident priests, so we look for these in the parish churches that were formerly abbeys or priories, or in collegiate churches. As they were always built by rich men no expense was spared, and at best the craftsmanship, as in the Beauchamp Chantry at Tewkesbury, is as charming as it is accomplished. Tewkesbury has three of these chantry chapels, all of the early Perpendicular period. But lovelier than any of them, as a work of art, is the slightly earlier Despencer tomb adjoining: delicate, complicated and subtle. The Perpendicular tombs look earthbound by comparison.

1. Wittering, Peterborough

112. Stow, Lincolnshire

EARLY CHANCEL ARCHES

3. Iffley, Oxfordshire

4. Tickencote, Rutland

115. Kilpeck, Herefordshire

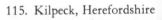

116. Eaton Bray, Bedfordshire

GOTHIC CAPITALS

117. Claypole, Lincolnshire

118. Patrington, Yorkshire

A VAULT AND A VAULT-LIKE ROOF

119. Cullompton, Devon: the Lane Aisle

120. Ludlow, Shropshire: under the Tower

121. Stansted Mountfitchet, Essex

122. Wheathampstead,
Hertfordshire

123. Ickenham, London (formerly
Middlesex)

TO THE DEAD

124. Swanton Morley, Norfo

All these grandees, needless to say, chose positions within a few feet of the high altar. One of the less grand summed it up neatly:

> Here *lie* I *at the Chancel door*,
> Here *lie* I *because I'm poor*:
> The *further in the more you pay*:
> Here *lie* I, *as warm as they*.

Important families would have their own burial chapels, achieved in various ways. At Spilsby in Lincolnshire a chantry was endowed in 1348 by the will of the first Lord Willoughby: his family took over the chancel but built another one. At Bottesford in Leicestershire the Manners family filled the chancel but did not provide a new one: the monuments include all the first eight Earls of Rutland, 1543 to 1684, but unhappily not one of them is a work of distinction. At Edenham in Lincolnshire it is the Bertie monuments that fill the chancel; that to the 1st Duke of Ancaster, represented life-size in Roman costume, by Henry Scheemakers (brother of Peter), is vast. A later one commemorates a Duchess (*ob.* 1743) 'whose death sealed the inimitable virtue of a useful and Pious Life'. At Warkton in Northamptonshire, about 1750, the 2nd Duke of Montagu cleared away the chancel altogether and substituted another in a classical style, planned to house four very large monuments, including two by Roubiliac. But aesthetically the best way of accommodating these family monuments was generally to concentrate them in a special chapel added for the purpose. This is what occurred at Warwick as early as the fifteenth century, when the lavish Beauchamp Chapel was added between 1443 and 1464. It is also what the Cecils did at Hatfield, where the big Salisbury Chapel, built in 1618, occupies the north-east angle of the church; since 1871 this has had an entirely Italianate interior, tolerable of its kind, but quite foreign to the building of which it is a part. The monuments here include not only a major one to the first Earl by Maximilian Colt, a tomb of European standing, with a cadaver lying below the main effigy, but a most original recumbent effigy in a shroud, by Nicholas Stone.

In France comparatively few funerary monuments survive intact, because at the Revolution the rage of the mob was directed against the aristocracy, as upholders of the *Ancien Régime*, and it was therefore their monuments which were shattered, whereas French religious sculpture, and stained glass, have had a somewhat less stormy passage than here. In England the fanatics always sought to destroy 'Popish images', or even, at times, anything richly coloured, which was equated with sensuous pleasure; thus nearly all our glass has gone, and almost all our religious statuary. Tombs, on the other hand, have suffered relatively less damage, and an immense quantity of funerary sculpture remains. This undoubtedly adds to the interest of church visiting, and is a valuable store-house of biographical history. It is a pity that aesthetically so much of it is pedestrian, and some incompetent. The really fine work, at any period, is not common. The following are no more than a few disjointed notes on monuments which seem to me to be in one way or another memorable.

Stowe-Nine-Churches in Northamptonshire (Church Stowe on the sign-posts), which incidentally had only five rectors between 1720 and 1921, is architecturally almost devoid of interest, but in addition to a handsome early Georgian wall monument, the church has two earlier life-size effigies of outstanding quality. The medieval one, in Purbeck marble, is believed to be Sir Gerald de l'Isle (*ob.* 1287). He wears chain mail and a surcoat, and the legs are crossed, which, contrary to an oft-repeated legend, has no ascertainable connection with the Crusades. The figure is sensitively carved and, apart from a new nose, remarkably well preserved. So is the other one, dating from 1620, which is of Elizabeth Lady Carey by Nicholas Stone. This is in off-white marble, and exhibits naturalism at its best. A gryphon lies at her feet and there is a good tomb-chest. In sum, these three monuments, so different in style and date, provide an excellent 'miniature anthology' of this kind of English sculpture.

Clifton Reynes in Buckinghamshire has two knights and their ladies in black oak; all are about 1300, sensitive again, and in excellent preservation. The same church has another more worn pair in stone on a chest, carved some eighty years later, with twelve mourners under cusped and crocketed ogee canopies. Some of these little figures have great charm, and their clothes are interesting.

From the fifteenth century probably no monument in a parish church equals that of Richard Beauchamp, Earl of Warwick (*ob.* 1439) in the Beauchamp Chapel, which is masterly. The brass effigy, not a portrait, is beautiful and so are the smaller figures, fourteen mourners and eighteen little angels, in gilt copper. The contemporary monument to Sir Ralph Gray (*ob.* 1443) and his lady at Chillingham in Northumberland is also unusually lavish for its date, but in comparing these two we have a perfect illustration of the key rôle played by material in the impact of a work of art. The effigies are of alabaster; all else is of a hard carboniferous sandstone, dun-coloured and rather coarse, so that, although vigorous and extremely well preserved, the fourteen saints and shield-holding angels which surround the chest are not delicate. The drapery folds are comparatively few and thick. But the characters are nicely differentiated, and they look the sort of people it would have been delightful to have known. The Grays were perhaps a little dull by comparison. Wholly of alabaster is the Cokayne monument at Youlgreave in Derbyshire. A very small table-tomb stands plumb in the middle of the chancel, and really deserves its prominent position. The fine effigy of Thomas Cokayne (*ob.*

1488) is about 4 feet long and in an admirable state of preservation. This is a lovely little monument, perfect of its kind.

Another alabaster tomb which occupies the centre of the chancel, an unusual position for a parish church monument, is that of Lord and Lady Williams at Thame. We are now in the sixteenth century; the date is 1559. This is a much more imposing tomb than Cokayne's, but the sculpture is more naturalistic and less enjoyable. From the Tudor period a much finer work, worthy indeed of a cathedral, is the Dacre monument at Herstmonceux, probably of about 1540. The principal material is chalkstone, lending itself, because so easily carved, to exuberant decoration, and there is a magnificent chest with cusped quatrefoils, canopied niches, and above, lively cresting in a kind of Gothic-Baroque. The effigies, however, appear to be earlier (c. 1480?), and it is thought that they were rescued from Battle Abbey at the Dissolution and reused. At Godshill in the Isle of Wight Sir John Leigh (ob. 1529: alabaster again) has two little monkish weepers pressed against the soles of his feet, to pray for his soul: a very pretty, and so far as I know unique, conceit.

Alabaster, so much used for effigies in the later Middle Ages and until well into the seventeenth century, becomes in time dirty and discoloured, but with skill and patience its pristine beauty can be recovered. To see how worth doing this is, one should visit Rushden in Northamptonshire, where a benefactor generously paid for the restoration and recolouring of the alabaster monument to Robert Pemberton (ob. 1608) and his wife. It was beautifully carried out. The contrast between this now lovely tomb and the soapy brown with pink streaks of the other Pemberton tomb in this church, also Jacobean, is not quickly forgotten. Where stone monuments were once coloured, discreet recolouring, leaving much of the stone untouched, can also be very rewarding, so long as it is performed with taste and care. At Leigh in Worcestershire the excellent recolouring of the Colles monuments may be compared with the amateurish repainting of the south aisle screen, in the fairground manner. Rather endearing is the coloured effigy of Hester Salusbury (ob. 1614) by Epiphanius Evesham at Stansted Mountfitchet in Essex (121). She reposes on a sarcophagus, also of alabaster, in all her finery: as Norman Scarfe remarks, 'ready for heaven'.

From the second Stuart period are two marble monuments to Claytons, as different as can be, but both outstanding. Ickenham in Middlesex has Robert Clayton, an infant who died in 1665 (123). The face is rendered with touching naturalism; the clothes are beautifully formalised; the preservation perfect. Bletchingley in Surrey has his parents, Sir Robert and Lady Clayton, by Richard Crutcher, of whom no other work is known: a remarkable fact, since Rupert Gunnis regarded this as 'the most important early eighteenth-century monument in England'. Sir Robert, who died in 1707, was not a Lord Mayor of London for nothing; the statues of him and his wife are larger than life, and their swaggering memorial leaves us oblivious of everything else at Bletchingley. There is a story that the statue was completed before Sir Robert's death so that he could admire it. Another Queen Anne monument in a church which has little else of interest is that to Sir William and Lady Villiers, who both died in 1711, at Brooksby in Leicestershire. The identity of its sculptor is unknown, but with its putti, coat of arms, vases and marble of two colours, white and grey, this is a work with plenty of style: not so large as that to the Claytons, but hardly less accomplished.

Although the monuments constitute an integral part of parish churches considered as works of art, it will be evident that another book would be needed to do justice to them. Indeed, the major part of Gunnis's *Dictionary of British Sculptors* is devoted to Georgian monuments, of which there are many thousands. Their quality varies greatly; the best, notably some of the works of John Michael Rysbrack and Louis François Roubiliac, are masterly. At the other extreme are those which are just over-sized and arrogant. It is worth observing that the most enjoyable Georgian memorials are by no means always the biggest. Many churches are the fortunate possessors of a Baroque wall-monument, so decorous beneath its broken pediment and within its frame of columns; or there may be a charming Rococo tablet, convex and beribboned; or only a prim neo-classical grieving maiden by a Flaxman or a Westmacott.

Victorian monuments, it must be admitted, are seldom of much artistic significance, for three reasons. The effigies are almost invariably over-naturalistic, much attention being paid to the exact representation (sometimes in 'streaky-bacon' alabaster) of such details as buttons, buckles and belts, Orders and Decorations; or, with female memorials especially, there is an excessive sentimentality; and there was a sharp decline in the standard of lettering. In this last respect at least, there has been since the time of Eric Gill a notable recovery; the lettering of contemporary tablets is not infrequently delightful.

Almost every amateur of churches will probably at some time or other have copied down an epitaph or an inscription, from either inside or outside a church. I have a whole anthology of them, and I will end by citing a few of my particular favourites. A priceless instance occurs at Bicknoller in Somerset, close to the north-east window:

> *Here lie 3 Saffords out of view*
> *Mabel, Mary, Bartholomew.*
> *Bartholomew Safford's flesh and bone,*
> *His wife, His Sister and his Son.*
> *Mabel became for worms a bait*

December 9th in forty-eight.
Mary was fitted for the bier
  on March 4th in that same year.
Death on Bartholomew did fixe
  on March the 2nd fifty-six.
Wife, Sister, Brother. Father dear,
  Christ's minister and pastor here.

Bartholomew Safford was vicar of Bicknoller 1646–62. Staying in the seventeenth century, we can picture Sir Francis Mannock (*ob.* 1634) of Stoke-by-Nayland, 'whose religious conversation made him reverenced by all'. Rutland has three tender inscriptions for those who died young. At Brooke:

Charles, son of Andrew Noel, brave and high,
His dust inhabits here, his soul, the sky:
Nature and Worth, Valour and Wisdom too,
In this one boy strove all their gifts to show.

He died in 1619, aged twenty-eight. Not many miles away, at Stoke Dry, rude lettering on a stone in the chancel floor tells us that 'Here lieth the body of Dorothy Stevens Virgin Age xi waiting for a ioyful resurrection, November x 1637'. And at Ryhall we encounter Sam Barker, who was 'of admirable sweetness of temper, of an erect and comely body, and of a most pregnant wit', who died in 1696, aged two years and fifteen days.

At Malmesbury in Wiltshire there is the following wording on the tombstone of a young woman killed by a tiger:

In memory of
Hannah Twynnoy
who died October 23rd 1703
aged 33 years
In bloom of Life
She's snatched from hence.
She had not room
To make defence;
For Tyger fierce
Took life away.
And here she lies
In a bed of Clay
Until the Resurrection Day.

The following very touching epitaph is to be found at Stanton Harcourt, in Oxfordshire, on a tablet on the south wall of the south transept:

> Near this place lie the bodies of
> JOHN HEWET AND SARAH DREW
> An industrious young man and
> virtuous maiden of this parish
> CONTRACTED IN MARRIAGE
> who being with many others at harvest
> work, were both in one instant killed
> by lightning on the last day of July
> 1718.
> *Think not by vigorous judgment seized*
> *A pair so faithful could expire:*
> *Victims so pure Heav'n saw well pleas'd*
> *And snatched them in celestial fire.*

According to Nikolaus Pevsner (*Oxfordshire* p. 781), this epitaph was written by Alexander Pope. The following charming inscription of 1730 is to be found at Edgcote in Northamptonshire:

> Under this marble stone lies whatsoever was mortall
> of Bridgett Chauney, of whom man was not worthy.

But it is to the Georgian period that we must look for the most delectable epitaphs. This is the age when, as Dr Johnson observed, 'in lapidary inscriptions a man is not upon oath'. Apart from the sentiments, the use of the English language is in itself a constant delight. For instance, at Wingham, in Kent:

> To the memory of WILLIAM NEWTON the dear and only son of WILLIAM NEWTON Minister of this Parish
> WHO in his early years made such discoveries of his Truly good and virtuous Disposition, Pregnant Parts, Promising Genius, and Proficiency of Learning Adorned with a most agreeable and modest Deportment as procured him the love and esteem of all who knew Him and caused him to be regarded by the best Judges as one of the Greatest Ornaments of ye Place of his Education.
> Born Sept. 1721 Died of small pox April 1737
> 'How blind is Hope, and how regardless Fate
> That so much WORTH should have so SHORT a date!'

A nautical epitaph can be found at Bosham in West Sussex, with a lively carving of a ship on a stormy sea, and a winged cherub's head on top of the stone:

> In Memory of THOMAS Son of Richard and ANN BARROW.
> Master of the Sloop Two Brothers who by the Breaking of the Horse fell into the Sea & was Drown'd October the 13, 1759 Aged 23 years.

Tho Boreass' Storms and Neptune's waves
have tos'd me to and fro
Yet I at length by God's decree
am harbour'd here below
Where at an anchor here I lay
with many of our Fleet
Yet once again I shall set Sail
my Saviour Christ to meet.

At Spelsbury in Oxfordshire we meet Robert Earl of Lichfield, 'whose social Disposition Amiable Condescension and unaffected Benevolence endeared him to all who had the Honor of his Acquaintance'. Died 1776. Aged seventy-one. At St Peter, Wolverhampton, we find Charles Claudius Phillips, (*ob.* 1732), 'whose absolute contempt of riches and inimitable performances upon the violin made him the admiration of all that knew him'. At Scotter in Lincolnshire we learn that Mrs Sarah Ashton, (*ob.* 1739), was, *inter alia*, 'Religious without Moroseness, Charitable without Ostentation, and Cheerfully obedient to her Husband'. The inscription ends with an exhortation: 'Go, female Reader, and imitate'. At Dunchideock in Devon there is Stringer Lawrence, (*ob.* 1775), 'the Father of the Indian Army', and Clive's master.

In vain this frail Memorial Friendship rears:
His dearest Monument's an Army's tears ...

And then, at Foxley in Norfolk, the poor invalid Mary Rudd, who died in 1771 at the age of thirty-five years:

Afflictions sore, long time I bore,
Physicians were in vain;
Till Death did please to give me ease
And free me of my pain.

In pointed contrast with these unsophisticated sentiments is the recondite inscription at Kempsey in Worcestershire on a tablet commemorating George Boulter, vicar there for thirty years, and his two wives, who predeceased him, the first in 1757, the second in 1774. Perhaps it was no accident that the year of his own death is not stated: 'He died January 30th, aged 81'.

Underneath the corruptible Parts of a Vicar, one Husband, two Helpmeets, both Wives, and both ANNs, a Triplicity of Persons in two Twains, but one Flesh, are interred.

After about 1800 the epitaphic art will be found to have shed much of its eighteenth-century lustre. A prize for banality might be given to the following from Potton in Bedfordshire:

Adieu, dear boy, short was thy stay
Just bloomed to youth, then called away.
Thy smiling face we all did see,
But soon we were deprived of thee.

(Will Parrott, 1856, aged 16). But examples can be found from this period that at least evoke pleasing pictures of a couple of estimable people. For both of these we step out into the churchyard. At Pott Shrigley in Cheshire a stone recalls Margaret Bowden, Widow, 'a pious Instructress of little children in this village. Died January 4 1812, aged 78',

Learn, village maids and rustic swains,
One lesson more from her remains,
Who taught with toil your heedless youth
To syllable the WORD of TRUTH ...

and quite a lot more, of less interest. At Corby in Lincolnshire an outsize slab of limestone, very well preserved, commemorates Joseph Wright, an Eminent Auctioneer, 'Whose irresistable humour and brilliant wit obtained for him an extensive circle of friends'. He died on October 11 1835, aged sixty years.

Beneath this stone facetious wight
Lies all that's left of poor Joe Wright.
Few hearts with greater kindness warmed,
Few heads with knowledge more informed.
With brilliant wit and humour broad
He pleased the Peasant, Squire and Lord.
At length old Death with visage queer
Assumed Joe's trade of Auctioneer,
Made him the lot to practise on
With going, going, and anon
He knocked him down, so poor Joe's gone.

A less witty example of the nineteenth-century epitaph can be found at Houghton in Huntingdonshire, to the memory of one Thomas Garner who died 30 September 1826, aged 77:

My sledge and hammers lie declined,
My bellows too have lost their wind.
My fires extinct, my forge decay'd,
My vice is in the dust all laid.
My coal is spent my iron gone,
My nails are drove my work is done.
My fire dried corpse here lies at rest
My soul smoke like soars to be blessed.

What, I wonder, would you wish to have for your own epitaph? Perhaps, at the end of a book which, I am prepared to believe, some readers may already have found excessively subjective, I may be permitted the final indulgence of setting down my own favourite: the epitaph, of all those that I have read, which I should like most for myself, if I were thought to be worthy of it. It commemorates, in the little church of Trusley in Derbyshire, on a beautifully engraved glass screen, Ronald Coke-Steel, (*ob.* 1963).

He honoured the past, rejoiced in the present, and built for the future.

Glossary

ANNULET A ring round a circular pier or shaft.

APSE A semi-circular or polygonal end to a church or chapel, usually vaulted.

ASHLAR Masonry of hewn or sawn stone, in blocks which are usually large but often quite thin, carefully squared and finely jointed in level courses.

AUMBRY A recessed cupboard for the sacred vessels used at Mass or Communion. Usually to the north of an altar.

BALL-FLOWER A form of ornament consisting of globular three-petalled flowers enclosing small balls: characteristic of the Decorated period.

BARGE-BOARD A wooden board, usually with decorative carving, fixed to the lower edge of a barge (the overhanging edge of a roof up the slope of a gable) in order to mask the ends of the horizontal roof timbers.

BATTER The slope of a wall backwards from the vertical.

BATTLEMENT An indented parapet, used on churches for its decorative effect (see also EMBRASURE and MERLON).

BOSS In ribbed vaulting, an ornamental projection, generally carved with foliage or figures, used to conceal the intersection of the ribs.

BRATTISHING Ornamental cresting found on late Gothic screens, etc., usually formed of conventional leaves.

BRESSUMMER A horizontal beam extending over a wide opening or series of openings and supporting a superstructure, such as the loft over a screen.

BROACH A sloping and usually elongated half-pyramid of masonry or wood, introduced above each angle of a square, unparapeted tower to effect the transition to a tapering octagonal spire.

CANONS REGULAR Canons who renounced private property and lived together in communities under rule (in fact, the rule of St Augustine): they were ordained priests but not monks.

CELURE Or 'canopy of honour'. That part of a roof over an altar or rood which receives special adornment.

CHANCEL The eastern limb of a parish church, so called because *cancelli*, or screens, separated it from the rest of the building.

CHEVRON A zigzag form of ornamentation characteristic of the Norman period.

CLERESTORY The upper part of the nave, choir and transepts, containing a series of windows clear of the roofs of the aisles.

COLLAR-BEAM A short beam linking a pair of principal rafters not far below their apex.

CORBEL A block of stone projecting from a wall in support of a roof, vault, parapet, shaft or other feature. Corbels were often adorned with carving.

CORBEL-TABLE A connected range of corbels beneath the roof of a building, or supporting a parapet.

CROCKETS In Gothic architecture, ornaments, usually in the form of buds or curled leaves, placed at regular intervals on the sloping sides of spires, gables, canopies, pinnacles, etc.

CURB An enclosing framework, e.g. of a group of wooden benches. See p. 150 and cf. KERB.

CUSPS In Gothic arches or tracery, the projecting points between the lobes or foils.

DIAPER An all-over pattern of squares or diamonds, incised or in low relief, covering a plain wall-surface.

DOG-TOOTH A form of ornament consisting of a succession of raised tooth-like pieces, arranged in pairs or groups of four, and set diagonally to each other, usually in a hollow moulding: characteristic of the Early English period.

DRIPSTONE A projecting moulding over the heads of doorways, windows and archways, to throw off rain. Also known as a 'hood-mould' and, when rectangular, as a 'label'.

EMBRASURE The space between two projecting merlons of a battlement.

EYE-CATCHER An architectural 'incident' in a landscape.

FAN VAULT A conoidal type of vault in which the length and curvature of all the ribs (which are decorative and not structural) are similar: confined to the Perpendicular period.

FINIAL A decorative termination to a pinnacle, canopy, etc.

FLUSHWORK The decorative use of knapped (i.e. split) flint in conjunction with dressed stone to form patterns, monograms, inscriptions, etc.

FREESTONE Stone which is homogeneous enough and of sufficiently fine grain to admit of being cut 'freely', in any direction, either with a saw or with mallet and chisel.

GRISAILLE Greyish-white glass, ornamented with monochrome decoration in neutral-coloured enamel used like paint and fired into the glass.

HAMMER-BEAMS Beams projecting at right angles, generally from the top of a wall, to provide support for the vertical members and/or arched braces of a wooden roof.

HOOD-MOULD See DRIPSTONE.

KERB An edging of stone bordering a grave (cf. CURB).

LABEL See DRIPSTONE.

LANCET WINDOW A narrow window terminating in a sharp point: characteristic of the Early English period.

LANTERN TOWER A tower in which the crossing space is extended upwards and lit from the upper windows.

LEDGER A flat stone covering a grave, and often forming part of a church floor.

LIERNE RIBS Short subsidiary vaulting ribs serving a purely decorative purpose: characteristic of the later Decorated and Perpendicular periods.

LIERNE VAULT A vault incorporating such ribs.

LITHIC Of or pertaining to stone.

LUCARNE (or SPIRE LIGHT) A vertical opening in the tapering surface of a spire, gabled and usually traceried but never glazed.

MERLON The raised portion of a battlement.

MINSTER A term indicative of a large church, but, surprisingly, with no precise signification. Apart from West Minster – i.e. the minster west of the city of

London – this lovely title is applied to several northern cathedrals and to two parish churches, St John, Beverley, and Wimborne.

MISERICORD A bracket on the underside of a hinged wooden seat in a choir stall, which, when turned up, afforded support during long periods of standing, and is often found to be enriched with lively carvings. Sometimes called a MISERERE.

MOULDINGS The varieties of contour given to piers, arches, etc., in order to obtain effects of richness through light and shade contrasts.

MULLION A vertical structural member subdividing a window.

NAVE The western arm of a church, eastwards from the inner door.

NOGGING Brickwork employed as infilling for timber-framed buildings.

OGEE A continuous double curve, concave above and convex below, or vice versa: specially characteristic of the later Decorated period.

PARCLOSE A screen separating a chapel or aisle from the body of the church.

PIER A solid masonry support designed to sustain vertical presure. Piers may be simple (round, square, rectangular) or compound, composite, multiform – i.e. of more complex profile, achieved by applying mouldings, engaged shafts, etc.

PISCINA A recess containing a shallow stone basin, with a drain, for washing sacred vessels. Almost always to the south of an altar.

POPPY-HEAD A finial used to decorate the tops of bench- or stall-ends, usually based on a kind of conventional fleur-de-lis. See p. 151, 152.

QUATREFOIL A four-lobed ornamental infilling for a circle or arch-head.

RAIL A horizontal member separating the compartments of a panelled wall, screen, etc.

RETICULATED TRACERY Tracery of net-like character, in which a single pattern, consisting of circles drawn out at top and bottom into ogee-shaped points, is repeated over a whole area.

RIB A length of stone or wood, generally moulded, dividing the compartments of a vault or roof.

ROMANESQUE The style of architecture prevalent in Western Europe from about the ninth to the twelfth centuries. In England the two phases are known as Saxon and Norman.

ROOD A cross or crucifix supported on a loft or beam at the entrance to the chancel.

ROOD LOFT A projecting gallery built over the rood screen (q.v.) to contain the rood and also for use by singers and musicians.

ROOD SCREEN A screen placed at the entry of the chancel, and usually of wood, on which was erected the rood loft or rood beam.

RUBBLESTONE Unsquared and undressed stone, laid either in rough courses or random.

SANCTUARY The part of a church in which the high altar is situated.

SEDILIA Seats (usually three) for the clergy on the south side of the chancel.

SHINGLES Thin pieces of wood, generally with parallel sides but one end thicker than the other, used for covering roofs and walls.

SPANDREL The area, approximately triangular, between the curve of an arch and the rectangle formed by the mouldings enclosing it; also double this area where there are two contiguous arches.

SPIRE LIGHT See LUCARNE.

SPLAY-FOOTED SPIRE A variant of the broach spire, in which the four cardinal faces are splayed out near their base to cover the corners, while the intermediate faces taper away to a point: principally occurring in the south-eastern counties.

STEEPLE The tower of a church together with its spire, cupola or other 'top-knot'.

STIFF-LEAF The foliage of conventional form, with stiff stems and lobed leaves, that characterises Early English ornament on mouldings, capitals, corbels, bosses, etc.

STRING COURSE A moulding or narrow projecting course running horizontally along the face of a wall.

STUD A vertical timber in the wall of a timber-framed building.

TIE-BEAM A beam at the base of a roof-truss, spanning the space from wall-plate to wall-plate.

TIERCERON RIBS Pairs of ribs with the same point of springing as the principal ribs but which meet obliquely instead of being carried across from one side of a vault to the other in a continuous line.

TIERCERON VAULT A vault incorporating such ribs.

TRACERY The intersecting ornamental ribwork in the upper parts of Gothic windows: also on walls, screens, vaults, etc. The earliest form, Plate tracery, in which decoratively shaped openings appear to be cut out of infillings of solid stone, soon (c. 1250) gave place to Bar tracery, in which the mullions are continued upwards to produce patterns of various kinds.

TRANSEPT An arm of the cross-piece of a cruciform church.

TRANSOM A horizontal structure member subdividing a window.

TREFOIL A three-lobed or trifoliate ornamental infilling for a circle or arch-head.

TRIBUNE A gallery extending over the whole roof – usually a stone vault – of an aisle.

TRIFORIUM An arcaded wall passage or area of blank arcading above the main arcade of a church and below the clerestory. In smaller churches and in some large ones of late-Gothic date the triforium stage was omitted.

TYMPANUM (plural TYMPANA): The area between the lintel and the arch of a doorway, often filled with relief sculpture.

VOUSSOIR A wedge-shaped stone for an arch.

WAGON ROOF A curved wooden rafter roof recalling, inside, the canvas tilt of awning over an old-fashioned wagon.

WALL-PLATE A timber running horizontally along a wall-top to receive and distribute the load from the roof-rafters.

WEATHER-BOARDING Boards providing an external covering for a wall-surface, usually fixed horizontally and generally overlapping.

Appendix A

Abbeys, Priories and Friaries
now serving as parish churches

THE FOLLOWING county list (based on the pre-1974 boundaries—see p. 12) aims at including all the parish churches which were formerly served by monks, canons regular or friars. In most cases the present church only occupies part of the medieval church, and often that part, the nave or an aisle, which was parochial long before the Dissolution. In a few cases the present church was once some other part of the monastic buildings.

A—Augustinian; B—Benedictine; C—Cistercian.

Bedfordshire
Dunstable Priory; A. Most of nave;
    N.W. tower
Elstow Abbey; B (nuns). Most of
    nave; detached tower

Berkshire
Hurley Priory; B. Nave
Reading, Greyfriars; Franciscan
    friars. Nave and transepts (almost
    all rebuilt)

Buckinghamshire
Chetwode Priory; A. Chancel (much
    rebuilt)

Cornwall
St Germans Priory; A. Nave and
    west towers

Cumberland
Holme Cultram Abbey; C. Most of
    nave
Lanercost Priory; A. Nave
St Bees Priory; B. Nave

Devon
Pilton Priory; B. Whole church

Dorset
Cranborne Priory; B. Whole church
Sherborne Abbey; B. Whole church

Durham
Jarrow Priory; B. Chancel (the
    original nave) and tower

Essex
Blackmore Priory; A. Nave
Hatfield Broad Oak Priory; B. Nave
    and W. tower
Hatfield Peverel Priory; B. Nave
Little Coggeshall Abbey; C. Chapel
    by the gate
Tilty Abbey; C. Chapel by the gate
Waltham Abbey; A. Nave

Gloucestershire
Bristol, St James's Priory; B. Nave
    (much altered)
Deerhurst Priory; B. Nave and W
    tower
Stanley St Leonard's (now Leonard
    Stanley) Priory; A; later B. Whole
    church
Tewkesbury Abbey; B. Whole church

Hampshire

Beaulieu Abbey; C. Refectory

Christchurch Priory; A. Whole church

Pamber (formerly Monk Sherborne) Priory; B. Crossing tower and chancel

Porchester Priory; A. Whole church

Romsey Abbey; B (nuns) Whole church

Herefordshire

Dore Abbey (now Abbey Dore); C. Chancel and transepts; tower

Leominster Priory; B. Nave and W. tower

Huntingdon and Peterborough

Thorney Abbey; B. Part of nave

Kent

Davington Priory; B (nuns). Nave and S.W. tower

Minster-in-Sheppey Abbey; B (nuns). Nave and part of chancel

Lancashire

Cartmel Priory; A. Whole church

Upholland Priory; B. Nave (the former choir)

Leicestershire

Breedon Priory; A. Chancel and central tower

Owston Priory; A. Chancel, tower and chapel

Lincolnshire

Bourne Priory; A. Nave and S.W. tower

Crowland Abbey; B. North aisle of nave

Deeping St James Priory; B. Nave

Frieston Priory; B. Nave and W. Tower

Heynings Priory; C (nuns). Transept part of Knaith church (since 1630)

Kirkstead Abbey; C. Chapel by the gate

Sempringham Abbey; Gilbertine. Nave and central tower

South Kyme Priory; A. S.W. corner only

London

Austin Friars; Austin friars. Nave (rebuilt after bombing)

St Bartholomew's Priory, Smithfield; A. Chancel and crossing

St Helen's Priory, Bishopsgate; B (nuns). Whole church

Norfolk

Binham Priory; B. Nave, without its aisles

Wymondham Abbey; B. Nave

Northamptonshire

Canons Ashby Priory; A. W. tower and part of nave

Northumberland

Blanchland Abbey; Premonstratensian. Nave, N. transept and N. tower (mostly rebuilt)

Brinkburn Priory; A. Whole church except S.W. corner (much rebuilt)

Hexham Priory; A. Chancel; transepts; central tower (nave 1907–09)

Nottinghamshire

Blyth Priory; B. Most of nave

Thurgarton Priory; A. Part of nave; N.W. tower

Worksop Priory; A. Nave and W. towers; Lady Chapel

Oxfordshire

Dorchester Abbey; A. Whole church

Shropshire

Bromfield Priory; B. Nave and N.W. tower

Chirbury Priory; A. Nave and W. tower

Shrewsbury Abbey; B. Nave and W. tower

Somerset
Bath Abbey; B. Whole church
Dunster Priory; B. Whole church
Stogursey Priory; B. Whole church

Staffordshire
Farewell (properly Fairwell) Priory;
  B (nuns). Chancel
Lapley Priory; B. Nave, central
tower and chancel
Tutbury Priory; B. Nave

Suffolk
Bungay Priory; B (nuns). Nave
Great Bricett Priory; A. Nave
Letheringham Priory; A. Nave; W.
  tower

Sussex
Boxgrove Priory; B. Chancel; central
  tower

Warwickshire
Atherstone; Austin friars. Chancel;
  central tower
Merevale Abbey; C. Chapel by the
  gate
Polesworth Abbey; B (nuns). Nave
  and N. tower
Wroxall Priory; B. N. aisle of nave

Wiltshire
Amesbury Priory; B (nuns). Whole
  church, except W. end of nave
Edington Priory; Bonshommes.
  Whole church
Malmesbury Abbey; B. Most of nave;
  S. porch

Worcestershire
Great Malvern Priory; B. Whole
  church except S. transept
Little Malvern Priory; B. Chancel
  and crossing tower
Pershore Abbey; B. Chancel, central
  tower (lantern) and S. transept

Yorkshire
Bolton Priory; A. Nave
Bridlington Priory; A. Nave
Malton Priory (now Old Malton
  church); Gilbertine. Part of nave;
  S.W. tower
Nun Monkton; B (nuns). Nave
Selby Abbey; B. Whole church
Swine Priory; C (nuns). Chancel
York: Holy Trinity Priory,
Micklegate; B. Nave and N.W.
tower

Appendix B

County Lists

THE COMPILATION of county lists of the 'best' English parish churches is a daunting undertaking which has nevertheless been several times attempted, notably in the *Collins Guide to English Parish Churches* edited by John Betjeman, which first appeared in 1958: in Charles W. Budden's *English Gothic Churches* (1927) and in Lawrence E. Jones's *Guide to some interesting old English Churches* (n.d.) for the Historic Churches Preservation Trust. I have been indebted to all these for suggested candidates. Finality is of course impossible, if only because standards of assessment differ considerably.

My own criteria, based mainly upon first-hand impact, are those which have prevailed throughout this book: which churches, I have asked myself, are the best worth visiting *from the artistic stand-point*? Since it has been necessary to be much more selective than in, say, the *Collins Guide*, it may perhaps be helpful if I mention a number of categories which figure sparsely or not at all in the lists that follow. (1) Churches of great archaeological or historical interest, like Brixworth or Great Paxton, which are nevertheless deficient in aesthetic qualities, are not included. Nor do small Saxon churches usually seem to qualify. (2) Churches often much lauded but so heavily restored as to offer little visual pleasure today, like Castle Rising or Stewkley, are likewise omitted. (3) This also goes for timber framing, which has almost always been drastically renewed: wooden structures figure only very seldom in these lists. (4) Churches more notable for their contents than for their architecture often find a place, yet it is possible that in recent years the taste for 'atmospherick' churches has been overworked. Any little stone or brick box which has escaped Victorian refurbishing and still preserves its box-pews, double-decker pulpit, white walls and clear glass is certain now to leave some church writers swooning with delight; but, charming as some of these little buildings are, they do not seem to me to deserve as many asterisks as it is now fashionable to accord them. Onibury in Shropshire, for example, gets a star in the *Collins Guide* for revealing 'a loving recapturing of village simplicity', while Lawrence Jones cites it to illustrate that 'the real interest in old English churches is often their quaintness and simplicity', which is not a view that I share. (5) Town churches, for reasons fully explained earlier, do not figure nearly so prominently as country churches. (6) Only a few Victorian churches are included, partly because the large majority *are* town churches, but still more for another reason: even in the finest Victorian churches one is generally conscious of a somewhat machine-made perfection which would no doubt have characterised those of earlier times too if the development of the necessary industrial processes had occurred long before it did. (7) Still fewer twentieth-century churches appear, if only because those which have not had to be built on the cheap, a disasterous recipe for churches as for any other architecture, are so scarce.

All these reservations will probably serve to put me out of court in various quarters. Equally the short summaries of the basic characteristics of the churches of each English county, inevitably superficial and incomplete, are certain to cast me into bad odour with some local patriots. The task has involved trying to look at England as a whole; and here it must be admitted that it has been impossible to adopt an all-embracing standard, for if one has to select only, say, the best two dozen churches in Norfolk or Lincolnshire and to apply the same standards elsewhere, the truth is that there are several counties which would not be able to produce even one church good enough for inclusion. Here therefore a certain flexibility has been essential. In some counties I have had to lower my sights.

Where a church has one outstanding feature but is otherwise unnotable, I have thought it helpful to indicate this in brackets; but it must be emphasised that where there are other good features as well the outstanding one will not be specifically designated.

Churches which are artistically quite outstanding, and on no account to be missed by the amateur of churches, are asterisked, but the county arrangement is alphabetical, as even within a single county it would usually be impossible to arrive at a satisfactory 'order of merit'.

Place-names in italics will also be found in Appendix A: these are churches, or much more often parts of churches, that were formerly served by monks, canons regular or friars.

Notice has been taken of the county changes made in 1965, when the Soke of Peterborough was detached from Northamptonshire and united with Huntingdonshire, and Middlesex was gobbled up, mainly by London; also in 1970, when after more than four centuries Monmouthshire was returned to Wales. But the far more drastic changes of 1974 have been ignored. Based on administrative convenience, these changes have been made without regard for history, and it seems likely that only the next generation will be able to accept them as normal. At present a vast corpus of topographical and other literature is based on the traditional county boundaries, and most of these books will certainly continue to be used for many years to come. It has seemed to me more sensible and less confusing to retain the traditional county classification, especially as the new one is not concerned with the character of parish churches.

Bedfordshire
The Bedfordshire churches are a mixed lot, with no specially distinctive character. The best built are where the limestone is: in the north-western part of the county. Farther south the builders had to make do with a coarse yellow-brown sandstone, the all-too-soft chalk from Totternhoe, or flint. But some fine things were done with the chalk internally, especially at Eaton Bray.
Chalgrave; Cockayne Hatley; *Dunstable Priory*; Eaton Bray*; *Elstow*; Felmersham (west front); Houghton Conquest; Luton; Marston Moretaine; Wymington.

Berkshire
A county almost devoid of good building stone, which meant an extensive

recourse to flint, and here and there to chalk: later, brick and tiles were used extensively. Until the nineteenth century, when for the first time the county became rich, the churches were mostly modest. Then they were all too often over-restored.

Avington; Charney Bassett (tympana); East Hagbourne; Padworth; Shottes-brooke; Theale; Uffington.

Buckinghamshire

The northern end, where this long county reaches the limestone, can offer some notable architectural pleasures, and some of the churches of the Vale of Aylesbury have enjoyable woodwork and good Norman fonts (Bledlow, Edlesborough, Great Kimble, Ivinghoe, Pitstone). South of the Chiltern escarpment, where there were only flint and chalk rubblestone, now often cement-rendered, there is not so much to see. Dorney is included for its charm rather than for architectural interest.

Bledlow; Clifton Reynes; Dinton; Dorney; Edlesborough; Gayhurst; Great Kimble (font); Hillesden; Ivinghoe; Maids Moreton; North Marston; Pitstone; Willen.

Cambridgeshire

A dearth of good building stone in Cambridgeshire involved either importing oolitic limestone by barge across the Fens, which freely occurred in the Isle of Ely, or resorting to clunch and flint. The southern part of the county has the greater number of churches, but for the best one should explore the area between Cambridge and the Suffolk border, and the Isle. Some of the Cambridgeshire churches have excellent woodwork.

Bottisham; Burwell; Cherry Hinton; Isleham; Over; Soham; Willingham; *Isle of Ely*: Elm; Leverington; March, St Wendreda; Sutton-in the-Isle; Whittlesey (steeple).

Cheshire

Except on the eastern fringes of the county, where there is some tough Millstone Grit, well displayed at Astbury, Cheshire's medieval churches were built of yellowish or red Triassic sandstone from the Keuper and Bunter beds. This is a most attractive stone when freshly quarried, but unfortunately not very weather-resistant, and prone to blacken. Despite some delightful towers, the chief appeal of the Cheshire churches tends therefore to be internal. This county has a number of buildings of considerable distinction and some very notable woodwork. Specially characteristic are the cambered tie-beam oak roofs of very low pitch, with ornamental square panels and many bosses. In addition to those listed, no one should miss one of the best of all the Cheshire-style churches, which is just across the border at Gresford in Denbighshire.

Acton; Astbury*; Bunbury; Chester, St John; Congleton; Gawsworth; Great Budworth; Malpas; Mobberley; Nantwich*; Nether Alderley; Northwich; Stockport, St George.

Cornwall

The typical Cornish church is of granite, with a low-pitched slate roof; at some places the walling is also slate. This accounts for the absence of carved stone ornamentation (the display at Launceston is a freakish exception, and none too successful either) and the simplicity of the window tracery. Porches are low and wide; towers may be squat or tall. Triple-gabled east ends are common. The low interiors lack clerestory windows and chancel arches, but some have well carved benches and screens, and almost invariably wagon roofs. Nearly all these churches belong to the Perpendicular period and there are some family likenesses. No major examples and no thrills, perhaps, but much that is quietly sensitive.

Altarnun; Blisland; Kilkhampton; Laneast; Lanreath; Launcells; Mullion; Probus (tower) St Buryan; St Ive; St Kew; St Neot.

Cumberland

Remote from centres of population and exposed to attacks from across the Border, there was no great incentive to build churches here, although Lanercost and Holme Cultram were once fine monastic establishments. Few churches in Cumberland have escaped drastic restoration.

Abbey Town, St Mary (a relic of *Holme Cultram Abbey*); Greystoke; *Lanercost Priory**; Millom.

Derbyshire

Not a very distinguished county for churches. Apart from Melbourne, the best are in the Decorated style; several have boldly conceived fourteenth-century chancels. But there was much insensitive Victorian restoration. So today the settings are sometimes more rewarding than the buildings.

Chesterfield; Melbourne; Morley; Norbury; Sandiacre; Trusley; Wirksworth.

Devon

This big county has a few churches of distinction and many which, though undistinguished, are very likeable, whether for the beauty of their often rough stonework (delightful sandstone colours) or for the richness of their screens (many with gorgeous lofts) and bench-ends. The large majority, as we now see them, belong to the fifteenth century. Although the fine austere towers are sometimes very lofty, the buildings are low, often wide and, because there are seldom any clerestory windows, inclined to be dark, especially when 'scraped'. The roofs are usually of wagon form, in the most pleasing examples with plaster infilling, and there are not many chancel arches. As in Cornwall, there are some strong family resemblances.

Ashton; Buckland-in-the-Moor; Chittlehampton; Coldridge; Cullompton*; Crediton; Dartmouth, St Saviour; Harberton; Hartland; Kentisbeare; Kenton; Lapford; Molland; Ottery St Mary; Parracombe, St Petrock; *Pilton*; Plymtree; Sampford Courtenay; Sutcombe; Swimbridge; Tawstock.

Dorset

Despite the possession of very fine limestones, Dorset, except for Sherborne Abbey, is not a great church county. (Milton Abbey is not now a parish church.) Few counties, however, can equal Dorset for beauty of siting, and these churches offer many gentle secondary pleasures.

Bere Regis; Blandford; Bradford Abbas; Cattistock (tower); Chalbury; Charlton Marshall; Hazelbury Bryan; Kingston-in-Purbeck; Piddletrenthide; Puddletown; *Sherborne Abbey**; Studland; Trent; Whitchurch Canonicorum; Wimborne Minster; Yetminster.

Durham

The sandstones from the Coal Measures and the Millstone Grit which provided the material for most of this county's churches are not rich in charm and in the industrial areas have blackened. But, in addition to half a dozen Saxon survivals not listed here, Durham has, in Darlington and Hartlepool, two most distinguished Early English churches, and, thanks to Bishop Cosin, some notable seventeenth-century carved wooden fittings. Undoubtedly the most rewarding of our four most northerly counties.

Brancepeth; Darlington; Hartlepool*; Haughton-le-Skerne; Roker; Sedgefield.

Essex

Essex churches include two highly distinctive features: the early employment of brick on a far wider scale than elsewhere, and the extensive use of timber, in particular for belfries. Both were the outcome of the county's acute shortage of serviceable stone. Chalk was used in the north-western area; flint, pudding-stone and ragstone from Kent elsewhere. So the building materials are very varied. Nevertheless, the county has some churches of real distinction, and, away from the London suburbs, many more with an unpretentious charm that has managed to survive to a quite surprising degree. Although with no Norman gem like Barfreston in Kent, Essex is the best of the Home counties for churches.

Blackmore (steeple); Clavering; Dedham; Great Baddow; Great Bromley; Great Coggeshall; Greensted (exterior); Hatfield Broad Oak; Ingatestone (tower); Layer Marney; Little Maplestead; Margaretting; Navestock; Newport; Saffron Walden; Sandon; Stock (steeple); Thaxted; Tilty; Waltham Abbey.

Gloucestershire

The Cotswolds are still almost untouched by modern industry and the 'wool' churches, built of exquisite limestone, are externally one of the great sights of England. Internally they are not all quite as satisfying as less beguiling churches elsewhere, but there are of course many good internal features too. Cotswold churchyards are easily the best that we have, and some of the villages provide the churches with settings of incomparable charm.

The Vale of Severn has some grand churches too, but of more varied character, including notable Saxon and Norman survivals. In the Forest of Dean and the north-west limestone gives place to somewhat coarser sandstones, and the achievements are less spectacular.

Berkeley; Bishops Cleeve; Bristol, Redland; Bristol, St Mary Redcliffe*; Chipping Campden*; Cirencester*; Deerhurst; Eastleach Turville; Elkstone; Fairford*; Kempley, St Mary; Leonard Stanley; Minchinhampton; Newland; North Cerney; Northleach; Painswick (churchyard); Southrop (font); Tetbury; Tewkesbury Abbey*; Toddington; Upleadon (tower); Winchcombe (exterior); Yate (tower).

Hampshire and the Isle of Wight

The grand monastic churches of Romsey and Christchurch and the imposing chapel of the Hospital of St Cross at Winchester, all now parish churches, bring distinction to a county otherwise notably short of it. Except for some rather soft sandstone close to the Sussex border the only materials available were flint, chalk, wood, thatch and, later, brick and tiles. A few of the smaller churches are enjoyable, but restoration in Hampshire has been drastic.

The Isle of Wight is better off for building stone, and, although unambitious, several of her churches have considerable charm.

Avington; *Christchurch Priory**; Idsworth; *Pamber Priory*; *Romsey Abbey**; Silchester; Stoke Charity; Warnford; Winchester, St Cross.

ISLE OF WIGHT: Godshill; Mottistone; Shorwell.

Herefordshire

In this beautiful and still extremely rural county the churches are nearly all built of sandstone, usually red-pink or brown and perfectly in tune with the countryside. Herefordshire is very strong in Norman survivals, whether fonts, tympana or even complete churches, as at Kilpeck, the most perfect Romanesque village church in England. Most Gothic churches are unspectacular (there is hardly any Perpendicular) but many contain old glass or good woodwork.

Abbey Dore*; Aymestrey; Brinsop; Brockhampton-by-Ross; Castle Frome (font); Eardisley (font); Eaton Bishop (stained glass); Fownhope (tympanum); Hereford, All Saints; Kilpeck*; Ledbury; *Leominster Priory*; Madley*; Pembridge; St Margarets (screen); Shobdon; Stretton Sugwas (tympanum).

Hertfordshire

'Hertfordshire', said E. M. Forster in *Howards End*, 'is England at its quietest, with little emphasis of river and hill; it is England meditative.' Her churches are the same: quiet and unspectacular, but not unenjoyable, with their little thin spirelets of wood sheathed with lead, the 'Hertfordshire spikes'. Chalk and flint are the only local building stones. Hemel Hempstead is the one major church.

Anstey; Ashwell; Barkway; Hemel Hempstead; St Paul's Walden; Stanstead Abbots; Wheathampstead.

Huntingdon and Peterborough

The Soke of Peterborough has some Saxon and early Norman survivals of special interest and quality. Huntingdonshire churches group with those of Northamptonshire in the north and west of the county, where good limestone was available, and there is a profusion of spires; in the south and east, with the notable exception of the great Perpendicular church of St Neots, the affinities are more with Cambridgeshire.

Barnack; Castor; Conington; Glatton; Keyston; Leighton Bromswold; Little Gidding; St Neots; Somersham; *Thorney*; Tilbrook; Wittering; Yaxley.

Kent

Kent has a lot of churches worth seeing but not so many worth going to see. The building materials range widely: they include flint, ragstone, Caen limestone from Normandy, Wealden sandstone, wood, brick and rich red roofing tiles. The towers are tall but plain, with prominent stair turrets; there are also over two dozen shingled spires. Clerestories are usually absent, and the east ends often have two, and sometimes three, gables of more or less equal size, as in Cornwall. In window tracery, Kent in the fourteenth century evolved her own distinctive style. There is some pleasing stained glass in the Canterbury neighbourhood. But everywhere much Victorianisation.

Barfreston*; Brookland; Chartham; Cobham; Graveney; High Halden (steeple and porch); Hythe; Ivychurch; Lullingstone; Minster-in-Thanet; New Romney; Patrixbourne; St Margaret-at-Cliffe; Selling; Shoreham; Stone; Tunbridge Wells; Upper Hardres; Woodchurch.

Lancashire
There is some white Carboniferous limestone in the north but most old churches in Lancashire are of sandstone, which in the industrial areas is now often nearly black. Sparsely populated in the Middle Ages, there are nevertheless a few buildings of distinction. But most of the large churches are Victorian, and a good many are of brick, now usually grimy.
Cartmel Priory; Halsall; Lancaster; Pendlebury, St Augustine; Sefton; *Upholland*; Whalley; Winwick.

Leicestershire
The eastern side of the county has the better stone and most of the better-looking churches, yet not many that are really memorable. The most beautiful church in Leicestershire, Staunton Harold, is not parochial, and belongs to the National Trust. Noseley Chapel, perhaps the second finest, is also not a parish church. Withcote Chapel, on the other hand, is, although there is no village! The Leicestershire churchyards contain many nicely lettered Swithland slate gravestones.
Appleby Magna; Bottesford; *Breedon-on-the-Hill*; Claybrooke; Gaddesby; King's Norton; Leicester, St Mary de Castro; Melton Mowbray; Stapleford; Stoke Golding; Twycross (stained glass); Withcote Chapel.

Lincolnshire
This enormous county, England's second largest, abounds in big, lonely churches which serve little purpose today but to delight the visitor, and it must be added, to fill him with anxiety. In eastern Lincolnshire the only materials available before the advent of brick were greensand stone and chalk, both dangerously soft; most of Lindsey's better churches are therefore weather-beaten, crumbling and patched. Elsewhere, with a few exceptions, the churches of Lindsey are not very ambitious. Kesteven, on the other hand, had plenty of fine limestone and (from wool) the resources to make good use of it, while Holland was able to obtain by water transport all the limestone she needed from the great quarries at Barnack. So in these parts of the shire there are many stately churches, mainly Decorated, with some of the noblest stone spires in the country. But although the quality of the building and of the carved detail is often superlative, that of the wooden furnishings may lag behind, and there has been much iconoclasm.
Algarkirk; Barton on-Humber, St Mary; Bicker; Boston*; Brant Broughton*; Burgh-le-Marsh; Claypole*; Croft; Ewerby; *Frieston*; Gainsborough; Gedney; Grantham; Heckington; *Kirkstead*; Kirton-in-Holland; Long Sutton; Louth (spire); Marsh Chapel; Northorpe; Rothwell; Silk Willoughby; Sleaford; Stow*; Swaton; Tattershall; Theddlethorpe All Saints; Weston; Winthorpe; Wrangle.

London (and Middlesex)

Once upon a time (for it seems as long ago as that) London was in Middlesex. Now the wheel has turned full circle: most of Middlesex is in London. Churches which until 1965 were in the county of Middlesex are indicated: (Mx). Not all those listed below are parish churches any longer.

From the Middle Ages little of note has survived. In London there is part of the Priory church of *St Bartholomew the Great, Smithfield*. Of country churches the most interesting is Harefield (Mx). Cranford (Mx) has great charm.

Two notable seventeenth-century churches in a partly Gothic idiom are St Katherine Cree (Laudian) and St Mary Aldermary (Wren).

In contrast to its paucity of Norman and Gothic buildings, London has by far the richest Renaissance collection in England: churches designed in a Classical style with some features that are mildly Baroque. Today's list differs considerably from that which would have been presented before 1940, for German bombs left fifteen of Wren's churches and one of Hawksmoor's as burnt-out shells. The best have all been restored. But six are now chiefly notable for their steeples: St Bride, Fleet Street; St Mary-le-Bow; St Michael Paternoster Royal; St Vedast, Foster Lane; St Anne, Limehouse (Hawksmoor); St George-in-the-East, Stepney (Hawksmoor).

The following should be seen for their sumptuous furnishing in wood, and in some cases also for ironwork and plasterwork: All Hallows, Twickenham (Mx); St James, Piccadilly; St Margaret, Lothbury; St Mary Abchurch; St Mary-at-Hill; St Peter, Cornhill.

The Wren churches which can now be best appreciated in their entirety, outside and in, are: St Benet, Paul's Wharf; St James, Garlickhythe; St Magnus the Martyr; St Stephen, Walbrook. To these should be added Hawksmoor's St Mary Woolnoth. St Lawrence Jewry has the most beautiful of the restored interiors.

Of eighteenth-century churches, apart from some of those mentioned above, the following are the best worth visiting: St Paul, Deptford (Archer); St Mary-le-Strand (Gibbs); St Martin-in-the-Fields (Gibbs); St Mary, Twickenham (Mx) (James); St Lawrence (Whitchurch), Little Stanmore, (Mx); St Giles-in-the-Fields (Flitcroft); All Hallows, London Wall (Dance, Jr.); St Mary, Paddington Green (Plaw).

A great many churches were built in London between 1815 and 1914. Before 1837 the three best, the first two Classical and the third Gothic, are: St Pancras New Church (Inwood); All Souls, Langham Place (Nash); St Luke, Chelsea (Savage).

Since the accession of Queen Victoria, the following are the most generally admired: All Saints, Margaret St (Butterfield); St Augustine, Kilburn (Pearson); Holy Trinity, Sloane St (Sedding); St Cyprian, Clarence Gate (Comper).

Like the rest of England, London has no memorable parish churches in the modern style.

Norfolk

The area known as the Norfolk Marshland, between King's Lynn and Wisbech, contains memorable churches in greater numbers than any other part of England of comparable extent. All of them, moreover, are built of oolitic limestone. These are the finest: Emneth; Terrington St Clement; Tilney All Saints; Upwell;

Walpole St Peter*; Walsoken*; West Walton*; Wiggenhall St German; Wiggenhall St Mary Magdalene; Wiggenhall St Mary the Virgin.

Were it not for the Marshland, one would feel less certain about placing Norfolk among the first three English counties for the beauty of her churches. In Lincolnshire, thanks to the stone, the fabrics are undoubtedly a good deal finer; in Somerset, though the churches are smaller, there is excellent woodwork as well as those superb towers which leave East Anglia far behind. The great glory of the Norfolk churches is their woodwork, and especially their roofs, but here the Suffolk churches are equally impressive. Screens (some with painted figures) and benches are also a delight in Norfolk, but still more so in Suffolk. Norfolk has a few early fonts and some fifteenth-century stained glass of a quality not found in Suffolk; but apart from the splendid woodwork what one specially remembers is the scale of these churches, which, although in no way remarkable by continental standards, is in the English countryside a source of perpetual wonder. Selection has proved very difficult, but it seems to me that no list should omit any of the following: Attleborough; *Binham*; Bressingham; Cawston*; Cley; East Harling; Gooderstone; Great Walsingham; Great Yarmouth, St George; Gunton; Hales; King's Lynn, St Margaret; North Creake; North Elmham; North Runcton; Norwich, St Peter Mancroft; Pulham St Mary; Ranworth (painted screen); Redenhall (tower); Salle*; Shelton; Shernborne (font); Snettisham; South Creake; Swaffham; Toftrees (font); Trunch*; Tunstead; *Wymondham*.

Northamptonshire
A county perhaps rather over-praised in the Victorian period because of its wealth of 'Middle Pointed' (i.e. Decorated) churches, with broach and lucarned spires and sometimes fascinating window tracery. The abundance of fine limestone is certainly a great blessing here: the quality of the masoncraft is extremely good, and externally Northamptonshire churches are often delightful, especially when roofed with Collyweston slates. Internally, however, these buildings are not usually memorable; arcades tend to be low and furnishings plain. The Victorian 'improvers' also wrought great havoc here.
Earls Barton; Finedon; Fotheringhay; Higham Ferrers; Kettering (steeple); King's Sutton (spire); Lowick; Middleton Cheney; Northampton, All Saints; Northampton, Holy Sepulchre; Northampton, St Peter; Oundle (steeple); Passenham; Rothwell; Stanford-on-Avon*; Titchmarsh (tower); Wellingborough, All Hallows; Wellingborough, St Mary; Whiston.

Northumberland
A county whose churches, usually austerely conceived in the first place, mostly suffered from punitive restoration in the Victorian period. The pleasures are therefore not widespread, but Hexham is a distinguished exception, and so is All Saints, Newcastle, which is a parish church no longer.
Hexham Priory; Newcastle-upon-Tyne, All Saints; Norham.

Nottinghamshire
Nottinghamshire is well endowed with stone, but since the elevation of Southwell Minster to cathedral rank in 1884, Newark and St Mary, Nottingham, have been the only big parish churches. There are some good spires south of the Trent, and in several of the Decorated churches some very notable ornamental

sculpture. But the usual Nottinghamshire church is not architecturally spectacular, and unhappily there has been a good deal of iconoclasm.

Blyth Priory; East Markham; Hawton; Holme-by-Newark; Newark; Nottingham, St Mary; Teversal; Willoughby-in-the-Wolds; *Worksop Priory*.

Oxfordshire

Oxfordshire has beautiful limestones at one end – the north-west – and only chalk and flint at the other, with a broad band of clay across the centre. Most, though not all, of the best churches are on or near the limestone, which ranges in colour from the palest yellow around Burford to a deep tawny brown towards Banbury. Architecturally most Oxfordshire churches, for all their quiet self-assurance, are reticent and chary of display: not many pierced parapets; very few pinnacles. Only with their spires, and in the carving of big gargoyles, do they occasionally become exuberant.

Adderbury; Bloxham; Burford; Chislehampton; Church Handborough; Churchill; *Dorchester*; Ducklington; Ewelme; Iffley; Kidlington; North Leigh; Oxford, St Mary the Virgin; Stanton Harcourt; Witney.

Rutland

England's smallest county (until 1974) has a building tradition based on the beautiful grey-buff oolitic and golden brown liassic limestones with which she is so plentifully endowed. Yet it must be said that a number of her externally most distinguished churches are of little interest within; among these are Empingham; Ketton; Langham; Lyddington; Oakham; Ryhall; Whissendine.

Those best worth a longer visit are: Brooke; Exton; Great Casterton; Stoke Dry; Tickencote.

Normanton church only survives as a folly on the shore of Rutland Water. Partially buried in concrete, it looks from a distance to be half-submerged.

Shropshire

Shropshire churches are mostly of sandstone and with few exceptions modest in scale, for this county has always been predominantly rural and not populous. None the less there are some delightful surprises scattered up and down the county, while St Mary, Shrewsbury, and Ludlow merit prolonged visits.

Acton Burnell; Hughley (screen); Ludlow; Lydbury North; Shrewsbury, St Chad; Shrewsbury, St Mary; Stottesdon (font); Tong; Whitchurch.

Somerset

One goes to Somerset primarily for the towers, which are of incomparable beauty; they include a high proportion of the finest parish church towers in England if not indeed in Europe, and their numbers are such that a tower tour alone would occupy several days. The thirteen finest are discussed on pages 99–102, and I would give a * to all of them. Were it not for their towers, seven of them – Batcombe; Chewton Mendip; Huish Episcopi; Mells; North Petherton; Staple Fitzpaine, and Wrington – would not qualify for inclusion in a select list of Somerset churches; but the remaining six have other attractions as well: Evercreech; Ile Abbots; Ilminster; Kingston St Mary; Leigh-on-Mendip; Wells, St Cuthbert.

There are more towers (e.g., among churches listed below, Taunton, St Mary Magdalene, Kingsbury Episcopi, Bruton) which in any other county would also be regarded as outstanding, although, it should be added, these towers are not all very big. But the prosperity of the county in the later Middle Ages and the lovely stone assured for Somerset churches a sumptuousness that is by no means confined to the towers; there are some splendid porches, windows and parapets, while for woodwork – roofs, screens, bench-ends – this is also a county of very high quality. Towards the western fringe, where the limestones have given place to mainly pink sandstone, most of the churches are closer in character to those of neighbouring Devon than to the rest of the county. Although the Norfolk and Lincolnshire churches are grander in scale and the former has the splendid Marshland group, it may well be that Somerset merits the first place among the English counties for parish churches considered as works of art. Other Somerset churches deserving special mention are:

Axbridge; Backwell; *Bath Abbey*; Bishops Lydeard; Brent Knoll; Broomfield; Bruton; Crowcombe; High Ham; Kingsbury Episcopi; Long Sutton; Martock; North Cadbury; Norton-sub-Hamdon; Shepton Mallet (roof); Taunton, St Mary Magdalene; Trull; Watchet, St Decuman; Weston Zoyland; Yatton.

Staffordshire
Another sandstone county. Some dignified buildings, but it would be difficult to point to a distinctive Staffordshire style. There are churches worth seeing, though, from almost every period.
Checkley; Clifton Campville; Enville; Gnosall; Hamstall Ridware; Hoar Cross; Ingestre*; Leigh; Rushton Spencer; Sandon; Tamworth; *Tutbury*; Wolverhampton, St Peter.

Suffolk
See under Norfolk. The attractions of the Suffolk churches are closely comparable to those of her neighbour, with flint the chief material, sometimes dressed and enriched with a fine display of flushwork (see Glossary, p. 223), and superlative woodwork as the great draw. Again, it has not been easy to choose from among so many.
Bacton; Badingham; Barningham; Blythburgh*; Bramfield; Cotton; Cretingham; Dennington; Denston*; Earl Soham; Earl Stonham; Framlingham; Fressingfield; Kedington; Lakenheath; Lavenham; Long Melford*; Mildenhall; Needham Market (roof); Rougham; Southwold*; Sudbury, St Gregory; Walsham-le-Willows (roof); Wingfield; Woolpit; Worlingworth.

Surrey
In the Middle Ages Surrey was short not only of stone but of financial resources. In the Victorian period she was rich, with a rapidly expanding population of regular churchgoers. Accordingly few old Surrey churches have escaped enlarging and refurbishing, and many have been entirely spoilt. In any of the good church counties not one of those listed below would have earned a mention.
Burstow; Chipstead; Lingfield; Littleton (Mx until 1965); Ockham; Shere; Stoke d'Abernon.

Sussex

The Normans built some notable churches on or near the coast of Sussex, but the Weald long remained thickly wooded and very scantily peopled. Gothic churches of the Weald, as of the Downs, are therefore mostly small and unimposing, although, when not enlarged and often spoilt by the Victorians, they can be very lovable. Special characteristics are the abundance of shingled spires and the heavy roofs of Horsham sandstone, beautiful alike in colour and texture. Brighton has several nineteenth-century churches of unusual character.

Arundel; Ashburnham; *Boxgrove Priory*; Brighton, St Bartholomew; Burton; Glynde; New Shoreham; Penhurst; Poynings; Sompting; Steyning; Warminghurst; Winchelsea; Worth.

Warwickshire

This county's churches have suffered considerably from the friability of the New Red sandstone which was the principal building material, and a good deal of restoration has been inevitable. Only towards the south-east was limestone used, admitting of good external details. But Warwickshire has a few exuberant examples of Gothic, and some interesting Georgian buildings.

Astley; Binley; Brailes; Castle Bromwich; Coleshill; Great Packington; Honington; Knowle; Lapworth; *Merevale*; Over Whitacre; Stratford-on-Avon; Tredington; Warwick, St Mary.

Westmorland

Small and until the nineteenth century sparsely populated. Very little here that is worth going to see. But the churchyard of Kirkby Stephen, almost cleared of gravestones, is a delight, and a specially good example of how artistically beneficial this clearance, so much condemned in some influential circles, can sometimes be.

Brougham, St Ninian; Kirkby Lonsdale; Kirkby Stephen.

Wiltshire

An interesting county architecturally but not a very coherent one. Nearly all the best churches are in or towards the north and west, where there is an abundance of fine oolitic limestone which was used by the well-to-do clothiers to splendid effect. But the excellent limestone which also occurs in the south (Chilmark, Tisbury) yielded few parish churches of much note outside Salisbury. Between these two areas lie the Plain and the Downs, always very thinly populated and in church-building unambitious.

Amesbury; Bishops Cannings; Bishopstone; Bradford-on-Avon, St Lawrence; Bromham; Devizes, St John; *Edington**; Farley; Inglesham; Lacock; Lydiard Tregoze; Maiden Bradley; *Malmesbury Abbey*; Marden; Mildenhall; Potterne; Salisbury, St Thomas; Steeple Ashton*; Urchfont.

Worcestershire

The churches of Worcestershire, like those of her neighbour Warwickshire, are mostly built of rather soft New Red sandstones which have had to undergo substantial patchings and refacings. The limestones on the Cotswold fringe in the south-eastern corner of the county have worn much better. But some of the sandstones have great charm of colour. Apart from the former monastic churches of Great Malvern and Pershore, Worcestershire's parish churches are not architecturally memorable, nor is there a special county style. But there are some delightful Georgian buildings.

Bredon; Broadway; Chaddesley Corbett; Croome d'Abitot; *Great Malvern Priory**; Great Witley; Overbury; *Pershore Abbey*; Strensham; Wickhamford; Worcester, St Swithun.

Yorkshire

England's largest county has memorable churches of almost every type and period. The finest area is scenically the least spectacular, the East Riding, which contains some magnificent church architecture. Much of the limestone was brought in barges from near Tadcaster. The West Riding, in addition to many sandstone churches which in the industrial regions have turned nearly black, can show notable white magnesian limestone buildings in its south-eastern area and rough but likeable structures in the Pennines. The North Riding has no churches of special distinction but a number that are well worth visiting, and in their settings the North Riding churches are the most fortunate of the three. It should not be forgotten that considerable parts of Yorkshire are still sparsely populated and have never needed more than small and widely scattered places of worship; whereas, on the other hand, the churches of the industrial districts, as in Lancashire, are mostly Victorian. The distribution of notable churches in Yorkshire is therefore very uneven.

City of York
All Saints, North Street; Holy Trinity, Goodramgate.

East Riding
Beverley Minster; Beverley, St Mary; Boynton; Great Driffield (tower); Hedon; Hemingbrough; Holme-on-Spalding-Moor; Howden*; Hull, Holy Tinity; North Newbald; Patrington*; Skipwith; South Dalton (spire); Welwick.

North Riding
Brandsby; Coxwold; Lastingham; *Old Malton*; Pickering; Skelton; Thirsk; Wensley; Whitby.

West Riding
Adel; Adlingfleet; Arksey; Birkin; Bolton Percy; Ecclesfield; Fishlake; Halifax; Hatfield; Leeds, St John; Leeds, St Peter; *Nun Monkton*; Rotherham; *Selby Abbey**; Sherburn-in-Elmet; Slaidburn; Sprotbrough; Tickhill.

Notes

1 It should perhaps be at once made clear that, for reasons explained on page 12, this book takes no cognizance of the redrawing of the county map of England in 1974.

2 Lytton Strachey, *Eminent Victorians* (1918). Essay on Cardinal Manning.

3 Cf. *The Cathedrals of England* (1967), p. 73.

4 This is by Samuel Chandler, a sculptor otherwise almost unknown.

5 By Gervase Jackson-Stops in *Country Life*, December 21, 1972.

6 Her epitaph describes her as 'A lady endowed with a natural disposition to vertue, a true understanding of honour, most noble behaviour, perpetual cheerfulness, most eligant conversation, and a more than ordinary conjugal affection'.

7 In much the same spirit, between the church and the house there used to be a monumental pedestal with some lines 'To the Memory of a Beautiful Mottled Peacock.'

8 Most of the guide books on sale in churches would at one time have probably informed us that 'the parish numbers fewer than two hundred souls': some may still do so. My mother once delighted me by remarking, 'Yes, but how many *bodies?*'

9 Frederick Burgess, *English Churchyard Memorials,* 1963: p. 109. The indispensable book on this subject.

10 It is ironical that the adjacent parish to Standish, Moreton Valence, possesses a collection of twentieth-century gravestones of a vulgarity that is specially shocking in Gloucestershire. Here can be seen, most of them prominently signed by the firms who supplied them, polished pink and grey granite, white marble employed for headstones, for crazy paving (!) and for chips, reconstituted stone, many heavy kerbs, *créme de menthe* chips and even bright blue tesserae. This deplorable churchyard constitutes an affront to the church itself, which has walls of Cotswold stone exquisitely masoned, and a roof of well-graded stone slates.

11 John Betjeman, *Poems in the Porch* (1955).

12 At Tugford in Shropshire a series of horrible white marble gravestones yields, in addition to the inevitable At Rest, the following, mostly in inverted commas: Thy will be done; Abide with me; In God's keeping; Peace, perfect peace; Jesus called a little child; Till we meet again; Father in thy gracious keeping Leave we now our loved one sleeping.

13 Nor, even today, is it accepted by all clergymen. Not many years ago, when a new crematorium was opened at a large industrial town in Lancashire, one of the local vicars wrote in his parish magazine: 'We are not prepared to conduct the committal ceremony at the crematorium. From the earliest times the Christian Church resisted anything but burial, partly because cremation had many heathen associations, partly because Our Lord was buried, and partly to emphasize the Church's belief in resurrection. The Church's traditional teaching on this matter has never wavered.'

14 The name adopted in 1972, Council for Places of Worship, seemed less happy. It has now reverted to the Council for the Care of Churches.

15 This passage is not included in The latest (third) edition of *The Churchyards Handbook* (1976).

16 It is also well hallowed by tradition, and not only for sheep. Frederick Burgess cited John Gay's *Dirge*:
With wicker rods we fenc'd her Tomb around,
To ward from Man and Beast the hallow'd ground:
Lest her new Grave the Parson's Cattle raze,
For both his Horse and Cow the church Yard graze.
He also pointed out that in 'Home from the Sea', by the Pre-Raphaelite painter Arthur Hughes (1857), there is a country churchyard with grazing sheep and a grave-mound pegged with withies.

17 Although many attempts have been made to proscribe the scattering of confetti, it can still be seen, soaked and sluttish-looking, at the entrances to some country churchyards. Confetti is litter, and not only to throw but to sell it should be a penal offence. My own view is that if people *must* throw something at weddings it should be maize, and that on all such occasions a troop of hens should be included among the guests.

18 In *The Pattern of English Building*, 3rd ed. (1972), pp. 205–207. Although that book is primarily concerned with domestic architecture, there are many references throughout to the building materials of the parish churches.

19 The degree of corrosion, however, often varies substantially from piece to piece. Why this should be so is not yet understood, but scientists from the University of York, in conjunction with the York Glazier Trust, are conducting a full inquiry into this problem. It is also hoped to find some means of arresting and preventing what has become a serious hazard for old glass.

20 Marvellous to relate, it is rumoured that these towers are soon to be removed.

21 Other examples of central towers that are internally obstructive include the following: Kingston-upon-Thames, Selling in Kent, St Michael at Southampton, Tisbury and Sherston in Wiltshire, South Petherton, Crewkerne and Stogursey in Somerset, Colyton in Devon, Staunton in Gloucestershire, Toddington in Bedfordshire, and Holy Trinity, Hull. This list is by no means exhaustive; but it should be added that in some churches the central tower seems to have presented no serious problems.

22 John Newman, in the 'Pevsner' volumes for the county gives the following statistics for Perpendicular towers in Kent: Central towers (apart from Bell Harry), 4; west towers, about 82; south-west, 2; north-west, 2.

23 Although the great Abbey did not attain cathedral rank until 1541.

24 William Golding, *The Spire* (1964).

25 The following are the more important parish churches that were formerly collegiate:
Berkshire Shottesbrooke
Cheshire Bunbury, Chester, St John
Cornwall Crantock, St Buryan
Cumberland Greystoke
Devon Crediton, Ottery St Mary and Tiverton
Dorset Wimborne Minster
Durham Chester-le-Street, Darlington, Lanchester, St Andrew Auckland and Staindrop
Gloucestershire Westbury-on-Trym
Kent Ashford, Cobham, Maidstone, Wingham and Wye
Lancashire Manchester (Cathedral since 1847)
Leicestershire Kirby Bellars and Leicester, St Mary-de-Castro
Lincolnshire Tattershall
Norfolk Attleborough and Thompson
Northamptonshire Cotterstock, Fotheringhay and Irthlingborough
Nottinghamshire Southwell Minster (Cathedral since 1884)
Shropshire Battlefield, Bridgnorth, and Tong
Staffordshire Gnosall, Penkridge, Stafford, Tamworth, Tettenhall and Wolverhampton
Suffolk Denston, Stoke-by-Clare, Sudbury, St Gregory and Wingfield
Surrey Lingfield
Sussex Arundel, Bosham, Etchingham and Steyning
Warwickshire Astley, Knowle, Stratford-on-Avon and Warwick
Yorkshire Beverley Minster, Hemingbrough, Howden and Ripon Minster (Cathedral since 1836)
There are a few others, such as Bredgar

in Kent, of less importance.

26 St Lawrence, Evesham (R), for example, has a cruel east window by Willement, brutally coloured, which does great damage to a rather charming Gothick interior.

27 It is necessary to write this in full as the adjacent parish, with its own church, is Wiggenhall St Mary Magdalene.

28 See N. E. Toke, 'Heraldic Ledgers in Kentish Churches', *Arch. Cantiana*, Vol. 41, pp. 187 *et seq.*

29 These were not invariably available for baptisms. In at least one village, where the parson was an ardent angler, the village boys were induced by suitable *pourboires* to catch minnows for his bait, and to pop them into water under the font cover, until he was ready to use them.

30 Information kindly provided by Norman Scarfe.

31 'Of both sexes', said Edward Croft-Murray. I know few problems more teasing than the proper determination of the sex of angels: a perfect subject for theologians.

32 Mention of this chancel arch prompts the reflection that Bosham is one of the many parish churches at which the chancel and the nave are not aligned on the same axis. Clergymen nearly always account for this in symbolic terms by referring to the inclination of Christ's head upon the Cross, regardless of the fact that in medieval art the head is always represented as drooping towards the right shoulder, whereas many chancels 'weep' to the left. There is no evidence whatever to support the symbolic 'explanation'. The fact is, as H. Munro Cautley observed, 'in the 12th, 13th and early 14th century churches, it is quite rare to find even an exact rectangle, and, as I have proved by measurement, towers, naves, aisles and chancels turn out to be irregular parallelograms, often indeed without any axis in common'. And the explanation? Simply the rough and ready methods of the early church-builders who were unconcerned with mathematical accuracy. When it came to rebuilding in the Perpendicular period, these earlier malalignments were, whenever possible, corrected; but of course many churches, of which Bosham was one, experienced no Perpendicular or later rebuilding.

Nothing, of course, is easier than to 'explain' deviations from the norm in symbolic terms without a shred of evidence, and some church guides are rich repositories of this nonsense. At St Martin's in Shropshire the current leaflet informs us that 'the inner walls are sloping and curved at the west end like a ship, being symbolic of the Ark, while the main aisle has a definite slope from the west up to the altar, symbolic of the ascent to Calvary'. It might be felt that the refutation of statements like these hardly merits even a footnote, but there is always a risk that the credulous may be taken in by such *ex cathedra* assertions.

Place Index

General Index

For individual churches please consult The Place Index